Discover Your Soul Template

"Marcus T. Anthony's new book moves with a wisdom and confidence that has the feeling of being channeled from that higher being within us so few of us ever manage to tap in to consciously. . . . It illuminates and demystifies the mystical. I heartily endorse this book and have no hesitation in recommending it highly."

DAVID LOYE, PH.D., SOCIAL PSYCHOLOGIST,
FUTURIST, SYSTEMS THEORIST, AND AUTHOR OF
DARWIN IN LOVE AND *DARWIN'S LOST THEORY*

"An easy-to-read and inspiring book on transmodern spirituality . . . deepens our understanding of spirituality and the nature of intelligence."

SOHAIL INAYATULLAH, PROFESSOR AT TAMKANG UNIVERSITY,
TAIWAN, AND THE UNIVERSITY OF THE SUNSHINE COAST, AND
AUTHOR OF *YOUTH FUTURES* AND *TRANSFORMING COMMUNICATION*

". . . very personal and contemporary examination of synchronicity as it visits our personal lives and enlivens our destinies."

ALLAN COMBS, AUTHOR OF *THE RADIANCE OF BEING*
AND *CONSCIOUSNESS EXPLAINED BETTER*

"Anthony not only describes in some detail the emotional and karmic obstacles that we bring to the struggle [of liberating ourselves] but also describes many practical tools that we can use to tune in to our own and

SIMON BU RRICULUM DEVELOPMENT,
STITUTE INTERNATIONAL

Discover Your Soul Template

14 Steps for Awakening Integrated Intelligence

Marcus T. Anthony, Ph.D.

Inner Traditions
Rochester, Vermont • Toronto, Canada

Inner Traditions
One Park Street
Rochester, Vermont 05767
www.InnerTraditions.com

SUSTAINABLE FORESTRY INITIATIVE · Certified Sourcing · www.sfiprogram.org · SFI-00854

Text stock is SFI certified

Library of Congress Cataloging-in-Publication Data
Anthony, Marcus T.
  Discover your soul template : 14 steps for awakening integrated intelligence / Marcus T. Anthony.
    p. cm.
  Includes bibliographical references and index.
  Summary: "How to create the life you want in alignment with your soul's purpose"—Provided by publisher.
  ISBN 978-1-59477-426-3 (pbk.) — ISBN 978-1-59477-805-6 (e-book)
  1. Intellect. 2. Self-actualization (Psychology) 3. Two thousand twelve, A.D. I. Title.
  BF431.A5774 2012
  131—dc23

                                                                2011051980

Printed and bound in the United States by Lake Book Manufacturing
The text stock is SFI certified. The Sustainable Forestry Initiative® program promotes sustainable forest management.

10 9 8 7 6 5 4 3 2 1

Text design by Priscilla H. Baker
Text layout by Virginia Scott Bowman
This book was typeset in Garamond Premier Pro and Gill Sans with Didot Linotype and Avant Garde used as display typefaces

To send correspondence to the author of this book, mail a first-class letter to the author c/o Inner Traditions • Bear & Company, One Park Street, Rochester, VT 05767, and we will forward the communication or contact the author directly at **mindfutures@yahoo.com** or through his website **www.mindfutures.com**.

For my teacher, Jessica—
You know who you are

Contents

PART 2

Living an Empowered Life

❡

Foreword

Ervin Laszlo, Ph.D.

Marcus T. Anthony writes that we live in a crucial time in human history, one where we stand at the edge of possible catastrophe. I can only concur. In thermodynamics there is a concept known as a bifurcation point, where a linear process breaks down and becomes nonlinear. This is true for both human and natural systems. Up to a certain point a system may run smoothly, but then it reaches a crucial stage. Many different outcomes are then possible, but change is inevitable. The system can completely break down. However, the system can continue in a new form. The process is inherently chaotic, not predictable, and a period of rapid change occurs. It is in this critical period that the future unfolds.

If we view the early twenty-first century as a bifurcation point, then we have to admit the absolute importance of our choices. Human beings are living beings with the possibility of conscious choice. Yet to choose consciously means to be informed; and to be informed requires access to information. In *Discover Your Soul Template,* Marcus T. Anthony shows us that we have at our disposal a potentially infinite source of information, and that we can apply that data through our innate Integrated Intelligence.

In my own writings I have talked about how nations, organizations, and groups can help bring about a WorldShift, a global breakthrough, which permits a more sustainable development of the planet we live on.

Discover Your Soul Template is perfectly compatible with the idea of sustainable futures. Its author comes from a slightly different angle than I do, however. He writes from personal experience, telling of the way that each of us can consciously tap in to the greater intelligence of the cosmos, and create lives of "bliss."

Most importantly from my perspective, is that his understanding of bliss entails a broader dimension than the mere needs of the individual. In chapter two of this book he refers to a human oversoul template, a body of data that encodes the required lessons of the human species. As he puts it, the idea of "love" lies at the heart of human choice, human consciousness, and human evolution. As David Loye has pointed out in his many books on Charles Darwin's "lost theory of love," even the greatest evolutionary theorist of them all understood this well. Somehow mainstream science has forgotten such a vital understanding.

Even the most skeptical of us must admit that at times he feels somehow connected to others, the world, perhaps even the cosmos. This sense of connectedness is something that transcends culture and ideology.

More often than not, it features an integral part of the worldview of societies both past and present. Indigenous societies have always lived with this awareness of mundane and subtle connection, and their lives are typically lived within a world that features a transpersonal connection with the land, the biosphere, and to the spirit world, including their ancestors. The ancient Greeks and their deep thinkers such as Socrates, Plato, and even Aristotle—far from being the adamant logicians they are sometimes erroneously depicted to be by some modern scholars—believed that mind and cosmos are intimately intertwined.

Further, the monotheistic religions have strong mystical traditions (though they have typically been suppressed because their direct connection to the divine often threatened the power hierarchies within their institutions). Despite the increasing societal influence and power of the "detached" scientist, in recent centuries the Romantics and the modern alternative spirituality movement have continued to burn this spiritual flame.

In my own research and publications, I have constantly referred to the connection between mind and cosmos by its ancient Hindu terminology: the Akashic Field. This subtle body of all-knowing information is what connects the individual with collective, lower with higher knowledge, and the mundane with the divine. Such statements are not mere philosophy, but increasingly vindicated by science.

Vacuum physics strongly suggests that the Akashic Field is real, and this is echoed in the concept of the quantum vacuum—or better, plenum—a cosmic information field that fills all of space. Its multiple energies give rise to our physical universe—from the microcosm of subatomic particles and up to the sprawling macrocosm of galaxies, stars, planets, biospheres, and even consciousness itself. This plenum-based Akashic Field contains within it the memory of all things past and future.

In parapsychology, we have had many enticing glimpses of cognitive abilities, which suggest the intimate entanglement of mind and environment. These include clairvoyance, telepathy, precognition, and even psychokinesis. Although the evidence is not definitive, we would be foolhardy to dismiss the data based purely upon an insistence that the cosmos is machine-like. Systems science has already shown us the folly of such ignorance.

With the exception of physics, much of mainstream science continues to ignore the ever-growing body of data of an interconnected universe, and an Integrated Intelligence. The connectivity hypothesis is the four-hundred-pound gorilla in the room that some scientists are unwilling to acknowledge, being too preoccupied with affirming their mechanistic predilections.

As Wordsworth famously stated, we murder to dissect, and the reductionism of the modern mechanistic paradigm has strangled the life—the spirit—from the world. Too busy counting, calculating, classifying, analyzing, and describing, many in the mainstream scientific community are still unable to connect the dots or to connect with the cosmos.

The modern world, alas, has also gone through a period where it has largely forgotten the wisdom and teachings of our spiritual forebears. Our economically developed societies are all too often worlds of glass and steel, their inhabitants endlessly chasing financial security, craving material satiation, or finding distraction in mass entertainment mediated by information technology. We have lost our roots. Mainstream culture has become spiritually impoverished, and the world disenchanted.

It is time for something different. It is time for change. In *Discover Your Soul Template,* Marcus T. Anthony calls you forward to embrace that difference. What is most exciting is that he shows you precisely how to do this. He shows you how to choose a life of bliss aligned with your spirit, and the greater good of the human species.

Ultimately, what is required is not merely to choose, but to choose wisely. As Marcus T. Anthony puts it so aptly, we have to become the Sage. Wisdom is not merely intelligence. Intelligence is successful application of knowledge, but wisdom entails sagacity, grace, and equanimity. For these things to occur we need to acknowledge the connectedness of all things. We do not act alone. We do not choose alone.

Our thoughts exist within a sea of cosmic intelligence—Integrated Intelligence. In a dynamic and interconnected system, everything affects everything else. This is the logical conclusion we can draw from systems science, and the mystics and sages of eras long gone came to the same conclusion through introspective means. Marcus Anthony agrees too.

We are not alone.

ERVIN LASZLO, PH.D., twice nominated for the Nobel Peace Prize, is the editor of the international periodical *World Futures: The Journal of General Evolution* and Chancellor-Designate of the newly formed GlobalShift University. He is the founder and president of the international think tanks the Club of Budapest and the General Evolution Research Group and the author of 83 books translated into 21 languages. (See the recommended reading for references to some of Ervin Laszlo's books.) He lives in Italy.

Acknowledgments

All writers know how lonely the art of prose can be at times. Fortunately, I have had some great help in bringing together the ideas you see in *Discover Your Soul Template.*

First, to all the spiritual teachers who have helped me over the years, I give a big thanks. I have had the good fortune to learn from some of the best. My good friend Simon Buckland read the whole manuscript, and gave tremendous support and encouragement to me. His guidance has been invaluable. Thanks too, to David Loye, for being an ongoing supporter, and for believing in what I do. A big "thank you" to Marisa Cohen, Steve Sims, and Nina Wegner for helping with the editing of the book at difference stages of its production.

This book is about Integrated Intelligence, and I cannot possibly conclude without thanking Spirit and the universe itself, for without their input, this book would never have been written. I have been constantly inspired and guided at every step of the journey, and I feel deeply blessed.

Putting the 14 Steps into Practice

The information contained in this book is the result of many years of diligent research and application, trial and error. However, the reader should be aware that time and care are required to develop the intuitive skills outlined here. It is recommended that the reader begin with small, relatively unimportant decisions and gradually build up to more significant choices. The author and publisher can take no responsibility for the actions the reader chooses to take after reading *Discover Your Soul Template.* If you suffer from any serious psychological problems, you should consult relevant mental health professionals before applying the principles in this book.

Personal Prelude

Why I Wrote This Book

My goal as a speaker, writer, and researcher has always been to let people know that there can be an expansion of our understanding of mind and intelligence. Our consciousness can be transformed into something extraordinary. Most of the writing I have done so far has been academic, in the field of futures studies. I am a futurist. That means I question the future, and I like to think carefully about where it is taking us.

In popular culture and advertising, the future is often depicted as being about more money, more machines, and more cool stuff for everyone. I call these "money and machines futures."

Deep down we know that there is more to the future than just acquiring more possessions and amusing ourselves in more innovative ways. There are futures beyond flying cars and a faster Internet.

I am particularly interested in how people think, feel, and relate. Relationship is at the heart of what it means to be human—relationship with self, with others, and with the universe we live in. Most important of all is the relationship with ourselves, and especially the way that our conscious mind interacts with the deep ocean of consciousness within—and beyond. I know of no better word for these relationships than "spirituality."

I am a futurist who is concerned with the spiritual futures of humanity.

When I started writing about futures* I was rather academic and theoretical. I was scared that if I got too far ahead of the parade, nobody would be able to see me. I was afraid nobody would give me a job. Luckily nobody gave me a job anyway, so I didn't need to worry about big brother looking over my shoulder. I soon got cheeky and started to introduce the personal, the esoteric, and the spiritual into my writing.

Discover Your Soul Template is thus the next step in a natural progression. The book has a smattering of the left-brained stuff, and the rest is personal and practical. And fun too. I confess to being very Australian. Where I come from, they start swinging at you if you take yourself too seriously. (We Aussies are very insecure.)

If you read some of my early academic papers, you might think I am purely an intellectual. In fact, many years ago I was a hard-line empiricist—just the facts, please. I had no idea as I was growing up about the kinds of concepts you will read of in this book. My father was a baker, and my family was very much working class. Beyond the odd trip to church, my childhood included no reference to spiritual experience. Chomping on a loaf of white bread was about as deep as it got for me.

Now I work with deep consciousness and the intuitive mind daily. The story of how I changed from being a left-brained intellectual philosopher to a whole-brained intuitive futurist will tell you a lot about me, this book, and why I wrote it.

In 1990, I was sitting in a lecture hall in the Department of Education at the University of Newcastle, Australia, waiting for another "Schools and Society" lecture to begin. Suddenly an impressive-looking man sporting a cool goatee and wearing fine Italian clothes strode magnificently to the lectern. The first thing I noted about the man was that the room was only just wide enough to contain his huge shoulders. The second was his voice.

"Hello, I'm Ronald Laura," he announced in a posh Boston accent.

---

*Futurists often prefer the word *futures* to the singular term *the future*, because we like to think of the future as being an unfolding field of potential. This is not just the case for mystically inclined futurists like me, but also for more conventional futurists, who tend to focus upon economics, technology, social systems, and so on.

Professor Laura is a brilliant philosopher and (to top it off) a former weightlifting and world arm-wrestling champion. On that day, he lectured for two hours about science, mysticism, physics, and philosophy in a way I had never heard before. As Ron Laura spoke, something deep within me stirred. I was developing enough self-awareness then, at twenty-four years of age, to know that when something moves you like that, you should take note. I had the merest stirrings of an appreciation of what it means to follow your excitement. That day, my Western materialist/scientific worldview was shaken. Still, I remained skeptical. It would take more than a few words of philosophy to crack this tough nut. In fact, it would take something absolutely extraordinary.

That incredible event occurred almost three years later. That was when I met a remarkable woman named Lesley Williams-Halverson, while I was living in the town of Coffs Harbour, in northern New South Wales. Lesley was very much the New Age spiritual woman, and I attended her meditation classes for a while. She possessed a type of mental ability that I had never encountered before.

She seemed to be able to intuit the general circumstances and emotional issues of people without physical evidence. I was intrigued, and I began to consider the possibility that human beings could "see" beyond the five senses.

Lesley inspired me to embark upon a disciplined study of my own mind. Every day, I recorded my dreams, meditated, and used self-taught trance states to tap in to the depths of my psyche. I found I was able to gather both simple and profound data, merely by relaxing deeply and directing specific questions to myself. I got "answers" in feelings, images, and sounds. These were things I had never learned in school. A fantastic inner world suddenly opened before me. I wondered why nobody had told me about this before.

One night I had a very profound dream. Just after I fell asleep, I "dreamed" that a dark-haired woman was standing beside my bed. By this time, I had developed the ability to remain conscious even as I dreamed, so I was completely aware of what was happening. The woman was moving her hands, holding them above my body. I knew some kind of healing process was occurring. She began to speak softly. She told me that I was using only 3 percent of my mental ability, and that there was much healing work for me to do on myself.

I awoke immediately, and remembered everything vividly. Reflecting upon the dream, I felt strongly that the experience was not merely imaginary. Yet if there were parts of my mind that I was not using, what were they? Or was all this the function of wishful thinking and an overactive imagination?

Then came the extraordinary. At the end of a group meditation session one evening, Lesley told everyone that she had dreamed a lot about "UFOs" the previous night.

"Whenever I have these dreams there are lots of UFO sightings around," she said. "So if you go out tonight, you may see something. I feel that about two in the morning would be the right time."

It was an outrageous claim that only a fool would take seriously. This undoubtedly explains why I dragged myself out of bed at a quarter to two that night to take a look.

My eyes almost popped out of my head when I swung my front door open five minutes later and looked up into the clear night sky. There I saw a large ball of luminous white light, about a third the size of a full moon. The thing was shimmering silently through the darkness, a few hundred yards in the air, gliding eastward at about ninety degrees above the horizon. It was eerily unearthly.

I watched it disappear over the neighbors' houses after about thirty seconds.

The ball of light was heading out over the ocean. Excitedly, I ran down to the beach a few hundred yards away and looked out over the dark water. But the ball of light was gone. I walked up and down the beach for an hour, the cool sea breeze brushing my face. I saw nothing more.

I started to walk home. Yet the strange night wasn't finished with me yet. As I was about to open my front door, I looked skyward one last time. My mouth must have dropped open, for directly above my head I saw a group of about twenty small, red, circular lights in a double "V" formation—one "V" inside the other. The objects were flying silently southward, parallel to the coast, and at a height of perhaps a few hundred yards. I stood there gaping, breathless. In less than a minute they disappeared behind trees on the opposite side of the road.

The questions deepened. What were those things I saw that night? How on earth did Lesley know that they were going to be there at that time, merely from a dream? Why are these kinds of subject matters still a taboo topic in modern science and education?

Despite these extraordinary events, up till that time I had seen but the tip of the iceberg. Almost four years later my worldview, and my ego, were shattered again. It was during a meditation in early 1996 that the image came to me. I saw a woman with dark hair. She was turned away from me, and on the back of her shirt were two letters: "NZ."

Brilliant as I am, I knew it must have something to do with New Zealand. Exactly what, I wasn't sure, as my knowledge of the Shaky Isles was restricted to knowing that their sheep are uglier than Australia's and that they dishonestly tried to claim credit for the Pavlova, a creamy cake, definitely invented in Australia.

The vision of the NZ woman remained perplexing.

A few weeks later, I was talking to a colleague of mine over lunch. He mentioned that an international school principal from New Zealand was coming to Australia to recruit teachers, and suggested I apply. I said I would think about it, said good-bye and walked over to buy a snack from the kiosk. When the cashier handed me the change, a coin jumped out at me like a punch in the nose. It was a New Zealand twenty-cent piece, somehow mixed in with the local currency.

I took the hint. I applied for the job, got an interview, and received an offer shortly afterward.

Had I known that this synchronicity was an invitation for a joyride to hell, I suspect I would have said "No." That is probably why the universe declined to give me that little bit of additional information. Still, the fact that my flat mate, Martin, had also received an offer from the same school, and accepted it, encouraged me. His position began three months before mine, so he flew out first.

On July 8, 1996, I stepped off the plane at Wellington airport. The hellish bit didn't start right away. It slowly got a bit warmer every day, until a certain point about three months later when the world as I knew it became a furnace of chaos.

At work, my department head literally would not acknowledge my existence, not even to say hello to me in the morning. She gossiped about me in staff meetings, conspired to turn other staff members against me, and nailed long lists of demands to my forehead—her preferred way of communicating. What was worse, I was told that she made fun of my clothes behind my back (and if anyone who tells you that trousers that are two inches too short are uncool, they don't know what they are talking about). My Australian flat mate Martin had already been bullied to such a degree that he resigned not long after I arrived. Australians were an endangered species at the school, and we hadn't even mentioned the Pavlova.

Then I met a wonderful but intense assemblage of advanced souls who worked as part of a group that drew people from all across New Zealand and the world. I told them what a bunch of bullies I worked with, and how bad they "done me wrong." I demanded some sympathy.

I didn't get any. My spiritual teachers took me aside and told me that I had to take complete responsibility for my work and life. I got slapped just hard enough to snap me out of my delusion—and the collective delusion of modern humanity. I was told I had lived my life as a victim, and had not yet healed, nor even addressed, the deep wounds that existed within me. They showed me how to begin. It would require some old-fashioned guts and a whole new way of using the body, mind, and soul. The worst part was that the journey would go via the road to hell. But, rather kindly of them, they said they would help me through the gates of the furnace and back out—if I made it.

Not content in seeing me being battered about the head and body at my place of employment, my teachers proceeded to see how far I could be pushed before I broke. They threw me into the fire, and looked on to see whether I'd burn alive or if I'd claw my way back out of the embers and construct myself anew.

Slowly, something special began to happen. I started to draw in the lost pieces of my soul, the light and the darkness within. I connected with the inner child, the part of me that had never been loved. In this emotional bonding, I began to develop acute perception. Soon I was able to draw information from past, present, and future, from within and without—in an instant.

I said it was hell. But it was really just a very, very big test because that was what I needed. It all came back to something I had asked for when I had first begun my spiritual journey. I had asked to be shown what it means to truly love. What I didn't know at the time of asking is that everything has a price. I didn't realize that genuine love requires healing parts of the mind that lie in shadow.

You never quite know how powerful you are until you have been stretched to the limit. Even as I went through the most challenging period of my life, I was given the most amazing gifts. Besides beginning to stand in my power as a human being, I met the most brilliant, incredible, and courageous people. These people became the inspiration for my doctoral thesis and my first book, *Integrated Intelligence.* Integrated Intelligence (INI) is the idea that we human beings have an innate capacity to draw upon knowledge that exists beyond the confines of the five senses.

Given the right environment and support, and with the personal courage and commitment to push personal boundaries, ordinary people can develop extraordinary intelligence—Integrated Intelligence. This includes the capacity for deep intuition, and the ability to perceive the profound meanings often hidden within life. It also includes being able to process information from spiritual realms currently not on the map of modern science. Integrated Intelligence can make you wise, by deepening your relationship with your inner Sage, the world, and the cosmos. It can help you perceive and understand synchronicities, the numerous fortuitous and deeply meaningful events that come into your life every day.

You might like to look upon this book as an adventure, a somewhat "in your face" challenge. Try to suspend disbelief for a few hours. *Discover Your Soul Template* is meant to shake you up, not make you feel as if your world is becoming increasingly certain and comfortable. I prefer my spiritual journeys to be shaken and stirred.

Now, I know what you are thinking. If this guy is taking me on a trip to hell, I'm going back to reading *People* magazine. Well, it isn't quite like that. My journey has been a difficult one. I have suffered at times (who doesn't?). But as the Buddhists have so wisely taught, suffering is largely a product of the mind. Much suffering is unnecessary. Quite a bit of my suffering—mostly the hellish bit—was that kind. The great news is that because of people like me, who have journeyed before you, you can skip that part, if you just make a commitment to discipline your mind. The other great news is that the suffering that is legitimate is not really suffering as we usually think of it, when it is experienced in the present moment, and the story that the the ego attempts to build around the pain is removed.

Nonetheless, what I outline in this book is no feel-good New Age philosophy. It goes much deeper than that. I am going to show you how to put yourself on the road to an empowered life: how to get what you really want and need. I am going to tell you about worlds and human abilities that mainstream science and society still refuse to acknowledge. And I am going to talk about the development of consciousness, the higher self, and a grand unifying love that underpins all of cosmic evolution.

This is the Sage's journey, and it requires more honesty, courage, and commitment than many populist approaches to creating your bliss. That bliss is not so much about material acquisition, finding your true calling, or even about reaching a destination. It is about a shift in consciousness, whereby the ego is brought into the right relationship with the wise Sage within you. It involves increasing amounts of your life being lived in the truth of the present moment. But as I mentioned, there is a price to pay for everything. The only question is whether you are willing to pay it.

Introduction

Synchronicity and the Soul Template

In 1999, I moved to Taiwan, and began work as an English teacher. I greatly enjoyed my time in Taiwan, but a year after I arrived there I suddenly realized that I was just about the only foreign guy in the town who didn't have a girlfriend. I had spent twelve months without so much as having a date, undoubtedly a record for a white guy in Taiwan.

One Saturday morning when I had just completed doing some inner work on myself, the realization hit me that this was not a situation that I preferred. I wanted to see a bit of action with the ladies. So, I sat down to seek guidance from Spirit. I meditated, entering a light trance state. I put a question out to the universe: "God, why is it that in a town where even the most awful rejects of Western humanity can get it on, I have failed to get lucky?"

God could have laughed in my face and called me a loser. But he must have been in a good mood that day, because straight away an image came into my mind. It was a picture of the little motor scooter that I drove around town (the standard means of transport in Taiwan). In particular the image zoomed in on the brand name of the motor scooter: "Charming." The bike was actually designed and marketed for women, but was perfectly fine for men to use.

Immediately I knew what the message meant, and it wasn't that a six-foot-five white guy riding a woman's motor scooter is uncool. I was not attracting women because I lacked charm. I was being too aloof, too serious. The solution was simple. I needed to learn to relax, smile more, and do a bit of good old-fashioned flirting. So I decided to change my behavior and attitude toward women. Soon after that I entered my first real relationship in Asia, dating a young Taiwanese lass by the name of Nini.

I tell this little story because it is a typical example of how I have long employed the intuitive mind in my life. When combined with a positive intention and focused action, this innate intelligence is life changing. And it is available to you as well as to me. You are a lot smarter than you think you are. An infinite stream of intelligence moves through you, connecting you with all the knowledge and wisdom of the universe. I like to call this Integrated Intelligence (INI), and this book is about utilizing this innate intelligence to create a more deeply meaningful and fulfilling life. Integrated Intelligence will help keep you *really* smart.

Integrated Intelligence implies an intelligent cosmos, which joins you in a kind of cosmic dance of creation. Wisdom born of Integrated Intelligence comes, in part, from listening to the universe, taking note of the fortuitous events that occur around you, then making smart choices. You too can make wise decisions in an instant, drawing upon the intelligence of the cosmos. Wisdom is not exclusive to elderly wise men and women living in temples and wafting incense. It is available to all of us, anywhere, any time. All learning is process, and learning to use INI is no exception.

I have learned much about how to apply Integrated Intelligence over the years. I have made wise decisions and some stupid ones, and I have learned from both. Slowly, I began to discern the way the human ego and Spirit interact. I came to see the way that Integrated Intelligence can be applied and misapplied in life.

The "law of attraction"—where ideas created first in the mind manifest in the external world in cooperation with the laws of creation—is something that has been talked about by many over the years. In recent times there have been quite a few successful books and videos on the subject. I am not going to focus on that law in this book. *Discover Your Soul Template* is more about the process of connecting with the intelligence that allows you to tap in to the law of attraction. The INI tools I will give you are the mental equipment missing from many other books. These tools take often-vague ideas about creativity, imagination, and inspiration, and turn them into real, practical technologies.

Discover Your Soul Template is for people who have at least some openness to embarking upon a spiritual journey. It will particularly benefit those who have explored some spiritual territory before, but are now looking for a path that involves more depth and substance than is often found in popular expressions of spirituality.

Just as you don't need to know how your computer works to surf the net, you don't need to know the precise mechanics of INI to apply it in your life. The proof of the pudding is in the eating, not in the lab report detailing the chemical composition of the cake. What I will tell you is everything you need to know to become competent at using INI. The part I cannot teach you is the bit where you learn through applying what I say.

Discover Your Soul Template thus differs from many New Age and popular self-help volumes in that the latter often begin by telling you that you can have it all, but explain little about how to establish your personal power to discern inner wisdom from inner trash. In *Discover Your Soul Template* I tell you how to build a solid platform that will allow you to actually live your soul purpose. You need to lay the groundwork before you can start erecting the superstructure of your dream. You first need to know your soul. The wisdom of the Sage has a price. Part 1, "Foundations of an Empowered Life," will tell you what that is. It begins with the chapter "Frontiers of the Mind," which outlines the idea of Integrated Intelligence in detail, including all the mental capacities it entails. An aim of this chapter is to introduce you to certain key concepts that will help you to understand the rest of the book. I explain why INI has been forgotten by mainstream science, and I introduce different ways of knowing. I also tell you about the competing voices within your mind and why being aware of them is so important if you want to live your dream.

Most notably, I redefine what it means to be human. Beyond your place in the consumer society, you have a far greater value: your capacity to express love and serve humanity and Spirit through the expression of your bliss. The rest of the chapter looks practically at how Integrated Intelligence can be used to express your empowerment—or the capacity to live life the way you need, when you need.

Chapter 2 is called "The Soul Template," and it is important. Any vision that you attempt to create in your life must be aligned with your soul template, the essential character of your soul, or it will lead to great difficulties. This chapter outlines how you can get to know your soul template, which contains three components: soul issues, the soul's self-limiting behavioral habits; karmic issues, soul habits that are carried over from one lifetime to the next; and soul aptitudes, which consist of the various abilities at which you excel. These are the key to expressing the creative nature of your spirit, and the love that is the essence of your journey.

Chapter 3, "The Fourteen Tools of Integrated Intelligence," presents the powerful tools that you can use to draw upon Integrated Intelligence, along with detailed guidance for their use. They are ranked in order of the proficiency required to use them effectively.

The purpose of chapter 4, "Standing in Your Power," is to explain the way that you can use INI and the natural wisdom of the Sage in practical ways to create real abundance in your life. This chapter defines empowerment, and addresses ways that human beings often deny or abuse their power. This leads to the idea of the karmic triangle, where people typically assume one of three tendencies in power plays: the victim, the rescuer, or the persecutor. The second part of this chapter explains that intuition is not simply a vague feeling, but can be developed and called upon at will. This chapter also outlines certain key attitudes that are necessary to create genuine abundance: commitment, self-discipline, passion, and the capacity to suspend doubt.

In Chapter 5, "Moment to Moment," you will learn why presence is the most noble and empowering goal of all. Without presence, your true empowerment is impossible, and all the physical power and control in the world is ultimately meaningless. This chapter is about the importance of your achieving presence and inner peace, and how you can do this. Presence allows a space for both the beautifully simple and the miraculous. In presence, serendipities flow. Presence is also necessary to use Integrated Intelligence optimally, and I explain why that is. INI works best in the silence of the present moment. It is least effective and least reliable where there is energy of fear, doubt, judgment, or haste.

This chapter explains how to work with your ego, which can be a roadblock standing between you and your soul purpose. The ego likes to create distraction and dramas; and may even be working stealthily to sabotage your dream. You will learn how to manage your inner trickster, avoid the dramas, and keep your dream alive.

Chapter 6, "The Real Secret," analyses popular spirituality and the New Age movement. I point out the strengths and weaknesses of this version of spirituality. The great truth is that we do have far greater power to create our dreams than we often imagine, while the great lie is that this power is not unlimited. The key distinction I point out is between the dreams that emerge from the ego and those that emerge from Spirit. Anyone who has tried or is interested in trying to apply the teachings of popular New Ageism in their lives should read this chapter.

"Doorways to the Soul" is chapter 7. In order for you to project a clear intention in your life and to work joyfully within your bliss, it is necessary to address the healing needs of your Spirit. These emerge from your soul issues. Simply focusing upon your dream is impossible while the psyche retains traumas from the past, including the negative belief structures they create.

There is a strong relationship between the deeply hurt parts of ourselves—what I call the wounded child—and the ego. Many of the false desires that are projected by your ego emerge from the pain within you. These desires often have little to do with your genuine soul purpose, and are typically associated with manipulating people and circumstances to gain power, control, and attention. The unconscious agenda of the ego and the wounded child is to avoid further suffering, rather than to create bliss. Chapter 7 tells you how to connect with these parts of the psyche and bring healing to them.

Part 2, "Living an Empowered Life," begins with chapter 8, where I talk about "Answering the Call"—*your* calling. Once you come to understand your soul template, much of the guesswork will be taken out of your life and your quest for bliss. The key to identifying your soul aptitudes is simply to follow your excitement. I explain how you can create a set of goals that align with your gifts, and how this allows Integrated Intelligence to direct you toward the fulfillment of those goals. The process is action-orientated, and I outline how you can harness the intelligence of the cosmos via the power of synchronicity. A key part of this chapter is practical, and I explain how the INI tools can be used at all steps of your journey.

Chapter 9, "Keeping the Dream Alive," outlines how to stay on track once you know what your calling is. I will show you how to intuitively assess the value of any decision before you take action. This will take a lot of the guesswork out of your life. The process centers upon the Wisdom Cycle, a formula to help you make wise decisions. It allows you to continue to connect with Spirit as you feel your way through life. This involves taking action with the help of Integrated Intelligence and learning from the results. The whole process is joyful, as your bliss is not simply your goal, but your journey too. Chapter 9 also explains how to deal with negative people and negative energy by keeping your consciousness field strong. Your consciousness field is the subtle stream of information in which your mind is embedded. You can think of the human auric field and chakras as being an essential part of this (though they are not exactly the same thing).

Creativity is essential as you live your dream. Chapter 10, "Inspiring," is about how you can use INI for inspiration and creativity. The brain is a self-organizing system, which can help you generate ideas, insights, and solutions. Yet, there are three key factors to creativity that are not acknowledged in mainstream psychology. First, your higher self—the part of you that is an expression of the soul—plays a key role. Second, your mind can access infinite knowledge. Finally, spirit guides can assist you. I will show you how you can deliberately develop your relationship with your guides and how to use the INI tools to these creative ends.

Chapter 10 also explains that there is a dark side to Integrated Intelligence. Your intuitive feelings can be affected by negative energy. These can include the human ego, interference from the fear of the human collective mind, and low-vibration spiritual entities. Such negative energies can interfere with your creative process by inputting distracting information and stopping the flow of positive inspiration. I will tell you how to protect yourself from such negative influences.

Love has always been the key desire of human beings, and in chapter 11, "Love Matters," I will show you how to create truly loving relationships that honor your spirit. This includes any human relationship—intimate, friendship, employment, and so on. INI is particularly useful in your relationships because it helps you intuit your own true feelings, attitudes, and motives as well as those of others.

You will learn several important skills in this chapter. I will show you how to measure the "energy" of particular decisions, such as whether to date a particular person, discontinue a relationship, ask for a raise, and so on. Second, I will teach you how to connect with your psyche to clearly see the ego projections and agendas that can harm your relationships. Finally, you will learn to intuitively "read" the motivations and projections of your friends and partners. These processes will help empower your personal relationships and minimize conflict within others.

This chapter also outlines more about "drama." Dramas are conflicts that exist either at a physical or psychic level within relationships. They involve unconscious struggles for power and control. At the superficial level these are ego projects, but under them lie the emotional scars that drive your ego. I will show you how to identify these, and pull out of energy-sapping conflicts. This all comes back to being aware of your soul template, which brings you a deep understanding of who you are, and why you are here. Working with such understanding will help you create the wellbeing and wisdom required to live your bliss.

"Sage Teachings" is chapter 12. The present chaotic state of world economics and politics is calling us to shift to a higher state of being. An unbalanced focus upon money and power has built up the collective human ego, widening the gap between society and Spirit. We need to understand that expressing a soul purpose does not require an unbalanced focus upon materialism. The wisdom of the Sage brings with it awareness that we are part of Spirit.

Once you have begun to develop the genuine empowerment of Spirit, you inevitably become a teacher. As a Sage, you have a responsibility to give consciousness back to the world. Chapter 12 identifies ways you can do this, ranging from merely being in presence (a great gift to all), to communicating your wisdom to those around you. I also give advice for those wishing to become spiritual counselors. Chapter 12 also addresses relationships with spiritual teachers. I outline ways that Integrated Intelligence can be used to find and work with the people who are right for you, and to avoid the common pitfall of giving power away to the guru.

Don't forget the important appendix at the end of the book. It will really assist you in reading the language of your mind: dreams, symbols, and images. There you will also find a glossary of certain significant terms used in the book, and the specific ways in which I intend them to be understood. I have also included a recommended reading section where you will find references to other books and articles of my own, as well as resources for further exploration, given by topic.

We all know that wisdom does not really happen in an instant. A fool will not likely become a Sage by adopting the philosophy and using the tools in this book, any more than giving a monkey the paintbrushes of Michelangelo will turn the primate into a master painter. However, what I say does offer you a way to bridge the gap between your ego and your higher mind, which opens up vast realms of possibility. In reality, it often takes us time to adjust to a new way of thinking, of being. So, don't push yourself too hard. You need to be gentle with yourself. This is the ideal loving attitude to self as you shift consciousness.

You will find support for that shift throughout the text, as this is not only a book of philosophy but also a "how to" book. Specifically, throughout the book you will find "In Practice" exercises that will guide your application of your new learning. These exercises are meant to be put into action. One way to approach *Discover Your Soul Template* would be to read the book right through the first time around to gain a general orientation, then go back through it and begin to apply the INI tools in your life. Or you can work through the exercises as you go along. Either way, it is by taking the actions Spirit is inviting you to that your soul purpose will be revealed and actualized.

PART 1

Foundations of an Empowered Life

I run on the road, long before
I dance under the lights.

MUHAMMAD ALI

one

Frontiers of the Mind

Intuition, Intelligence, and Your Future

In 1988, I left the University of Newcastle in Australia with an honors' degree in Modern History and wondered what the hell to do with my life. I couldn't get a job right away, which confused me, as I knew all the key dates in recent Indian history. What was worse, I was very shy, and my people skills were one step below that of a developmentally delayed garden worm. I could have tried to get an office job or land a cushy position with the public service to hide away from the world. Instead I stopped for a moment and thought to myself: "Considering that I am socially challenged, how can I learn better people skills?" After some deep reflection, I did the only logical thing I could think of, which was to take a job selling vacuum cleaners door-to-door.

After finishing the Dusty vacuum cleaner sales training program, I was driven out into the 'burbs with a bunch of pimply-faced high school dropouts and thrown out of the company van and onto a block of houses with another young kid. Our mission—as we had chosen to accept it—was to give away company cards and take people's phone numbers. This would help set up in-house demonstrations later on for our unsuspecting householders. My young friend and I were told to go in opposite directions, knocking on each door until we met on the other side of the block, whereupon we would be picked up by the Dusty van.

Now, I was pretty fired up, as any chronically shy young man would be when out on the street knocking on doors and trying to sell superexpensive dust collectors valued at two thousand bucks each (and remember it was the '80s!). I did pretty well, and by the time I got to the other side of the block to greet my colleague, I had collected more than a few phone numbers. However, my pimply friend wore the harrowed look of a man whose pet goldfish had just been diagnosed with a swimming disorder.

He began to moan, "This is all bullshit! I'm quittin'!"

And so he did.

But not me. No. I hung in there for another seven months, until I worked out that it really was all bullshit, and quit too.

Now, you might say that I am a slow learner, but the truth was that I had a strong motivation to stay in a job that literally sucked. The bigger picture was that even as I worked a hundred-hour week for a few lousy bucks, I was learning what I wanted to learn. My people skills got upgraded, and I learned a thing or two about self-discipline and selling. Some things are worth more than the cash.

The reason I begin with this story is that you might be thinking of skipping this chapter because it looks a bit "intellectual," especially considering the title "Frontiers of the Mind." However, if you do, you will miss something vitally important.

The fact is that it's very difficult to rise above the dominant beliefs and attitudes of your culture. You really need to see things from a distance. You need to see the big picture. You are part of the evolution of the consciousness of the human race, and of the universe. You must appreciate that this is a unique moment in history, and the present is just one of many possible futures that could have unfolded from the past.

That's what I mean by "the big picture." You were socially constructed as a human being, not unlike the way Toyota makes its cars. You were built to be a cog in the consumer machine and—not knowing any better—you bought this big lie. The problem is that the essence of your spirit, and your soul purpose, isn't much good for cranking the handles of the cash machine. So your teachers and leaders forgot to tell you the part about your soul. They forgot because they also were programmed to be cogs. They bought the big lie, and then sold it down the line, to you.

Armed with an awareness of your social status as a screw in the engine, you will be less likely to throw your arms up in the air when you get to the end of the first block, start moaning that "This is all BS!" and quit.

MORE ABOUT THE BIG PICTURE

As human beings, we have an innate capacity for Integrated Intelligence. We can access knowledge beyond the boundaries of the individual brain. We are in a constant state of data "retrieval and transmission" with people, environment, spirit realms, and the cosmos itself. Throughout history, the wisest people have been able to tap in to infinite wisdom to create lives of deep meaning and purpose.

> *You were built to be a cog in the consumer machine*
> *and—not knowing any better—you bought the big lie.*

Strange it is, then, that we are not taught this concept in modern public education systems. Instructing children to memorize the words to the national anthem is more important to curriculum designers than teaching them to operate their minds to full potential. People are not taught how to live an empowered life. There is a general taboo in modern public education about mentioning Integrated Intelligence. Chances are that by the time you have graduated from high school you will have sung the national anthem thousands of times—and spent precisely zero seconds learning about using your intuition.

Let's step back for a moment and examine the reasons for this astounding silence about the intuitive mind.* Educational, government,

---

*I have written a more academic book called *Integrated Intelligence* that address the reasons for this silence about INI. It goes into much more detail than this chapter. See the Recommended Reading section. You can also find a summary of what I call "the Western rationalist hegemony" online, in an article I wrote for *The Journal of Futures Studies* at www.jfs.tku.edu.tw/pdf/A_3.pdf.

and corporate institutions express a culture of rationalism, where brain-based cognition is the only model of mind seriously discussed. Further, modern developed societies have created scientific and finance-based cultures, which mostly ignore inner worlds and the mystical and spiritual aspects of mind. The consumer society has constructed human beings as gratification-seeking automatons without Spirit.

In other words, modern life has turned us into a bunch of zombies. It's not so much invasion of the body snatchers, as hegemony of the soul snatchers.

Historically speaking, the scientific revolution of the seventeenth century eventually led to the ideas of the mystics and Romantics being extinguished; along with that dismissal the human soul was also jettisoned. In mainstream media and culture, science and education, references to so-called psychic phenomena and spiritual intelligence gradually became taboo. The dominant paradigm in much of science became that of a mechanical universe structured according to the laws of science. Ideas about spirituality, God, and even consciousness became suppressed (though there has been some resurgence since the late twentieth century).

Free will is the absolute essence of human consciousness.

Finally, there is the issue of levels of consciousness. As the ego relaxes into deep presence and processes the psychological and karmic issues that keep it imprisoned in the illusions of mind, personal consciousness expands and incorporates direct intuitive knowledge. The individual is then able to freely acknowledge and access Integrated Intelligence much more readily. We are ruled and taught by people who have not fully developed their minds to this level. They are stuck in the limited perceptions of the "rational" mind, chronically dissociated from body and spirit, and—to make matters worse—their minds resonate at a low-frequency level* dominated

---

*This is a metaphor. Sometimes I use the terms "low-density," "low vibration," and "low frequency" to refer to low-level consciousness fields. The metaphors are based on my experience of them, not research. Many other writers have used similar metaphors.

by fear, anger, blame, shame, and guilt. In short, they live in the world of the ego.

This psychological dissociation is what I call the *alienated mind.* Our leaders and teachers are severely restricted in their capacity to understand and access high-frequency knowledge. How are they to understand it, let alone acknowledge and teach it, if they are not even aware of it?

ENTER THE ZOMBIE

One recent strain of thought in cognitive science maintains that we are not really conscious, and that there is no such thing as free will. We think we have choices, but it's all a delusion. We are really just zombies.

These cognitive scientists have gotten it all wrong. Free will is the absolute essence of human consciousness. However, in a sense, we *have* become a bunch of zombies. Yet the zombie state is not innate to humanity. It's just that we have forgotten how to think, and especially how to feel, and other zombies keep telling us not to think about anything too important or to feel anything too deeply. Last time I checked, zombies were not usually too good at teaching anyone how to live and think. And just quietly, don't ever tell a zombie that he's a zombie. Zombies get offended, and the next thing you know, they want your brain. All these factors have created the *zombie delusion,* as shown in figure 1.1.

WHAT IS INTEGRATED INTELLIGENCE?

Before we even begin to define *Integrated Intelligence* (INI), we should stop for a moment to ask what intelligence is. *Intelligence* is the mental ability that allows you to function successfully in a given situation. That's about it, really. Academics have been arguing about this for centuries and still can't agree on much more than that.

It's from this definition of *intelligence* that I define *Integrated Intelligence* as the ability to draw on the extended mind and all its intuitive capacities to function successfully and solve problems in your life. The extended mind, in turn, is consciousness that extends beyond

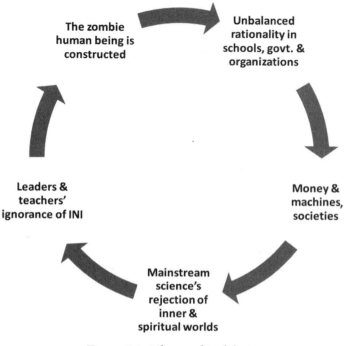

The zombie human being is constructed

Unbalanced rationality in schools, govt. & organizations

Money & machines, societies

Mainstream science's rejection of inner & spiritual worlds

Leaders & teachers' ignorance of INI

Figure 1.1. The zombie delusion

the individual's brain, and connects us with spiritual realms. So, in a nutshell, Integrated Intelligence is using all the abilities of the mind, including the psychic, to live the life you want.

INI allows you to perform at least seven core mental functions.

Integrated connection is the ability to sense the connections between and among things. Integrated perception includes the higher order enlightenment experiences where the individual's sense of self expands out beyond the immediate body.

Integrated location is the capacity to sense where things are, without having prior information.

Integrated diagnosis is the ability to intuitively find the cause of problems.

Integrated recognition is being able to immediately know somebody or something without ever being told about them or it.

Foresense is when you sense what is going to happen in the future.

Integrated evaluation involves being able to intuitively determine the wisdom or value of different options and choices.

Inspiration refers to creative knowledge and ideas that come from spiritual sources, not the conscious mind.

There are also two outcomes, which emerge from the successful application of INI.

Wisdom, which results from the capacity to use INI to create a life that is deeply meaningful and in alignment with your highest needs.

Transformation. This is a core shift, lifting you toward greater wisdom and intelligence and creating a higher level of consciousness. This causes a transformation of your entire being.

WHERE INTEGRATED INTELLIGENCE COMES FROM

To speak in slightly simplistic terms, the knowledge in your mind arises from two sources. The first is mundane knowledge gleaned from life experience, and the way your mind processes that experience. A lot is known and has been written about this in mainstream psychology. You can find out about it by opening any psychology textbook. The second source is beyond the brain, the home of the INI. This extended mind incorporates several different sources of information. First, there are the energy fields contained within each individual thing and the universe itself. The second source of transpersonal knowledge is the information that is given to you by Spirit.

*Spirit will is the absolute essence of human consciousness
and power until you show you can handle it.*

Spirit, in turn, consists of two channels of information. The first are spiritual entities, sometimes known as spirit guides, who have chosen to oversee part or all of your life, and guide you through it. We all have them, although many people are completely unaware of this fact.

The kind of information you are given by Spirit depends on your spiritual maturity, and how much you need it. The second category of Spirit is the wisdom of the universe itself. Personally, I like to call this intelligence "God," but this word has different meanings for different people. I tend to think of it in impersonal terms, rather than the personal God of religious lore. When you access the wisdom of God you will have transcended the need for spirit guides, because you will have become one with whatever it is you are perceiving, and all the knowledge that you require will open up to you in that present moment.

Now, even though the voice of Spirit is not in your immediate control, you can actively ask it for help. You can, and should, develop a relationship with Spirit. The more you actively seek out the assistance of Spirit, the more Spirit is able to work with you.

If you show that you are a person of wisdom, Spirit will repay you by giving you more knowledge, and by implication, more power. When I first began my spiritual journey, I met an Australian Aboriginal woman named Maria, who clarified this point for me. Maria was an intuitive counselor and a clairvoyant. Being young and naive, I sought her out for help. I have never forgotten what she told me. She said, "You will be given power by Spirit. But not yet." I asked her why. She said, "Because you are not ready for it. If it was given to you now, you might destroy it." That was almost two decades ago.

What she told me was true—for all of us. Spirit will not grant you higher knowledge and power until you show you are ready to work with the power in a responsible way.

SPIRIT AND THE SAGE

What you *can* do, regardless of where you are on your journey, is to take small steps, and work with Spirit in the only place you will find it—the here and now. This book is about those small steps. All it takes is a moment for you to connect with your Integrated Intelligence and its innate wisdom. The wisdom comes in the process of applying that information to life and learning from the process.

Spirit will give you tests.

Mastering INI takes time, application, and discipline. Spirit will give you many tests. Thankfully, they usually come one at a time. So you can work your way through them, step by step. Even Sages get an apprenticeship.

It is said that in the journey toward Spirit, the person who arrives at the destination is never the same as the person who starts out. Each step of the way will transform you a little.

Your wants and needs will change too, and become less ego-centered. Your goals will transform along with you. It is not necessarily a bad thing that we start out a little narcissistic. To some degree this is inevitable, so don't beat yourself up whenever you catch yourself being a show pony. Have a good laugh instead. Like it or not, a large part of your mind exists in the alienated ego state, and your dreams and desires are often a projection of the ego's pain, hurt, and insecurity. If you are completely honest, eventually you will see these egoic goals for what they are, and simply let them go. That's not quite as easily done as said. Ego is a trickster. Relax with that truth, hold gently to your desires, but be willing to let them go when they no longer serve you.

In the end the world will be the better for it. Both personal and planetary transformation will result from your application of Integrated Intelligence. Isn't that a wonderful thing?

THE MANY VOICES FROM WITHIN

Before you can use INI to live your soul purpose, you will have to learn more about how your mind works. There are multiple voices competing for attention within your mind, and it is imperative that you learn to distinguish among them. It is not difficult to let go and receive information from within. However, identifying the voice behind the idea is not so easy.

This confusion comes from the fact that we tend to identify with the personality construct—the ego. A prime function of your ego is to maintain the status quo. When the Sage begins to rise from within you, your ego will begin to lose power. This process represents death to the ego, and it thus will resist with all its might. This is something you really have to appreciate if you are to truly connect with your Sage. If you don't, instead of becoming the Sage, you just might become the silly old twit. Just between you and me, there are enough of those folks around already.

How can you distinguish the voice of the ego from that of the Sage? There are recurring themes, which tend to give the ego's game away. Take a look at the list in table 1.1 below, and note the distinctions between ego and the Sage.

TABLE 1.1. THE EGO VS. THE SAGE

THE EGO	THE SAGE
Sees itself as the center of the universe, and tries to establish observers.	Knows that he or she is part of a greater whole.
Insecure. Needs constant approval from others.	Knows himself or herself. Releases needs of approval from others.
Lives in a state of constant desire, in the past or future.	Lives within peace and presence.
Seeks control and power over situations and people. Pushes for outcomes.	Knows when to let go and listen to Spirit. Takes gentle action that honors all.
Runs from pain, uses it for attention and emotional leverage.	Takes responsibility for pain and allows a healthy expression of pain.
Blames and seeks revenge.	Uses anger responsibly, including as a spur to take appropriate action.
Death-denying. Seeks to maintain things as they are, or return to the past.	Permits change and transformation, understands all things are impermanent.

When you listen to your inner voice, simply ask yourself whether the intention behind it is Sage-like or ego-like. If it tries to tell you that you are the star, or that you can have it all, that is your inner silly twit speaking. Tell it to sit down and behave itself. But do it gently. The best way to know the ego is to develop a close relationship with it.

> *The best way to know the ego is to develop a close relationship with it. Befriend it. Love yourself.*

Befriend it. Don't try to pretend ego is not there. That will just drive it into the shadows, where it will gain more power over you. Remember, each time you judge yourself or deny parts of yourself, you retract from the unconditional love that is your birthright. So it is a case of loving self-discipline. In the following chapters you will learn how to discipline the ego while retaining a loving relationship with it.

WAYS OF KNOWING

We have several ways of knowing, which can be roughly divided into two categories: rational and intuitive. Figure 1.2 shows the main ways of knowing we can use to journey the road to our bliss.

Rational Ways of Knowing

Rational ways of knowing are well known to most people, so I will just mention them briefly here. *Classification* is the process of determining the common qualities of physical things and concepts, and placing them into categories. This emerged as a dominant way of knowing about half a century ago in Europe. *Analysis* necessitates breaking things down in order to understand how they function. It really gained a foothold in Western society around 1800. *Experimentation,* which caught on around 1850, involves testing things under controlled conditions. In modern science, repeating those tests to the satisfaction of trained peers is required in order for the conclusions to be deemed valid.

Mathematical/logical and *verbal/linguistic* ways of knowing have

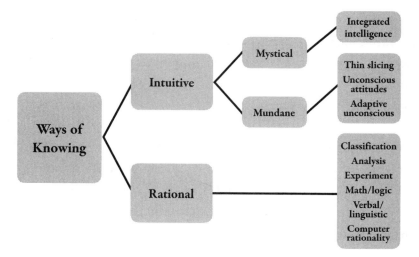

Figure 1.2. Rational and Intuitive Ways of Knowing

been around a long time, and underpin the first three ways of knowing. Math and logic are rules based. They allow us to make sense of much of the world through the rational mind. Language allows us to name things, and communicate more effectively. Both of these two ways of knowing bring us into the left brain, and create distance from the thing we are observing or talking about. Finally, computer rationality is a relatively recent development. In essence it is processing reality through electronic media. For example, whereas once meteorologists would go outside to look at a wind vane or a rain gauge (feeling the elements directly), they now receive their information online, with the data being processed via computer models.

The development of all these rational ways of knowing has led to the alienated mind becoming even more dissociated in modern cultures, because they disconnect us from the world.

Intuitive Ways of Knowing

In contrast to the rational, intuitive ways of knowing are not well understood in modern cultures. If we define *intuition* as "subtle inner feelings that prompt us toward a certain perception, attitude, or action," then intuition has more than one voice and various sources.

I divide intuition into two broad categories: mundane and mystical. Both contain useful types of insight, which you can use to your advantage as you move through life. However, both may also contain prompts that can be negative or distracting. We need to learn how to discriminate between them.

Mundane Intuition

Mundane intuition is the brain's way of communicating information through subtle feelings. The mind is, in part, a kind of self-organizing, data-processing machine. The data goes into the brain via the five senses, and then the mind-computer crunches it. The mind organizes the information all by itself, and we don't have to think about it. The unconscious mind communicates its "understanding" to the conscious mind via subtle feelings—intuitions.

Mundane intuition is brain-based. It contains no ESP.

There is nothing mystical or extrasensory about mundane intuition, so you can find references to it in mainstream psychology. Mundane intuition includes our unconscious attitudes. These are beliefs and judgments that we hold. They may, for example, lead us to size people up in the first few seconds that we see them.

Mundane intuition can serve a positive function, as some general perceptions about kinds of people, places, and things can protect us, or allow us to sense an advantage in a certain situation. A policeman seeing someone shuffling along nervously while lowering his gaze might intuit that the person is somebody with a guilty conscience.

Another kind of mundane intuition is "thin-slicing."* Thin-slicing is when we make an unconscious judgment about something based on a small sample of data. When we meet someone for the first time we may form judgments in the first few moments, based on what we see,

_____

*Malcolm Gladwell uses this term in his book *Blink,* which is all about mundane intuition. You can find Gladwell's book and others about mundane intuition in the Recommended Reading section.

hear, smell, and so on. The information we receive may be barely conscious, and may pass in milliseconds, but we process the information nonetheless.

The final kind of mundane intuition I will refer to is implicit knowledge, where we have learned something, and it becomes habitual and unconscious. Implicit learning can help us perform certain activities, such as when we drive a car without having to think about what we are doing. However, the negative aspect of implicit knowledge is when we apply the wrong procedures or behaviors when we misread a situation.

Mundane intuition is useful and real. I recommend that you take some time to understand it. Take advantage of it, as I do in my life. The more conscious you are of the feelings prompted by mundane intuition, the greater will be your wisdom in any given situation.

However, mundane intuition does not explain a great many kinds of intuition, and certainly doesn't explain Integrated Intelligence as I have outlined it. Some mundane intuition writers go to great lengths to distance themselves from any concepts related to mysticism and ESP. In doing so they lose the opportunity to explore and understand INI.

Mystical Intuition

Mystical intuition has a source beyond the physical brain. It involves ESP. It has both positive and negative expressions. The positive expressions include guidance from spiritual guides (trustworthy spiritual entities), the inner Sage, the universal reservoir of information, and from memories preserved within the consciousness fields of places.

We all have spirit guides. They give you information
to help you in your life. You can cultivate your
relationship with them.

We all have spirit guides. Yours can give you information, which will help you through your life's problems. It is not just one-way communication, though. The more you ask for help, the more assistance your guides will give you. If you want to take full advantage of INI, you should cultivate your relationship with your guides. You do this by asking them questions, listening for their guidance, and then applying it to your life.

By connecting with the Sage you will discover your soul template, which encodes your calling.

The second source of mystical intuition comes from your inner Sage. Although most of us identify ourselves with our personalities and ego, we each have a wiser self. Your Sage will, from time to time, prompt you with feelings and intuitions to help you out. Again, you can cultivate the relationship with your Sage by detaching from the ego. It is also important to stop believing that your mind chatter is really "you."

It is your higher self that will call you toward your bliss. By connecting with the Sage, you will learn about your soul template, as we shall discuss in the next chapter. The soul template encodes your calling.

The universe contains a vast reservoir of recorded information, sometimes referred to as the Akashic Field, after the Hindu term. This information is the third kind of positive mystical intuition. The "memory" of past and present is at your disposal. However, your capacity to tap in to it depends upon your intuitive development, the state of your mind at any given time, and also on whether you are given permission to access the data. There is some data that is not permitted for ordinary human beings, or those not ready to see it. One time, for example, I was trying to use a Light Trance (one of the INI tools, described in chapter 3) to "look" at the life of Jesus. I was subtly told I would not be allowed to see it. I have not tried since. Jesus may well be your friend, as many Christians like to say, but that doesn't mean he likes you snooping into his personal stuff.

The fourth kind of mystical intuition occurs when we receive a direct stream of information from the environment, including places and all of nature (plants and animals, Gaia and cosmos). Every place we enter contains information about its history at a psychic level. The most typical way this is communicated is via subtle feelings as we enter the place. Some might call this the "vibe." In every culture if there is a dwelling where a murder has occurred, the value of the house plummets. Why? Logically, if the past remains locked in the past, it should not matter even if it was the Yorkshire Ripper's holiday home. Everything that ever occurred there, bloody murders and rapes included, would be "finished." But it isn't, and that's what we intuit. Places have memories.

"Negative" Mystical Intuition

Simply because you have a gut feeling, a vision, or a voice tells you something, it doesn't make it the word of God. Mystical intuitions can become distorted by negative influences, and some of them simply come from the bad guys.

The first and most common cause of distortion comes from the mental projections of other people. Your mind is being constantly bombarded with the thoughts and emotional energies of others. The strongest are almost always negative, because it is when people want to control or disempower another person that their psychic "intention" becomes strongest.

This is hard for some people to accept, because we want to believe that the people around us love us and want the best for us. In certain ways, this is true. However, we all have fears and unacknowledged pain. Our egos try to arrange things so that they do not have to deal with those fears and pains. Our psychic projections are therefore mostly about control and power over others. If you are planning to relocate to another country, for example, your mother's abandonment issues may get triggered. She may send you a stream of manipulative psychic energy to try to "dissuade" you from going.

The negative psychic projections coming from family, friends, and others are usually unconscious. They would be shocked if they knew how destructive their thoughts often are.

These projections are often completely unconscious, and people would be shocked if they knew how destructive their mental projections often are. Recently for example, I have been dealing with some very destructive psychic energy from a female relative. Let's call her Wendy. This has been an ongoing situation. I rang her up just a few days ago, and she was as jovial as ever—"loving," even. At the same time, she cannot bear the idea of my achieving success in my work and profession. My ongoing self-work also threatens her. She wants to retain control of me, and she does retain some control of me via my "wounded" child, the part of me that she psychically manipulates. Although she may not be consciously aware of it, Wendy constantly pushes me down, because a higher degree of self-empowerment changes the psychic relationship between us.

You are also influenced by the collective energy fields around you. For example, major events in your family will influence the consciousness field of the family. If you have been working in one workplace long enough, your energy field will be partly embedded within it, and the dramas of the workplace will affect your psyche.

Collective consciousness fields incorporate all groups, from small gatherings of people, right through to the collective energy of humanity. The longer a group has been together, and the stronger their emotional bond, the more powerful is the field of connectivity. For example, with the downturn in the world's economic system at the time of the writing of this book, great psychic pressures have been placed on all of us. These relate to our beliefs about money and lack of abundance. Another theme that runs through the human collective psyche, and is returning big time, is the idea of Armageddon, the terror of the end of the world. Whenever the boat starts to rock a bit, that theme begins to ooze its way out of the collective mind of humanity. The human species' energy field begins to destabilize, and fear and anger become elevated. In such times, you really have to watch your mind to see if you are becoming ensnared in the collective muck.

Ideally, the leaders of this world could take preventive measures during difficult times to ensure that they don't get caught up in collective darkness. Unfortunately, the average garden snail knows more about quantum physics than your typical politician knows about Integrated Intelligence.

Negative Entities

Another "negative" source of mystical intuition is discarnate entities. This is one of the less pleasant things to learn and experience as you develop INI. Mommy and Daddy told us years ago that there were no monsters under the bed. They were trying to make you feel safe, and that is good. Unfortunately Ma and Pa weren't too attuned to the subtle energies that move through the shadows of the mind. The truth is that there are dark nonphysical entities, which affect human consciousness.

First, there are the souls of those who have passed away. The bad news is that people who die do not suddenly gravitate to paradise, as some religious and spiritual traditions suggest. Greatly disappointing as it is to have to accept, there will be no bevy of vestal virgins awaiting you if you've been really good. The energy of the departed remains fixed at the level of consciousness they developed in their lives, and they move to a realm that resonates at that same level. God doesn't send you to the top of the class simply because you drop dead.

The other bad news is that Grandpa is probably still hanging around. The psychic interaction between the deceased and those they have left behind often remains unchanged by their physical death. This is due in part to unresolved issues that remain. For example, I have from time to time experienced a great deal of psychic interaction with my father, despite his having passed away over a dozen years ago.

If you retain guilt, blame, anger, sadness, and so forth
toward someone who has died, your "relationship" will
continue at an energetic level.

Much of this energetic exchange is unconscious and emerges from codependence, typically involving needs to take and give away power.

If you retain lingering guilt, blame, anger, sadness, and so forth toward someone who has died, or if they retain similar attitudes toward you after death, your "relationship" will continue at an energetic level.

There are also what I might refer to as "dark energies." These are spiritual entities that have been emotionally damaged and retain little spiritual light. They range from the human, to the humanlike, and to those that are not human at all. These entities may try to draw you into their darkness.

Now, before you run out of the room screaming . . . it is true that some people will be greatly affected by such energies in their lifetimes. Still, I am not going to deal with this subject in depth in this book. Let me just emphasize that as you travel along your spiritual journey, you may become aware of them. However, you do not need to worry because if that time comes, you will already have developed enough power and wisdom to deal with them.* I am not going to pretend that this may not be quite a demanding test for those who have to face it.

Meanwhile, take one step at a time. The best protection against dark energy is to keep your ego in check (dark energy loves to build up and feed off egos). Refine your emotional energy by maintaining a mind-set of gratitude and positivity, and by releasing negative emotional attitudes. And do your healing work. Make sure you address your psychological or spiritual issues, and pay special attention to the needs of the wounded child within. Most of all, work at bringing your mind into the peace and surrender of presence. In that state you will receive all the knowledge you need to deal with your soul and karmic issues. In the remainder of part 1 you will find more information about the specific applications of the INI Connecting tool, which will help to protect you from the less pleasant energies of a connected universe.

Negative influences on your consciousness tend to be at their most pronounced when you are making a big shift in your life—changing jobs, starting up a business, establishing new relationships (or leaving

---

*At a later point, I may write another book for those who have used Integrated Intelligence over an extended period, and go into this in more depth.

old ones behind), working hard on spiritual issues, and so on. This is because the energy shifts within your mind are greatest at these times, and any shift in your psyche affects the energy fields within which your mind is embedded. That especially means those of your family, close friends, and lovers, past and present.

> *Dark energy enters your energy field through emotional pain. It also builds up and feeds off egos. The best protection against dark energy is to heal the hurt within and to keep your ego in check, and to bring the mind into presence. In presence your mind will be fully connected to the body, which ironically is absolutely vital for full spiritual realization. It is when parts of our consciousness split from the body that dark entities can exploit open doorways into our minds.*

Times of marked change always involve a "test," where your consciousness field becomes destabilized as you process emotional and spiritual issues. If you "pass" the test, the energy shifts and the issues may be resolved. Your psychic connections with others may then change. The psychic control that others have had over you will be diminished, and your need to exist in a state of co-dysfunction will be lessened.

Your energy field will then vibrate at a slightly higher level. However, if you do not process the energy (that is, you "fail" the test), your energy patterns will not shift. Chances are that the goal you were trying to achieve at a physical level—the relationship, the business, or the healing process—will also fail.

INTUITION IN A NUTSHELL

I summarize the various types of intuition below, moving from the most readily verifiable and mundane to the most mystical and spiritual.

- Unconscious attitudes and judgments
- Thin-slicing (rapid, unconscious judgments based on small amounts of data)
- Implicit knowledge related to automatic responses, from habit and conditioning
- Psychic projections from other people, collectives of people, and discarnate entities
- The consciousness fields from the environment, including places, and all of nature (plants and animals, Gaia and cosmos)
- The higher self/Sage; the call of the human spirit to align itself with its purpose
- Spirit guides; personal spiritual guidance including creative inspiration
- The Universe/God (however you define "It")

It is often hard to distinguish between these. However, you will get better at it as you work more closely with INI. The more grounded you are in the body and in presence, the easier it is to "know."

START SWIMMING

I developed the theory of Integrated Intelligence based upon years of work with people who exhibit these cognitive capacities. I have employed all of them to some degree in my own life journey. Speaking scientifically, there is no definitive proof for any of the mental capacities of INI. If you look into the field of parapsychology (PSI), you will find both hardcore skeptics and vociferous proponents. Their preferred intellectual position is one of beating each other over the head with blunt, heavy instruments.

I'm obviously a proponent of psi experience, such as clairvoyance, telepathy, ESP, precognition, and psychokinesis, but you will be glad to hear that I have put away my blunt instrument, at least for the duration of the writing of this book. There are valid arguments on both sides of the fence. I realized that I could spend a lifetime arguing the science and philosophy of all this, and still be none the wiser. So, I decided to put away the books for several years, and just jump in and test the water. After about five years of swimming in the volatile currents of the human consciousness field, I discovered the knowledge that you find in this book. I then swam ashore and once again dipped my head into a few books of science and philosophy, attended conferences (blunt instruments provided), and produced a Ph.D. dissertation and a few academic books and papers about INI.

All the while though, I have avoided getting lost in the human intellect. Without the nourishment of Spirit, rationality is a desert for the human soul. I keep returning to the waters of Spirit, to grounded presence. I took the best of both worlds, threw away the unhelpful bits, and the result is what you see in this book.

> *Without the nourishment of Spirit, rationality is a desert for the human soul.*

Nowadays I use INI every day of my life. I make few decisions, large or small, without it. I am very conscious that as I write this book, I am being guided and inspired through every page. For example, even as I began writing this section, I suddenly noticed that a song was playing in the back of my mind. It was the Australian band Midnight Oil's '80s song, "Best of Both Worlds." I think you can see how it helped me.

In the end, you will learn more about INI and your soul purpose by working with INI directly. The intellectual part is fine, but intellectualism without hands-on practice is just head stuff. I suggest you start swimming right away.

FINAL WORDS

Integrated Intelligence is the lifeblood of humanity. However, we have been sold the lie that it doesn't exist. Over a period of centuries, we have cut ourselves off from this essence of our being. It is a setback, to be sure, but merely a temporary one.

Rationality without intuition produces greatly impoverished human beings. Zombies. The intuition of our place in the cosmos has become muddled. Yet Integrated Intelligence has not gone away. The capacity to activate it has simply become diminished. We can rekindle its fire to empower our bliss.

two
The Soul Template
What It Means for Your Journey

The secret, they say in the New Age movement, is that you can have whatever you want, be whatever you want, if you just believe it enough. What they don't usually tell you is that each human being has a soul template with very specific needs.

For the soul, any old goal will not do. It has to be something that is aligned with your aptitudes and your unique spiritual "issues." What's more, the big picture is that you are part of a greater context—the evolution of humanity and cosmos. You need to work within a framework that is not just about freedom, but also about responsibility to the greater dynamic within which your ego exists.

In this chapter you are going to learn about the soul template and how to identify its nature. And you are going to learn about its cosmic context. As I will explain in more detail in chapter 8, your calling is not a job. It is a creative expression that meets the deep needs of your soul. And because each soul is different, that calling varies from person to person. There is no destiny and no life plan in any more than a general sense.

Imagine being on a ship in rough seas. You can't see much but the blackness of midnight. Suddenly the captain tells you to get out and start swimming for Jamaica, because the weather is nice there. You ask him where Jamaica is, and how far. He says, "I'm the one who asks questions around here, now get moving!" He gives you a good kick in the butt and overboard you go.

So there you are sucking in water in the dark in the middle of the ocean, clueless about where you are, and swimming round and round in circles, getting really tired. You start thinking all is lost, and begin fiddling round in your trousers, because that's what an awful lot of people do when they have too much time on their hands. That's when you find that the captain has kindly strapped a little guidance device round your waist, which responds to your input. It's a bit hard to work out at first, but because your life depends on it, you soon get the hang of it. You tap in the coordinates, and it gives you information about direction and weather conditions—although at times they seem annoyingly cryptic. Before you know it you are making good speed toward the Caribbean.

Life is a bit like that. You arrive clueless and have to start swimming real quick. The guidance device is Integrated Intelligence. It's time to stop fiddling around in your trousers and start using it.

THE SOUL TEMPLATE

Your soul template is the body of information encoded at the core of your soul, which consists of three aspects.

Soul issues. These are belief structures, ingrained patterns of behavior and attitudes that you tend to carry with you from life to life. They emerge from the biography of all the lives you have lived.

Karmic record. This is the record of your past lives and the actions you have taken in them. In particular it relates to relationships with other souls. You will tend to incarnate with the same souls with whom you have developed your soul issues. Therefore, karma is directly related to your soul issues.

Soul aptitudes. These are your key physical, mental, and creative abilities. To some degree they may change from lifetime to lifetime, but will tend to remain fixed around a core theme, such as music, writing, physical expression, and so forth. It is possible that they may change radically, if that is deemed necessary to achieve your soul purpose: to heal and grow in your capacity to create and love.

As figure 2.1 indicates, beyond the soul template are the group oversoul template and the human oversoul template. These consist of the psychological and spiritual issues contained within collective energies of your soul group and of humanity itself.

Each of us has a soul group, which consists of perhaps several hundred souls. These souls have long-standing relationships with each other, and tend to share a lot of karma. When you meet someone from your soul group, you will automatically be attracted to them if you are attuned to your intuition. This is *integrated recognition,* one of the core mental functions of INI. When Paul Potts, the winner of *Britain's Got Talent,* first saw his wife-to-be in a crowded restaurant (it was an Internet date), he knew who she was straightaway, even though he had never seen a photo of her. There was a soul connection.

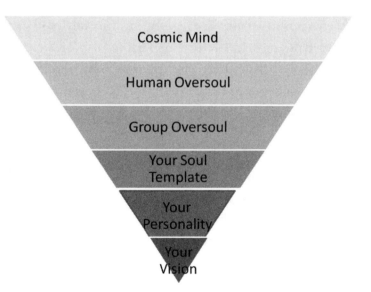

Figure 2.1. Your vision in the context of cosmic evolution

Begin by listening to Spirit and developing a basic understanding of your soul template. Then you can step off on the right foot and avoid a lot of wasted time trying to figure out who you are and where you are going.

It is helpful to understand the prime issues of the human oversoul, because that will enable you to understand the big picture in which you are embedded. The central issue of the human oversoul template can be summed up in one word: *love.* The movement of all souls and soul groups is toward the integration of the alienated mind, and in particular the shadow (consciousness centered in judgment, fear, blame, and anger). Our collective karmic issue is a tendency to cut ourselves off from the light, and then to go into fear, control, and separation, from which arise the innumerable expressions of the abuse of power that define so much of human history.

Certain New Age spiritual and religious philosophies do not address these aspects of living an empowered life. Being told you can manifest a Ferrari by imagining it hard enough doesn't tell you much about the evolution of humanity. The spiritual journey is not simply about what you as a personality (ego) want, nor how you can get it fast and at a bargain price. It is about being part of a greater purpose. Once you understand the soul template and the human oversoul, then you can begin to create the specific life you want with full integrity. It is so much easier when you know who you really are, who we really are.

First, know thyself.

Many people go about life the opposite way. They step off onto life's journey and wait for life to show them who they are, while all the time trying to impose the ego's view of things on circumstances. Besides being more honoring to yourself and your species, it is more efficient to begin by listening to Spirit and developing a basic understanding of your soul template. Then you can step off on the right foot and avoid an awful lot of wasted time. As you will be listening to your inner Sage, life will teach you infinitely more, and your capacity

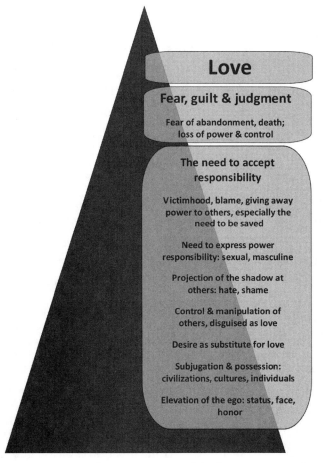

Figure 2.2. The prime issues of the human oversoul

for wisdom will be much greater. Your actions will be aligned with Spirit.

In Practice 2.1

℮ *Listening to Spirit First*

This exercise will particularly benefit those who are just beginning to work through the ideas of this book, and who want to get a greater sense of their inner world and INI.

Each morning make time for a short meditation of five minutes. For the first four minutes or so (there is no need to make it mathematically precise), relax, focusing upon your breath and allowing yourself to let go. In this space you are releasing the ego and its desires, which create a tension within the mind that shuts off the voice of the Sage.

Use some short affirmations, and release whatever wants and expectations have been clouding your mind. Affirm: "I now release my desire for (goal/expectation)" and "I surrender to the will of Spirit."

At the end of the four minutes make a single minute of time for listening to Spirit. Simply allow your mind to become quiet and pay attention. You can use a small affirmation or prayer such as "I allow this moment for the voice of Spirit." Note any words, feelings, or images that come to mind during that time, and simply allow them to be, without judgment or attachment. If you receive no intuition, then give thanks, for a silent mind is a great gift in itself.

Finally, take a minute or so to feel yourself fully connected with your body. Feel your breath moving in and out. Feel your consciousness fully embedded within your feet, legs, abdomen, arms and so on.

If done regularly, this little meditation will help you begin your daily journey in alignment with Spirit, and keep you moving steadily along the road of bliss.

The existence of the soul template brings something crucial to attention. If you get nothing else from this book, please get this: if you choose goals that are not aligned with your soul template, you will set up an internal conflict as the ego struggles to enforce its will, while the inner Sage is telling you to go another way. You will become spiritually disoriented.

Second, if you have an internal contradiction it is unlikely that you will put out the positive creative energy capable of sustaining you on the path to those goals. Internal contradiction is inevitable if you do not acknowledge your soul aptitudes and address your soul issues.

You do not necessarily need to have first-hand knowledge of your karmic record because karma is directly related to your soul issues, which tend to emerge from the karma of past lives. In the greater scheme of things, Spirit is more concerned with addressing soul issues than getting even for karmic impropriety. The main purpose of karma is merely for you to learn as a soul, not for Big Daddy in the Sky to punish you for your misdeeds. The essence of the spiritual journey is learning to relax into the present moment, and getting caught up in past life recall may be a hindrance to that. If there is a necessity for you to know about some past life incident, it will be made known to you. Finally, remember that the single greatest function of remembering lost pasts is to release them.

> *If you choose goals that are not aligned with your soul template, you will set up an internal conflict between your ego and Spirit.*

The upshot is this. No matter how positive and determined you are at a conscious level as you try to live your dream, no matter how many "manifestation" visualizations you do, or how much "love 'n light" you put out into the universe, if you are unaware of your soul template, your deep mind may contradict your conscious intention. The affirmative action you take and the "good vibes" you consciously generate will be negated by the chaos within your psyche. You have to work with your inner world at a deep level even as you create your bliss.

Soul Issues

Soul issues reflect karmic issues. They are the habits of the soul. Inevitably they center upon the appropriate expression of power, because this is a prime theme of the human oversoul. When the soul is balanced and the Sage has come to the fore of the personality, we are able to express power in ways that enhance the development of our self and humanity. We learn to align our personal intentions with the higher self and cosmic intention. The need to gain power and control over others and life situations is greatly reduced.

We tend to adopt one of three common positions when we feel disempowered. I call this archetypal situation the *karmic triangle*. These positions are the victim, rescuer, and the persecutor. Although it may not appear so at first glance, all are attempts at gaining power and control, albeit misguided attempts. The victim feels powerless to direct his life, or is too frightened to act, so gains a sense of control by ensuring he gets a regular supply of Nazi boots to the face, just to make him feel at home. He then proceeds to weep (attention-seeking as a substitute for love) or just moans and groans a lot. He gets a great deal of satisfaction out of knowing that he has been done wrong and that it is not his fault.

The rescuer is happy to join in this game. He also feels lost and out of control, can't deal with his own stuff or get what he wants. Instead, he seeks to make himself feel good by saving the world, especially its victims. Before you know it, he has a tribe of victims in tow. On the surface the rescuer looks all nice and kind, but he is a possessor of souls. He needs to control others and keep them down, so that he is not left alone to look at his own stuff. If he ever ran out of a steady supply of victims, he'd be completely lost.

The final player in the karmic triangle is the persecutor. He's the one who gets all the bad press, because he's dressed in a Nazi uniform with nice shiny steel-capped boots. He's a bully who likes nothing better than crushing skulls, but deep down he's a wimp. Typically, the persecutor was a victim of bullying in his childhood, and his deep anger and rage at his own powerlessness is projected out onto the world.

*The key to transcending soul issues is recognizing
the patterns, healing the pain and false beliefs,
then taking right actions.*

We all play each role at different times, but many people have a tendency to gravitate toward one. My soul issues resonate at about 70 percent victim, 20 percent rescuer, and 10 percent persecutor. When I am confronted with difficult passages in my life, I tend to revert back to that kind of pattern.

Soul issues are not a life sentence. They tend to reflect karmic habits, which can be effectively managed and even broken. The Sage is aware of these patterns; luckily she has a little bag of tricks she can use to return to a position of genuine power. The key to transcending karma is recognizing the patterns, healing the pain and false beliefs that lie behind them, taking the correct actions that show newfound wisdom, then bringing the mind into the present.

You will learn more about the karmic triangle in chapter 11, when we discuss relationships in greater depth.

The Karmic Record

Your karmic record is the total of unresolved energies from previous incarnations. This includes unfinished business with other souls.

It can be helpful to get a sense of your karmic record, but it is not necessary to have a full past-life recollection of all the stuff that has gone on before. That would just clutter up your mind, and probably leave you with more guilt, blame, and pain than you could possibly deal with. That is why the memory of these things is erased from our minds at birth.

You will get a feel for your karmic record by paying attention to your soul issues. Pay attention also to your dreams, as these often contain narratives from past lives. Occurrences from past lives are usually in symbolic form, but sometimes they are literal.

Recently I had a dream that contained a symbolic narrative of past lives. I was walking past a line of dead, preserved bodies lying on the ground. They were dead soldiers, and for some reason they had chosen to have their bodies preserved in grotesque positions, with their faces contorted and parts of their abdomens extruding, as if releasing the fetid gases that all corpses do.

This was not a pleasant dream, but touches upon my past lives as both soldier and warrior in different incarnations. As a little boy of less than five years old, I recall having horrifying dreams that army tanks and jeeps were rolling down the road to come and take me away to war. They were accompanied by a sense of fear, horror, and helplessness.

I have also had graphic actual past-life dreams. In one past-life recall, which I experienced while I was sleeping (calling it a "dream" would be a misnomer), I found myself lying on a hillside amid some very green vegetation, screaming in utter agony, having received a mortal wound through the lower abdomen. I was dying alone and in excruciating pain. I knew it was a war zone, and I had just been in some kind of combat. The distinction from an ordinary dream was the completely realistic emotional content, experienced as if it was a real-life event.

I saw no actual details of being wounded, and had no idea whether it was a bullet, bayonet, or other kind of weapon that had wounded me. I did sense that it was a relatively modern war. What is important is the emotional energy of the event. This is what leaves a lasting scar on the soul template, and becomes core to soul issues.

The abuse of power expressed via the mass death and destruction of war is one of the prime themes within the human oversoul. The hundreds of millions of horrifying war deaths, both civilian and military, throughout history are part of our collective energy. It is thus part of the karma of the human oversoul. It is something we need to appreciate and integrate. Just as the abuse of power and control is the essence of our personal soul issues, the abuse of power and control is a core theme of human consciousness evolution, as figure 2.2 indicates. Right now this theme is emerging again from the depths of the collective. A strong fear and sense of powerlessness, along with a tendency toward irresponsible expression in blaming the other, is being triggered by the global economic crisis.

Typically, the people with whom you now live your life were also involved in your past lives. We tend to play out the karmic triangle, with roles as victim, rescuer, and persecutor in games of power and control. We all retain a subtle sense of our past lives and relationships, even if we do not consciously remember them. This can create exchanges of psychic energy between the individuals involved, and typically such exchanges are completely unconscious (although they may spill over into real life "dramas," as I shall relate in the following chapters).

Karma plays out not just at the physical level.
There are battles for power and control at

an energetic level that are just as crucial
to the evolution of humanity and our souls.

From what I have been able to sense, I believe that in one past life I raped and killed a certain relative of mine, a woman again in this lifetime. I have not seen her for a dozen or more years, and in fact was not aware of this karma until about five years ago. What I have been long aware of is that her psychic energy tends to follow me around, trying its best to castrate me, which is quite a logical expression of revenge when you come to think about it. My male power is a threat to her, and since she is part of my group oversoul, she senses when I am more fully expressing my masculine power. Unfortunately, she has been deeply hurt again in this lifetime (she was raped at least one time that I know of), and her wounded child cannot distinguish between genuine male empowerment and abusive male power. So I have a real battle with her energy whenever I want to step forward in my life.

Karma thus plays out not just at a physical level. There are battles for power and control at an energetic level that are just as crucial to the evolution of humanity and our souls. This is all quite perfect. You can see that these psychic dramas center upon the responsible expression of power, and in particular of sexuality. The two often go hand in hand. When I got shafted in battle in a past life, through the lower abdomen, I was the one being penetrated, violated.

When you are about to be re-born into a physical body, you come to some agreement with your spirit guides about the overall essence of your journey. It is very likely that members of your immediate family, and your close relatives, will have karmic issues with you. Beyond that, there is a general life plan of the people you will meet and interact with over the course of the upcoming lifetime. The integrated recognition of INI informs us, albeit subtly, when we bump into karmic friends and foes. The Sage's greater level of Integrated Intelligence often allows him to feel the depth of such connections.

The same stories tend to get repeated in some form over several lifetimes, until you transcend that energy pattern. As you transcend your soul issues, you will alleviate your karma. However, there may be some requirement for you to feel the emotions you helped generate in others, as well as the energy that you have created within the human collective energy field. How this is expressed will vary. Sometimes it may simply occur through a spontaneous visionary experience of great intensity. Other times it may require a physical incident or even a lifetime or more of experiencing equivalent situations that allow you to fully experience the energy involved.

Soul Aptitudes

Soul aptitudes are the particular physical and mental abilities that we have a capacity and passion for expressing. These are our gifts. They are determined, in part, by physical attributes, including genetics. However, they are also influenced by general abilities and habits acquired in past lifetimes. If you have played a stringed instrument in a previous life, then you will tend to pick it up more easily in this lifetime.

I believe that we all have a brilliance that we are meant to express. However, simply because you are really good at something does not mean that you should turn it into a career. It would be a mistake to think that you should become a professional gambler simply because you are good at playing cards. Sometimes it is simply not practical to turn an aptitude into a job. The key to distinguishing soul aptitudes from simple skills and abilities is to be aware of that which generates excitement within you. That's the note to listen for. Remember my story from the prelude, where my excitement hit high fever in a lecture by Ron Laura at the University of Newcastle? I never forgot that moment, and I let it direct me forward. Because I didn't have the understanding that I have now, I slipped off the path a few times, but I always returned.

THE SOUL TEMPLATE AND LIFE PURPOSE

Your soul seeks to achieve certain goals in each life. Mostly, these are related to soul issues and karma, while your soul aptitudes come into play as you express your brilliance. Ultimately all this comes down to the expression of power: its use and abuse, and the spirit's requirement that we learn to use it responsibly.

> *There is no destiny. You are free to create a*
> *life in alignment with your soul template and*
> *the collective human oversoul.*

There is no such thing as a concrete life purpose, as in the idea of destiny. Once you get that out of your system, you are free to go about expressing your life in a way that resonates with your spirit, and is in alignment with your soul template. To that extent, you are free—within the bounds of the evolution of the human oversoul and the cosmos we live within.

The Sages have always said that the soul speaks to you, but only if you listen. It will set you on the right path, tell you when to leave, when to rest, when to stop, and correct you when you get off track. How can we make the soul's voice clearer? How can we invite the soul to be with us whenever we need its guidance? And what actions can we take to honor its voice? In short, how can we exercise real power in this world? The rest of this book, particularly the next two chapters, will show you how.

In Practice 2.2

℮ Remembering Your Excitement

Before you go any further in this book, stop and do this short fifteen-minute exercise. Discovering the essence of your calling is simple, and this exercise will help clarify things for you.

Take a pen and paper and sit quietly somewhere alone. Now, going back as far as you can remember in your life, quickly list all the events that deeply moved you or excited your soul. These could be movies and books that really moved you, speeches that rocked your socks off, songs that made you weep or soar, people you met who deeply inspired you, images and pictures that jumped out at you from a shop window or a TV screen, or anything else that comes to mind. They could even be dreams and synchronicities, amazing and deeply meaningful coincidences. The events can be as big or small as you like. Sometimes the tiniest, most transient thing has the deepest meaning for us.

When you have finished, sit back and look over your list. What are the common themes and ideas? The dominant feelings? The recurring activities? What skills and aptitudes run through these seminal life events? What does it all mean to you? What is your excitement telling you? Write down the answers to these questions.

Reflect on this experience over the coming days and weeks. Your innate capacity for integrated recognition will automatically go to work to connect the dots. The patterns and meanings will become clearer. It is not necessary to name your calling from all this. You are just getting in touch with your excitement, beginning to really listen to your soul.

three

The Fourteen Tools of Integrated Intelligence

As soon as I realized that selling vacuum cleaners wasn't my soul calling, I was in a dilemma. I was going to quit Dusty, but what would I do next? Then the hand of God descended and delivered the message (or so it seemed). For it was then that I was whisked by the Dusty van into a large, multistoried house in a posh suburb of Newcastle, Australia, to try to sell my vacuum cleaner. When I stepped through the front door for the prearranged demonstration, a handsome, bearded Indian gentleman of early middle age introduced himself and his wife.

"Hello, I am Doctor Nanra, and this is my wife, Doctor Nanra."

I said "G'day."

His wife briefly acknowledged my existence, and showed me the room to vacuum. After I finished, I attempted to get my pitch started, but they pushed me out the door and drove away in their BMW before I could get a word out. That's why I had about an hour sitting on the curb waiting for the Dusty van to return and pick me up. At that moment in time the only friend I had was the unwieldy metal contraption at my side. I looked up at the fancy houses all around me on the leafy street, with their pretty front gardens and manicured trees. Suddenly it hit me! I knew what I wanted to be! I would become a doctor, just like the Dr. Nanras. Then I too would be rich, drive a BMW, and be able to push vacuum cleaner salesmen around. I was excited! It was a great idea. And at twenty-three years of age I wasn't too old to give it a go. I ended up sitting through the entrance exam for the medical degree at the University of Newcastle three years in succession. I recall one particular question on the paper, the last time round. They wanted to test the candidates' capacities for innovative thinking. My paper implored me to suggest 101 possible uses of a carrot. I came up with 102, and my last hypothetical innovation, which required the participation of a willing female of the human species, probably explains why they didn't let me anywhere near the medical degree program. And just as well for the sick people of Australia.

If I had known then what I know today, I could have saved myself some fruitless struggle. My desire to be a doctor was born of ego, not of Spirit. I had little awareness of my Sage at that age, and I did not know how to listen to the voice of Spirit. It would take me another ten years before I would really know how to actively engage that inner voice, and even longer to appreciate what intuition really is. And because I was coming mostly from ego, I had little true power. I was not able to get what I wanted, because I didn't even know what I really wanted.

But in the years since then I have discovered that there are specific tools we can use to develop intuition, and to empower our life—the key tools of Integrated Intelligence. One of my main goals in writing this book is to take often-vague mystical concepts, and provide simple tools you can use to tap in to the intuitive wisdom of Integrated Intelligence. The INI tools are genuine empowerment techniques because they will assist you in clarifying what you really want, avoiding what you don't want, and taking the right actions to get where you want to go. If you apply them in committed fashion over an extended period, you will be able to relax into the wisdom of the Sage, and make wise choices in an instant.

I learned much about these tools from other teachers. But I also innovated and invented things for myself. You can do the same. Because

Integrated Intelligence is everywhere all of the time, there are innumerable possibilities. Don't let my toolkit limit your thinking and your practice.

THE INI TOOLS

I am presenting the INI tools in order of their difficulty. You will not need much practice to develop proficiency with the easier ones, while the harder ones require more work. The final aspect of Tool 14, Connecting with the Wounded Child/Karmic Child, really requires a facilitator or counselor to be present, at least until you have developed a greater understanding of what is required.*

Tool 1. Five Breaths

Five Breaths is a presence technique, whose purpose is to bring your mind fully into the present moment and quiet the ego. To do this technique, simply stop whatever you are doing. You will need just a minute or so for the whole process, so make sure you are not doing anything that requires prolonged and careful attention.

You can do this with your eyes open or closed. Take a deep breath, and bring your attention to your breath moving in and out of your nose. Take a second breath, this time just a normal one, but still paying careful but relaxed attention to the feeling of the air moving through your nose. You may notice your chest rising and falling as you do this, and that is fine. If your attention is distracted by thoughts, just gently acknowledge them, and return to your breath. Remember, you are not your thoughts. Do this for a total of five breaths. It will bring you into presence.

That is Five Breaths in its entirety. It's very simple. You can do it as often as you want. It is a kind of mini-mindfulness meditation.

---

*I originally outlined several of these INI tools in an article I wrote for *Foresight* journal in February 2009. That article was a guide for researchers, about how to use Integrated Intelligence during research. It is titled "Futures Research at the Frontiers of Mind." You will find it listed in the recommended reading section.

Tool 2. Oneness Technique

This presence technique involves allowing yourself to become present "with that which is already present." Virtually every nonhuman form on this planet is present. The simpler the object, the better—best not to use a surrealist painting! Plants, books (close them first!), coffee cups, chairs, pencils, and so on are great. Just stop and allow yourself to feel the presence of a tree, flower, or potted plant. Animals and birds likewise exist in a state of presence. You can bring the mind to attention by observing them. As far as we humans go, children tend to be the most present. Without judgment, observe a child playing for a moment, and just allow the mind to become silent.

You can do the Oneness Technique for a minute or so, or you can prolong it if you want to turn it into a meditation. Spiritual teacher Leonard Jacobson taught this to me.* After doing the Five Breaths or the Oneness Technique you will be centered and present, so it is a good time to do energy readings, such as the Quick Check and the Feeling Sense (Tools 10 and 12).

Tool 3. Deliberate Feeling

These are procedures for actively changing your feelings to create a desired emotional state. They positively affect your energy field. They include just about any activity that changes your mental state: music, dancing, reading poetry, and so on. Deliberate feeling is a little different than just doing something that makes you feel good. It's more active than that.

First, choose the feeling you wish to develop, and second the activity that you are going to do. Make sure the feeling and the activity are compatible. The chart on page 53 provides a short list.

---

*You can see references to some of Leonard's books in the Recommended Reading section. Leonard Jacobson is a deceptively powerful teacher. The transformative power of his message can be missed by some because of its simplicity. Eckhart Tolle is another teacher with a similar message. In his book, *A New Earth*, he refers to a method very similar to the Five Breaths tool.

FEELING	ACTIVITY
Joy	Listen to joyful music, sing a joyful song, dance joyfully, or play with a child.
Confident, empowered, energized	Listen and move to empowering music, such as the theme from *The Power of One* or *Chariots of Fire*. Go jogging, work out at the gym, or dance.
Relaxed, peaceful	Listen to a CD of relaxing music, or relaxing sounds, such as running water. Watch a sunset, have a bath, go swimming, or get a massage.
Light-hearted, humorous	Talk to someone who you know is funny or watch a funny movie or TV show. Listen to recordings of silly laughter.
Excited, inspired, motivated	Jump up and down, skip like a child, listen to some inspiring music, read/listen/watch an inspirational book, CD, or movie. Do an inspiration meditation, where you imagine inspiration as light pouring down on to you from above.

You can use an affirmation before or during your Deliberate Feeling activity. Make it short, simple, and in the present tense. For example, "I stand in my power as a woman," "I now feel relaxed and peaceful," or "I allow myself to feel joyously happy." I suggest that your Deliberate Feeling sessions be about three to five minutes, but you can make them longer if you want. Repeat the process regularly, and it will begin to condition your brain and physiology.

Tool 4. Nonjudgmental Reframing
This process involves deliberately assigning nonjudgmental and positive meanings to events, people, and things with the aim of maintaining a positive, compassionate, and loving relationship with the world, and

a high-vibration energy field. It enables you to actualize an extremely empowering understanding that all spiritual seekers should become aware of: What happens in your life is not as important as the meanings you assign to what happens, and the subsequent state of mind you create. The vast majority of human suffering on this planet occurs not through events themselves—past, present, or future—but from the judgments made about them.

This is not to deny than a certain degree of suffering is inevitable for anyone living in a human body. It probably is. Throughout your life, you will face some, maybe many, difficult situations. Some of them will involve physical and emotional suffering, which is pretty much unavoidable. For example, the people you love dearest will all pass in time, as will you. There is nothing you can do about it. Some degree of mourning occurs as we let go. Yet even that will lessen or pass in time, if the emotions are allowed to express themselves fully, and you do not assign any unnecessarily negative meanings to the event. In fact it is attachment to the past that creates the suffering. Leonard Jacobson states that he felt no sorrow when his parents died, because his mind was completely present.

Let's say you are late for work and running for the bus. The bus driver is in a bad mood, sees you, accelerates with a wicked grin, and the bus disappears down the road. You have to wait ten minutes for the next bus. You can't believe it.

Now, at this point you have a choice. The choice is the meaning you assign to the event. You can move into blame and judgment: "Did you see that! My God, that driver is a complete and utter bastard! Now I'm late for work! The boss will be angry. This is another terrible day. Why can't I get organized! My life is a mess!" And so on. The feelings that go with this interpretation of events are anger, fear, blame, and self-loathing. This is a very unpleasant experience.

Another way to deal with the same event is to avoid judgment, blame, and self-persecution. "That driver must be having a bad day. Maybe he has problems at home. So I'm going to be late again. Now, how can I avoid this in future? Okay, I'll make sure the kids' lunches are packed the night before, and leave for the bus by 7:30 a.m. sharp. I'll apologize to the boss, and tell him I have changed my schedule so that it won't happen again. Anyway, I'm grateful that the next bus is only ten minutes away. It's not much difference. I can work twenty minutes late to show the boss I'm committed to my work." The feeling here is one of a more relaxed assertiveness.

The first of these responses is the victim stance, the second the stance of the Sage. The victim blames, while the empowered person takes responsibility for the actions, the results, the meanings he assigns, and for his emotions.

Now, if you accept that almost all the time it is not what happens that is causing your suffering—your anxiety, fear, dread, anger, sadness, frustration, and so on—it leaves you in a very, very, powerful position. It means nothing less than that your bliss is right here, right now. Think about that.

To employ Nonjudgmental Reframing, you can connect with your ego, the part of you that is doing all the blaming and cursing. Let the ego speak, and then gently correct it.

Your ego says, "I hate that driver! I wanna kill that SOB!"

You (as Sage and loving parent) say, "No, that doesn't help. He's gone, and that's that. It's okay. The next bus is here in ten."

The ego then says "Shit! The boss will have me strung up! It's the third time this week I've been late. This is the end!"

You as Sage say, "That probably won't happen. We'll apologize, and tomorrow we'll make sure we are on time. We'll have to organize the mornings a bit better. And we'll stay late after work to make up for the lost time. Let's make this a great day!" And so on. The key is that you identify with the Sage, and not the victim.

When you see and feel your inner victim rising, dialogue with it. Just as a parent has to be forceful with an angry or emotional child, you have to be forceful but gentle with the victim in you. The victim is very stubborn. It is the part of you that emerges from the hurts and beliefs of the wounded child. When you find yourself in the victim state, you can also stop and bring yourself into the here and now with either of the presence techniques. That will shut the victim up real fast.

This is a mental discipline. Simply witness any thoughts that come to mind and let them pass. Don't struggle with them. You, as Sage, are learning to develop the right relationship with your mind and your ego. The ideal attitude toward your ego is one of gentle parenting, not harsh condemnation. You are worthy of complete love; that means all of you, including your ego!

Tool 5. Intuitive Diary

The Intuitive Diary is a notebook where you record your intuitive feelings, images, prompts, synchronicities, and so on. I consider it to be the most important of all the tools for those people just beginning to use intuitive ways of knowing. It is the one that will most easily establish a close link between left- and right-brain thinking, and get you in touch with the subtleties of the intuitive mind.

You will need a good-size hardcover diary. It is worth buying a good one, because you want it to last. All the things you record in it may not make sense at the time of writing, but when you look back later, maybe even years later, you may find your recordings invaluable. Alternatively, you can put your Intuitive Diary on your computer, but—as with all important writings—make sure you have at least one backup file saved elsewhere!

I recommend that you use your Intuitive Diary to record your dreams, intuitions, the synchronicities you experience from day to day, impressions of meditations, and any auditory, visual, or feeling impressions that come to you at any time during the research process. I like to record not only my dreams, images, and feelings, but also my interpretations of them.

When I started keeping an Intuitive Diary many years ago, I wrote in it almost every day. As time went by I found I needed to write less. It is up to you how much time you want to invest in it. But do it as often as possible.

Tool 6. Affirmations

Affirmations are pro-active statements repeated to yourself, with the aim of creating positive belief structures, affirming desired goals, and enhancing your state of being. You can repeat Affirmations silently or out loud, depending on where you are. You can do them just about anywhere, anytime. But the best times are when you are relaxed. In particular, use them during Light Trances (see Tool 12), or just before and after sleep, for your deep mind will be most receptive and open at these times. Also, use them during Creative Imagination (Tool 7) and after the Connecting exercises (Tool 14) to condition desired beliefs or goals.

There are certain general rules for Affirmations.

- Keep them short and simple. Stick to one idea at a time, and generally speaking, use only one short sentence at a time, and repeat it at least three times. You can, of course, then move on to another affirmation when the first is complete.

- Write Affirmations down. You can write them on small cards and carry them in your wallet, pocket, or purse, and then read and repeat them whenever you want during the day. You can also write them on larger sheets of paper and place them on walls and mirrors. Alternatively, you can record them onto your MP3 player, and listen to them on public transport, or before you go to sleep.

- Keep Affirmations in the present tense, as if the thing is already extant or completed. Use "I am . . ." not "I will . . ." and "I have . . ." not "I want . . ."

- Keep them positive. Phrase them in terms of what you want, not what you don't want, or wish to avoid. "I enjoy flying, and find it exciting" is fine; "I am not scared of flying anymore" is not. If the affirmation contains the idea of what you don't want, your mind will gravitate toward that idea, not away from it. You cannot not think of a red sports car by saying "I am not thinking of a red sports car."

Tool 7. Creative Imagination and Feeling

This process involves deliberately putting images and feelings into your mind to imagine playing out desired scenarios, goals, and actions. I cannot emphasize how important the imagination is in creating your life the way you want. Everybody uses Creative Imagination every day. It's just that most people don't know it. Instead of using the imagination to create, they allow the mind to create them. Left to its own devices, the imagination comes under the control of the ego, and especially the ingrained beliefs of the mind. This means that all the negative and controlling energies from within can dictate your life.

Creative Imagination is one way to help overcome this dilemma. Creative Imagination is most powerful when it is done in conjunction with healing, and within the present moment. If you do not work on your healing, then Creative Imagination is not as powerful. Your mind cannot be fully in the moment if the wounded child is trapped in pain, feeling a lot of doubt and fear, and projecting a belief in scarcity. Using Creative Imagination without working on the psyche is a bit like having the car in first gear and reverse at the same time—they cancel each other out.

The rules of Creative Imagination are similar to those for Affirmation. Imagine yourself in the present, from the first person position (not as an outside observer), as if the action is being completed successfully by you within the present moment. Make sure that you work on the feelings as well as the images and sounds within your mind. The deep psyche responds most rapidly to feelings. Don't just imagine yourself rock climbing—feel the rock, feel the wind, feel the sun, and allow yourself to experience the feeling of calm, relaxed empowerment it brings.

Remember not to get lost in creative imagination. The real world you experience here and now is more important than the world of imagination. The real world is where the joy and beauty of Spirit comes to life. Creative imagination is a means to an end, not an end in itself.

Tool 8. Active Dreaming

Active Dreaming consists of recording dreams (in your Intuitive Diary), and learning to decipher and intuit their meanings. It may include the experience of lucid dreaming (where you are dreaming and aware you are in a dream). You will find the appendix "Interpreting Dreams and Visions" most helpful. There isn't too much that I can tell you here that you will not find out from referring to it or working it out for yourself. I will just mention a few things Active Dreaming will foster.

- It will assist with learning to distinguish among the many voices of the psyche. The different types of dreams are quite similar to the various sources of intuition, which I outlined in chapter 1.
- It will help you learn the language of the psyche—its symbols and intuitive prompts.
- It will help you identify your soul issues. The narratives of many dreams involve issues that are crucial to your spiritual journey.
- It will improve the connection between the logical and intuitive parts of your mind.
- It will get you in touch with your spiritual guidance.

Tool 9. Embracing Synchronicity

Embracing Synchronicity is using life's meaningful coincidences to guide you. Some things that happen to you are the universe's way of telling you something, or just helping you along your way toward your bliss. Life presents "clues" in the dance of creation. You can learn to notice meaningful coincidences as they occur, and intuit their meaning.

It is my experience that a serendipitous and adventurous approach to life facilitates synchronicities. A key point is bringing the mind fully into the present moment. Mystic Leonard Jacobson describes this beautifully in the video *Bridging Heaven and Earth.** In the exalted state of

*www.youtube.com/watch?v=eg6ONEmJNiU

complete presence, it is as if the cosmos comes alive. The deeper meaning and purpose of things becomes known as they unfold, and as the psyche and cosmos are in open dialogue. This is somewhat akin to the state of "flow," which is usually reported in mainstream psychology in mundane and reductionist terms.

The experience of synchronicity is, in its most exalted form, almost a kind of spiritual rapture. It is a direct affront to the critical/rational worldview. If you can suspend disbelief, synchronicity contains messages that will help guide your spiritual journey.

There's no need to go fishing for synchronicities, or to try to read more into things than are there. Worrying about the meaning of things will just take you out of presence, and presence is too important to lose through worrying that there might be a hidden meaning in something.

Keep present. Allow the universe to speak to you. It is a soft, gentle, and receptive process. Your inner Sage will let you know when something is meaningful. Any time you overanalyze, you go into the mind and into the ego. Then you are off the path of Spirit.*

You do not harness synchronicity. You allow it and embrace it.

Tool 10. The Quick Check

The Quick Check is a simple and incredibly useful tool, where you take a reading of the "energy" of an intended decision. The simplest way to do this is to draw a line across a page and write "0%" on the left-hand end of the line, and "100%" on the right-hand side. Then ask "What is the energy on my (doing this or that)?" For example, "What is the energy on my watching this movie?" and "What is the energy on my going to . . . for my holiday this year?" As with any form of divination, make sure the question is simple and clear. To take a percentage measurement, run a finger from your nondominant hand (left hand for right-handers, and reverse for left-handers) across the

---

*A great website dealing with synchronicities is Rob and Trish MacGregor's www.synchrosecrets.com. Some of my own synchronicities appear there.

line until you feel it stop. You might feel a tingle in your finger, or hit an invisible wall.

You can also do a Quick Check by running the same finger across the palm of your dominant hand. Hold your dominant hand sideways in front of you (i.e., with your fingers pointing sideways, not upward). In this case, the length of your palm replaces the line on the paper.

Run your finger from left to right (or right to left—it doesn't make any difference). You will feel a slight tingling sensation or pressure at the correct point on the line. I believe that there is an actual "energy" or force of some kind that forms at that point. I often feel it in quite a physical way. People who are just starting out with this technique need to be patient. It may take time to begin to feel the energy. The skill will build up slowly. I encourage you to persist. It is very easy to use the Quick Check and requires virtually no time commitment. As your finger flicks across the page during the Quick Check, you are connecting with the innate Integrated Intelligence you were born with. All the Quick Check does is translate that intelligence into a simple technology.

Use the Quick Check every day for a month, testing the energy on small decisions you are making. After a while it will become second nature. That does not mean that the readings will be perfect. This is an approximation process, and is open to distortion from the ego, external influences, and plain bad execution. Use it carefully.

You can also use the Feeling Sense or a Light Trance to further test the results. However don't do too much divination. In the end, you need to trust the reading you get. My experience is that the first reading is usually the most accurate. You will probably just confuse yourself if you mix up too many INI tools in one go.

There are numerous other ways you can use the Quick Check. Here are just a few.

- You can use the Quick Check to assess your own or another's need for approval or the level of responsibility you or they are taking for themselves.

- It can be used to assess whether an action you are considering taking to resolve a drama in your life is appropriate and will be effective.
- The Quick Check also offers you a way to measure the consciousness level at which a spiritual teacher, book, or teaching resonates. For instance, the percentage readings of the consciousness levels of people, groups, and humanity that you see in this book are all taken from my use of the Quick Check. When using the Quick Check, be careful not to go into ego and judge those whom you are reading. Think of it this way. You are not measuring people's intrinsic worth, but the amount of spiritual light moving through them. Remember also that this is a somewhat crude tool and measurement. It is one-dimensional, while the reality is that human beings are multidimensional and multifaceted.

Tool 11. Free-Form Writing

With Free-Form Writing, you take a theme, problem, or question, write it down, then just let go and begin writing whatever comes to mind. It is a bit like jumping into a car's passenger seat and being driven off. You lose control, but you can just relax and enjoy the ride. Stream of consciousness writing is used to enhance your creativity and to "flow" insight and wisdom. One way to develop this channeling process is to use it for writing, at least five minutes every day, no matter what. The word *channeling* may put some people off, but all it really means is to let go and allow information to flow through you.

Before your writing session, say a prayer or affirmation to Spirit, either to yourself or out loud. It may go something like this: "Spirit, lead me through this writing process, so that my words may be in alignment with Spirit."

Free-Form Writing can be used to address just about any issue or problem, for inspirational ideas, for personal business problems, for spiritual guidance, and so on. It can also be used by researchers. I used Free-Form Writing extensively throughout the writing of my doctoral thesis, but particularly in the first two years. A book that inspired me greatly in developing this process was Joan Bolker's *Writing Your Dissertation in Fifteen Minutes a Day*. Bolker's book is about writing a thesis through approximately four stages: the zero draft, first draft, second draft, and beyond.

In something of a synchronicity, I first came across the book while scrolling through Amazon.com. Even before I had formally enrolled in my doctoral program in Australia, a friend told me about Phillips and Pugh's *How to Get a Ph.D.*, and so I went to Amazon to check it out. I did in fact buy Phillips and Pugh's book, but just happened to see Bolker's book there too. The title looked a bit gimmicky, but I felt a strong urge to buy it (a case of The Feeling Sense, as below), so I did.*

Previously, I had used Free-Form Writing when writing poetry and stories. I just wrote whatever came to me, and went back later to see if it was any good. Bolker made me realize I could use a similar process in the early stages of thesis writing—or any academic writing for that matter. Thus, when I actually began typing, I simply allowed myself to enter a fluid stream of consciousness and let the words pour out. I typically found that there was so much wanting to be released from my mind that fifteen minutes was just not enough. I adapted the system so that I set myself a goal of writing 500 words a day, every day, first thing in the morning.

Just as Bolker argues, I found that the writing process really clarified my thinking. As I wrote, ideas came together; links between people, ideas, and historical and philosophical concepts suddenly began to make sense. I did not stop to check if the ideas were valid. I just kept writing. This is thinking as you write, not thinking before you write.

My policy of using Free-Form Writing for my thesis paid off. I completed my doctorate in less than four years while working full time as a teacher. When I enrolled in August 2002, I had not a single academic publication. By the time I was granted my Ph.D., I had well over

---

*I highly recommend Bolker's book for anybody in the early stages of writing a thesis. In fact, I highly recommend it to any researcher in any discipline.

a dozen publication credits (either published or about to be published), including several book chapters. Further, I had completed the writing for my book *Integrated Intelligence.*

Bolker does not link her idea of a "zero draft" to mystical intuition. However, I adapted Bolker's method to my understanding of Integrated Intelligence. I continue to use Free-Form Writing today, for all of my writing.

Tool 12. The Feeling Sense

The Feeling Sense consists of the subtle feelings that are provided by intuition. It is the ability to feel the energy within people, things, and situations, including the outcomes of intended actions. This is an absolutely crucial INI tool, and the one that you will use the most often as you apply the knowledge in *Discover Your Soul Template.* The good news is that it is also quite simple. The Feeling Sense is innate, and anybody can learn to use it. I have taught people to use the Feeling Sense in two minutes flat.

As children we were better at employing the Feeling Sense, but as we get older, our modern educational systems diminish this capacity, because of the delimiting way we are taught to think. Not to fear, however, as the Feeling Sense simply remains latent, and never disappears. All you have to do is learn how to turn on the tap again.

The more you become comfortable with looking within yourself, the easier it will be to distinguish your many subtle feelings. You have to learn the difference between a "true" intuitive pull and other competing voices of the psyche—the ego, desire, wishful thinking, fear of the unknown, and so on. This is not really something that can be taught from a book like this. It is something you learn by trial and error.

You can use the Feeling Sense to pull data from people, objects, places, futures, and pasts. As far as I am aware there are few limits. It truly is the doorway to the Akashic Field of Hindu lore, that part of the intelligent universe that contains a reservoir of infinite knowledge.

Here are a few possible applications.

People. Imagine reaching out with your hand and into the body of the person you wish to "read." Then just let go and allow that person's thoughts and feelings to move through you. Alternatively, you can imagine your body merging with theirs, repeating the same process. Always let go of the person as you finish the process. Otherwise, you may find your energy entangled with theirs.

Objects. You can also reach out with your mind to touch an object and feel its energy. Use the same process as for people, as described above. This is something that is relatively easy to do.

Places. Imagine moving out of your body and finding yourself in the place you want to know more about. Here you are looking for any feelings about the place. Of course, you may get images of words coming to you. If so, take note of them.

Futures. The future is not set in stone, but you can get a sense of probable futures. The further away in time, and more small-scale the event, the less predictable it is. For major events, such as economic shifts or ethnic conflicts, the results are more reliable. To sense a possible future, feel yourself moving into the future choice you are thinking of making (e.g., accepting a job). What does it feel like? You can use this to imagine the futures of career choices, products you buy, places you visit, and so on.

Pasts. Generally speaking, the past is set; however, the way that you relate to your past can have a great effect on the energy of the past as it is represented in the present. You can read another person's past, in precisely the same way you read another person's energy in the present. As you move your energy outward, you are generally picking up the emotional experience of the past event, rather than the literal event itself. Any emotional energy that is trapped in the psyche of a person is relatively easy to read, as emotional energy is "loud."

The following example illustrates the Feeling Sense well. At one time I had a slightly problematic situation. I was living in Hong Kong and had decided not to renew the contract at the school where I was working. No new position emerged by the time I finished my job, and I was left with just a few weeks to find a new one. I was undecided whether to stay in Hong Kong or return to Australia. It was a big decision, so it caused me some stress.

What I did was put the question out to the universe in prayer. The next day I sat down on the toilet (a great place for inspiration!), thinking of nothing in particular. Suddenly the words from the chorus of a song from the '80s band the Traveling Wilburys came into my mind. The song and the words were *At the End of the Line*. After many years of working with such guidance, I knew exactly what it meant, immediately. I had seen a job advertisement two days before from a school at the very end of the subway line in eastern Hong Kong. I had been unsure about whether to apply, but when those words came into my mind, I felt a certainty within myself. I rang the school and went for an interview. It was the school holidays, so there were no students around, no classes to check, and no kids' faces to look at as a guide to the energy of the place. But as an office assistant showed me around the school, I was filled with a very positive feeling. There was something almost feminine about the energy of the school, a very rare thing in Hong Kong's hypercompetitive education system! There was just a good vibe about the place.

As it turned out, I was offered a job. Based solely on my positive feelings, I accepted it. I knew that I would fit in there, and that I would be treated well. My intuition turned out to be spot on. It was indeed a good place to work, and the students and the staff were the best I'd ever worked with.

A good way to begin honoring the Feeling Sense is to regularly repeat the following exercise. Think of a decision you want to make, one that involves two or three possible options (choose a new one each time you do this). Write each option down on a separate piece of paper, and sit with the papers in front of you. Breathe deeply and relax. Ask yourself one question about the choice, such as "Which of these options is the best for my spirit?" or "Which of these options is most likely to be successful?" (be careful—these are not the same thing). Then place your nondominant hand over one of the papers/ options. Allow yourself to get a feeling about it. Do this for each option, in turn.

You may get a subtle sense of excitement. If it feels "exciting," it is a good bet that there is good energy in the option. This process is a little like the understanding that eighteenth- and nineteenth-century Romantics had of the merging of subject and object (they believed the knower could merge with the thing they were trying to know). You can imagine yourself connecting with the choice (the place, the object, the person . . .), and sensing the energy of it. The more you honor your intuitive feelings, the more they will speak to you. This really is too valuable of an advantage to pass up. Don't ignore this simple tool. It can cut a lot of hassle out of the decision-making process, while saving much time and energy.

Tool 13. Light Trances

The process for Light Trances is to quiet the mind, put yourself into a drowsy, dream-like state, pose questions, and wait for the answers to come in any sensory modality—images, inner voices, subtle feelings, and so on. Light Trances are of great benefit to the Sage. You can cultivate meditative and nonordinary states of consciousness as a deliberate means of accessing the intuitive mind, insight, and inspiration. It is well appreciated by mystics and many parapsychologists that cultivating nonordinary states of consciousness is invaluable in accessing intuitive and spiritual knowledge.

Throughout my life after my midtwenties, I have used these states very deliberately to glean data from transpersonal sources and my subconscious. Light Trances are a potentially invaluable part of the development of Integrated Intelligence. However, in my personal experience, as my mind has become more grounded in presence, I have come to rely less on visionary information, which can be difficult to interpret. I now find that the Feeling Sense is all I need, most of the time.

You can familiarize yourself with Light Trances through deliberate meditation, or by taking advantage of the drowsy state between sleeping and waking—the hypnogogic state. This state occurs naturally when you are falling asleep and waking up. But you can enter it deliberately through meditation also.

To bring about the sleepy state, sit quietly in a chair (or wherever you feel comfortable) and relax. Focus on your breath, and breathe deeply in and out. As thoughts move into your mind, just allow them to pass. If you like, you can imagine them being placed inside balloons and floating away. A good time to do this is when you are actually feeling tired, such as in the middle of the afternoon or just before bed. This way you will naturally tend to drift toward sleep when you sit and relax deeply. After some practice, you will be able to do it more readily even when you are feeling alert.

Light Trances are a little different from some other forms of meditation, in that you are deliberately trying to begin to fall to sleep. In most forms of meditation, it is important to remain alert as you enter deep states of consciousness, and the images that come before the mind may be seen as a distraction. But this is not the case with the Light Trances that I am referring to here. As you relax, you may find yourself becoming too drowsy or nodding off. If so, simply persist in bringing yourself awake—but not fully awake. If you practice this meditative process regularly, you will become adept at moving toward sleep, but not quite succumbing to it.

When you find yourself just shy of sleep, put questions out to Spirit/ the subconscious mind (as you prefer). Then observe what comes before your awareness in the form of feelings, images, sounds, and words. Be patient with this process. If you don't receive definite answers, simply repeat the questioning process every minute or so. Even if you get no answer during the entire meditation, one may spring into your mind at a later time or during a dream. A synchronicity in your everyday life may answer the question for you. Regardless, your subconscious will go to work on the problem and begin to pull information and data together, both from mundane and (I believe) spiritual sources. Just trust that the answer is on its way.

Some questions and problems have complex answers. A full understanding of them may take some time, maybe even years with some big issues (but hopefully not that long!). Many issues and problems will require further life experience and maturity before you can really understand them. Some questions have no definitive answer, and merely present an opportunity for a deepening appreciation of the problem. Other answers may come in an instant. As you develop wisdom and come to understand how this Integrated Intelligence works more fully, you will be able to discern more easily how such "answers" develop, often as a process.

I recommend you employ Light Trances in short bursts. These could be as short as a minute or two for "lighter" questions, or ten to fifteen minutes for more in-depth issues. When you finish the meditation, record what you have experienced in your Intuitive Diary. If you want, you can later analyze the meaning of what you have "seen" or experienced. You will not be able to do this during the meditation, because the analytical mind cannot operate effectively while in deep states of relaxation, and vice versa.

There is one thing you will notice as you use Light Trances. After some time, you will be able to slow the mind and access these deeper states of consciousness in very little time, perhaps even instantly. You will also become more aware of the way the subconscious mind is constantly operating, even during "normal" states of waking consciousness. Bits and pieces will sneak through from the deeper levels of mind even as you are going about your everyday life.

Tool 14. Connecting

This tool has three components: Connecting with the Ego, Connecting with the Sage, and Connecting with the Wounded Child/Karmic Child.

Connecting with the Ego

This involves allowing normally disconnected parts of your mind to speak, through entering a Light Trance state. Connecting with the Ego is done by letting go, and simply allowing the voice to move through you. You will need to be somewhere private to do this. First, identify the situation you want to deal with: a work drama, your intention to do something, your relationship, and so on. Then simply imagine yourself in that situation, or facing that person, and really letting them know what you think and feel.

Do not censor anything. If you are in a drama, there will be some dark stuff there. This might involve subtle and strong judgments, a desire to harm or even kill, and perhaps shaming. Shaming is where you project a shameful idea or energy at the other. Examples are: "You are fat/stupid/ugly/nobody likes you." Much shame involves sexual issues, especially sexual preference ("You are probably gay/lesbian"), lack of desirability ("Who'd want you?") and so on.

The good thing about seeing the shadow is that it is downright embarrassing. It makes you see that it is not only the other person who has a dark side (a common delusion of the ego). That in itself should help to start dissolving the drama.

But to really take responsibility, set up a dialogue with the ego. Let it talk, and then respond to it. You can do this in front of a mirror. First play the role of the ego, while watching yourself in the mirror. Then play the role of the parent, gently disciplining the ego. The mirror will help you fully acknowledge the ego and its projections (but be careful not to judge the ego). Another excellent way to work with ego is by getting a soft toy and pretending that it is your ego, and letting it speak. Let it know that you, as parent or Sage, are the boss. Like any good parent, do it firmly, but lovingly. Reassure the ego that it is safe, and that you are going to take actions to deal with the situation.

Decide what those actions are, and use the Quick Check to see if they are appropriate. Remember, "actions" might not be concrete things, nor do you need to confront the other real world person involved in your drama (this may actually make things worse). The actions might be more subtle things like changing your attitude or the way you are thinking about the problem.

Connecting with the Sage

As with Connecting with the Ego, you allow yourself to sense the wise man/woman within you, and permit him or her to bring forth wisdom from the soul. When you try this initially, you might like to imagine yourself as your future self, as a wise old man or woman, in an enlightened state. Stand up, and then channel the energy of the Sage. Ask your Sage questions, and listen to the answers. After you have done this a few times, it should come naturally, and you will not have to use the imagination so much to get in touch with your Sage.

Connecting with the
Wounded Child/Karmic Child

This is the most difficult aspect of the Connecting tool, as it involves channeling not only ideas and information, but the trapped emotional energy that lies within the psyche. It requires a great deal of skill—and courage. Typically it should be done after Connecting with the Ego, as that process takes you into the shadow. To connect with the inner child, you just have to go a bit deeper, learn to relax, and allow the emotional vulnerability required.

The wounded child is the total of all the unexpressed pain energy within your psyche. A karmic child is not really a child as such; rather, your karmic children are packets of nonintegrated energy left over from previous lives. In every lifetime your psyche carries with it the energy of the wounds of previous incarnations. Thinking of them as children helps remind us that we need to be nurturing—loving and gentle—to ourselves.

Connecting with the Wounded Child/Karmic Child is a subtle and precise process, and might require some work with a regression therapist or an alternative healing process such as rebirthing. It is quite possible to make things worse if you don't know what you are doing. The key point is to remember that the purpose of this Connecting tool is not to feel pain for its own sake, but to relax and allow whatever emotions are present within the moment to arise and have full expression.

Beyond seeking help from a professional, there is something that you can do that will help you move in the right direction. What I am about to suggest should be done in a private setting where you feel safe to express strong emotions. If, after Connecting with the Ego, you feel strong emotional energy arising, permit those feelings to find expression. If you feel sad, cry. If you feel angry, beat a pillow or scream into it. If you feel scared, just let yourself feel that fear. If you need to curl up into a ball on the floor and express the terror of a helpless, abused infant, do it. Say and feel whatever moves through your mind. You can use appropriate music to help express the feelings—for example sad songs for grief, and loud music for anger. I suggest you do this for no more than five to ten minutes.

Please note. Do not force feelings during this process, and do not try to get rid of any feelings. Genuine emotional pain only heals when it is gently loved and accepted in the present moment. Trying to get rid of such pain is a subtle rejection of the wounded child. It is thus self-defeating.

Very importantly, after expressing what you need to feel, set up a dialogue with that emotionally hurt part of yourself. You can do this by letting a soft toy represent the wounded child. Let it speak, then be the parent, reassuring it that it is okay to feel angry, sad, afraid, and so on. You can reassure that part of yourself that the fear is unnecessary, that staying angry at the boss, mother, father, sister, brother, or whomever is not helpful.

As the wounded child lets forth its emotional torrent, it will tell you how terrible and hurt it is, how the world is to blame, and how people cannot be trusted. *Do not for a moment believe that story.* It is your attachment to this story that keeps you locked in the past. As long as you are attached to the story, you are attached to the pain. Reassure the wounded child by bringing yourself fully present, and pointing out to the wounded child that it is safe in the present moment.

Your wounded child may not be able to quite believe what you say. Actually, that is okay. Just allow yourself to find love and acceptance for yourself the way you are. I find it is good to acknowledge all the false beliefs and hurt emotions within, by simply giving them to God. For example, you might pray: "Dear God, I confess there is anger and blame. I confess that there is a belief that life is suffering and that people are cruel. Now, I choose to release them to you." This is not a confession of guilt, but a relaxation into truth. If done correctly it should be a joyous process.

Finally, you might like to use Affirmations and Creative Imagination to imagine desirable futures, as if they are present now. You can also put on a CD with some reassuring lyrics.

POWER IN PRACTICE

All the tools and methods mentioned in this chapter are within ready grasp (with the possible exception of the last). It may be true that some people have a greater propensity for the "psychic," but it is my firm belief, from experience, that just about all people have the potential to develop these skills in a practical way. The exception may be people with mental disorders. Obviously, individuals with major psychological issues need to seek professional help.

If you are not experienced with these kinds of intuitive tools and processes, begin with the first few tools in the list. As I have listed them in increasing order of difficulty, one way to begin experimenting with them is to go through them sequentially. Tools like Five Breaths, the Oneness Technique, and Deliberate Feeling can be begun immediately, because they are very easy and require little time. Over time you will know which tools you feel most comfortable with and prefer to use.

As with all cognitive skills, practice is required. It does take some time to open the intuitive centers of the brain. Don't give up after just one or two attempts with any particular tool. It takes persistence and commitment to learn skills that move you out of your comfort zone. You probably spent at least a dozen years in the public education system developing your rational mind. It will take a certain amount of unlearning to develop Integrated Intelligence.

To speak in general terms, most rational ways of knowing involve the control of the conscious mind in tangent with the ego, while mystical ways of knowing require a letting go. I call this "receptivity," where you relax and allow the answer to come to you, rather than actively controlling the process. With rationality you are the center of the universe, but with mysticism your boundaries soften and you become part of something greater. Having worked extensively with both the rational mind and the intuitive mind, I have come to see that much of the resistance to the idea of intuitive perception within mainstream science and education is because it involves this relaxation of control, and dissolution of self. To the ego, this represents death. Modern science and education remain in the tight grip of ego.

You can therefore expect some resistance from your ego as you practice INI and release the control of the rational mind. When I first began to explore other ways of knowing many years ago, I had recurring terrifying dreams of being attacked by UFOs firing intense laser beams and threatening to annihilate me. For the ego, the light of Spirit spells doom. The key is simply to acknowledge this fear, but gently persist with your INI practice.

You can develop Integrated Intelligence too. The only requirement is that you want to do it badly enough, and are prepared to take the required leap of faith.

There was a time when I did not use any of these tools or the other ways of knowing that underpin them. I was totally left-brained. Then one day, at the age of twenty-six, I met an Aboriginal *kadaicha* (medicine woman) named Maria, whom I mentioned in chapter 1. Maria was trained in the shamanic traditions of her people. She told me that I was "very psychic." I literally laughed out loud. I did not consider myself to be remotely gifted with any such ability. Despite my skepticism, I did one thing she told me to do, and that made all the difference. She told me to listen to the words of songs that came into my head, because that was how my guides would begin to communicate with me. After a few weeks of listening, I realized what she had said was correct, and slowly over time I acknowledged other innate abilities that I have.

Eventually, I became determined to develop the capacity for Integrated Intelligence, and persisted with the tools over many years. You can develop your INI too. The main requirement is that you want to do it enough, and are willing to take the required leap of faith. Integrated Intelligence is your relationship with the cosmos, and with the divine. Like all relationships, it has to be nurtured. So there is some limitation to what I can explain and teach within the constraints of the written word. The real issue is whether you are going to get out there and start using these tools. I learned by practice, and if you are serious about progressing, that's how you are going to learn too.

Theory into Practice

Here's an example of how I put these tools to work. Not long after I received my Ph.D., while living in China, I was involved in a negotiation regarding a university job with one of Taiwan's best universities. Via e-mail, the dean of the department was clarifying what subjects I would be able to teach. Something didn't feel right about the situation, so I got out a bit of paper, and drew a horizontal line across the page. I put a question to the universe: "What is the energy on my accepting a position to work at this university?"

Then I ran the index finger of my left hand across the line, from left to right, measuring the energy on making the jump across the Taiwan Strait. My finger just wouldn't go anywhere much past the beginning of the line, indicating that there was no energy on my going there. This was not as I'd expected. I was excited by the prospect of working at a university, and being rewarded for all my years of hard study.

I wasn't dissuaded just yet, however, so to check the energy reading I sat down, closed my eyes and focused upon my breath, putting myself into a Light Trance state. Then, when I was sufficiently relaxed, I projected my energy into the campus of the Taiwanese university, feeling my future self walking about there.

I was pulling the future toward me, merging my consciousness field with my possible future self in Taiwan. I immediately felt lost, disconnected, like I was not meant to be there. I felt myself wondering over and over, "What am I doing here?" There was an overwhelming sense of frustration, because I was in the wrong place at the wrong time. I kept myself in the trance state for a few minutes, but the feeling didn't change.

It wasn't meant to be.

I opened my eyes and brought my self back to full waking consciousness. I then wrote down the results of my experience in my diary. The next day I sent an e-mail to the dean, thanking him for his help, but telling him I would not be able to accept any offer he might give me.

This anecdote is typical of the way that Integrated Intelligence can permit you to peer into possible and probable futures, and sense the results of decisions you are making. Here I used several of the tools of Integrated Intelligence—the Quick Check, the Feeling Sense, a Light Trance, and the Intuitive Diary.

Of course I don't know what really would have happened if I'd gone to Taiwan. One piece of affirming information that I did get was that shortly after I had turned down the job, that department dean resigned. Apparently all was not well there.

MEANING, PURPOSE, AND ENERGY

You might be asking how it can possibly be that a person can read the energy of a decision from a line on a page, or by "feeling" possible futures. Those with a more academic mind might argue that decisions have no intrinsic value, there is no destiny, that all desires and choices are products of the mind, and have no intrinsic value to "the universe."

Values are a product of human culture, and have no existence in nature. How then, could the universe possibly interact with a person in this way to suggest the best way forward?

The truth is that this relativist stance emerges from the alienated mind. Cut off from the deep connection of Integrated Intelligence, the mind is unable to intuit that the cosmos has an innate intelligence and a kind of volition. As we saw in chapter 2, the soul template and the human oversoul template are all part of the cosmic dance of creation. They are the greater purpose of humanity.

During the twentieth century, a culture of relativism developed in the academic and philosophical arenas. Sometimes called the postmodern worldview, this relativism insists that all values are equal, and that history and evolution have no intrinsic purpose.

> *The prime value of the cosmos is love,*
> *the integration of darkness and light. So, any decision*
> *you make has the potential to take you closer to,*
> *or further from, cosmic purpose.*

In fact, the word *purpose* became forbidden in many areas of science and philosophy. It effectively remains so to this day. In current evolutionary theory, any mention of an organism or system having some kind of goal is to invite ridicule, and perhaps academic exclusion. And the French postmodern philosophers, led by Foucault, insisted that history had neither purpose nor destiny, and all attempts to suggest so were attempts to manipulate and control people.

There is much truth to all these claims. As far as I am aware, history isn't directed by a deity, nor is the biosphere. Nonetheless, there is an intelligence that exists within and beyond it all. But you cannot "think" it, analyze it, or experiment on it. You have to *feel* it with your soul. Try telling the guy eating a steel-capped Nazi boot that all values are equal. They are not. The prime value of the cosmos is love, or the integration of darkness into light. In this context, any decision you make has the potential to take you closer to love or further away from it. So, when you read energy, feel consciousness, and sense the possible futures unfolding before you, you are intuiting whether your intended decision is in line with your soul purpose and the evolution of the cosmos. In the broader context, that little decision you are making takes your soul group, humanity, and the cosmos closer to or further away from love.

four

Standing in Your Power

The Strength of the Sage

In this chapter I am going to define what real power is, and indicate the common ways that it is denied and abused.

EMPOWERMENT

The Sage walks in quiet power. A weak Sage is a contradiction in terms. Yet the Sage's power is not the same kind of power that we may think of when we think of powerful men and women in the modern world. Chinese mystic Lao Tsu stated two and a half millennia ago that although the Sage's body might appear weak, she can walk through the forest and remain unharmed by the tiger. Lao Tsu is saying that the wise person is granted protection via her acute perception. When the tiger appears on the path, the Sage will be at the jungle diner munching on a sandwich.

Just as I was writing up this chapter in Hong Kong, a leading news story broke around the world about a new and seemingly deadly flu strain. The swine flu was first spotted in Mexico, and in no time at all news of it spread around the world. In Hong Kong, just the day before I wrote this paragraph, the first four pages of the daily English-language newspaper were all on this topic. This is not too surprising, given that the 2003 SARS epidemic hit the city so hard. As you can imagine, with the media beginning to focus in on the possibility of a devastating pandemic, tensions were rising. A sense of fear was beginning to emerge.

I am in a somewhat fortunate position as an intuitive. I simply projected my feelings into the energy of the flu. I immediately saw that the swine flu would have no immediate significant impact on the world, at least not within the time frame of the reading. The feeling I got was definite and strong. There was no energy at all on the flu being a major problem. In a pandemic, the energy of the suffering is enormous, and I would have picked it up immediately. I even wrote to a good friend in North America and told him not to worry about the flu, as it had been exaggerated by the media and the authorities had overreacted.

The essence of empowerment is an unshakable belief in yourself, founded upon the conviction that your inner knowing is sound.

This capacity to sense what is going to happen in the future, which I call *foresense,* arising from the application of Integrated Intelligence, gives the Sage a great advantage in many life situations. It offers her protection and adds to her power in this world.

SELF-BELIEF

The essence of empowerment is being able to stand firm in your power. It involves an unshakable belief in yourself, founded upon the conviction that your inner knowing is sound. Being empowered also incorporates an absolute honesty that permits acknowledgment of your limitations, mistakes, and shortcomings.

There is a firm distinction between this kind of self-belief and an ego-centered self-belief, which may be founded upon the idea that you can have whatever you want, and that you are strong enough to get it. Egoic wishes for control and power are typically self-centered—a projection of the alienated mind. Ironically, this mind-set often emerges from a sense of weakness and the fear it engenders. Spiritual empowerment, on the other hand, emerges from the integrated mind and acknowledges that we are part of something greater. The alienated ego tends to seek power over others because it will not surrender to Spirit. It is fundamentally distrusting, and believes that it has to do everything all by itself. So power is sought over life circumstances and others, rather than with them. Much of the evil in this world incorporates this mind-set.

One of the greatest strengths of modern developed societies is the increased presence of an attitude of "can-do." This is nowhere more apparent than in the United States. It explains a great deal of America's surging to the position of undisputed world superpower in the twentieth century. The consciousness behind the New Age movement emerges from this awareness, bringing together traditional spiritual understanding with modern materialism and self-belief. We see it in the idea that you can manifest what you want in your life.

> *The alienated ego will not surrender to Spirit. It is distrusting. So power is sought over life circumstances and others, rather than with them.*

In what seems to be a contradiction, this same mentality can be a great weakness. It has created an impasse in the collective consciousness of humanity, even as we reach a plateau in our psychospiritual development. The confluence of the "can-do" mentality with materialism and our modern consumer/advertising society has generated the delusion that we can have anything we like if we just want it bad enough and believe it hard enough. It has elevated the alienated ego-state and exacerbated the split from Spirit.

It is true that the possibilities for human creativity, intelligence, and human consciousness are much vaster than what we have been told by our modern media, educational systems, and society in general. Human beings have cognitive potentials that are so mind-boggling that mainstream science and culture prefer to relegate them to the realm of the "paranormal." Yet Integrated Intelligence is not paranormal. It is part of our innate connection with Spirit and cosmos. It is perfectly normal. In fact, we need to understand that mainstream culture and society are not "normal," in the sense that they have lost touch with an essential component of human consciousness (indeed, the most important part). For it is the awareness of the integration of self and other, self and soul, self and cosmos, which provides us with the opportunity to love at the deepest level, and in turn express true power.

THE NEED FOR APPROVAL

The Sage knows who he is. He has no need to seek affirmation from those around him. The wimpy one doesn't know who he is and has his eyes darting left and right, trying to gather as much information as he can about what everyone thinks of him. Many of the office fights and dramas that people get into stem from this need to seek approval from others. Then when criticism, judgments, or gossip get going, it is easy to lose it. That's pretty wimpy.

The ideas of status, prestige, face, honor, and so forth are part of this weak expression of self. It's all about setting up onlookers to tell us that we are okay.

In certain countries men have been known to kill their daughters because they believe they have brought dishonor to the family by having an affair. But what is this dishonor? Ultimately, it doesn't exist. It is nothing more than a belief that someone else's opinion is more important than your own, more important than the life of your child.

In East Asia, you have to give people "face" (respect) all over the place. Flattery can sometimes get out of control. I was out buying a shirt the other day in Hong Kong. As I was trying on the shirt the young salesman said, "Sir, you are unbelievably strong!" Some time before that another Hong Kong lad told me, "You must be Superman's son!" (More like his father, these days!) On the other hand, in "face-based" cultures, criticism sends some people into sheer panic and often outrage.

The need for approval stands between you and your empowerment. When you seek approval outside of yourself, you are all too easily tripped up when others criticize you or threaten to disapprove of what you do.

Seeking approval outside of yourself is normal, but dumb. It's normal because it is part of the identity-formation process of the child. Children who are not loved and accepted by their parents become deeply damaged. The growing child's mind, including its sense of self, is plastic: it will tend to take on whatever messages are given to it by the outside world. It doesn't know any better. For the child, acceptance and approval are ultimately a life and death issue, because it is helpless and completely dependent upon its parents for support. Rejection by the parents may mean abandonment and even death. This is how we become conditioned into seeking approval from others. Ironically, it is those who fail to get approval as children who tend to have the greatest need in adulthood to give their power away to others by seeking their approval. The fear of rejection and abandonment lies at the heart of this disempowering process.

Assessing your own or another's need for approval can be approximated using the Quick Check. This is done in precisely the same manner as all other Quick Checks, by first asking the relevant question, then running the finger of the nondominant hand across a line, or alternatively, across the dominant hand. The average need for approval varies from country to country. More individualistic countries have people with generally lower levels of approval-seeking, while countries with more collective mentalities have higher levels. In Hong Kong, where I am writing this right now, the need for approval is close to 100 percent. In Australia, it is about 60 to 70 percent. This gap reflects differences in social conditioning and social mores. Many times I have sat in meetings in Hong Kong and witnessed completely passive employees being lectured to for hours, often on a Friday night, by bosses who were able to say and do virtually whatever they pleased. Typically, no staff member ever asked so much as a single question. If the boss tried to pull that stunt in Australia, there would be a riot!

Socially, high needs for approval make for more integrated

societies. People are willing to go with the group, although often blindly. In Western societies where people are more individualistic, there is a greater degree of institutional chaos and egotism can be more pronounced.

In Practice 4.1

ꙮ *Moving Beyond Needing Approval*

This exercise shows you how to use the Quick Check to measure your need for approval in general, and within a given situation. You will then use the Connecting with Ego tool to channel the energy behind that need for approval. You will need your Intuitive Diary and a pen.

ꙮ Quick Check

Draw a horizontal line across a page in your Intuitive Diary, and write "0%" on the left-hand end of the line, and "100%" on the right-hand side. Now ask the question to the universe. "What is my average level of need for approval at this time in my life?"

Run a finger from your nondominant hand across the line until you feel it stop. Chances are, your finger will stop much closer to the right-hand side of the line.

Repeat this several times till you feel the right place. As an indication, the average level of need for approval in people reading this edition of *Discover Your Soul Template* is about 25 to 30 percent, or around one quarter of the way along the line. Some readers will get much higher or lower levels, however. Be as honest as you can.

Mark the point where your finger stopped with a small "X."

ꙮ Connect with the Ego

The next step is to feel the energy in the space between that "X" and the end of the line. Using the same finger you used to make the reading, physically place it into that space on the line. Relax, let go, and allow the energy of that space to come to your mind. You can assist this by imagining the energy coming from the page and filling your abdomen. That energy will consist of self-doubt, fear, a sense of helplessness, or similar feelings. Allow that part of your mind to speak. If the feeling could speak, what would it say?

Write down the words and feelings in your Intuitive Diary, under the Quick Check line. This should just take a few minutes, till you feel there is nothing more left to say or feel. You may also get a sense of punitive presence—this will most likely be the energy of a parent or caregiver from childhood, but could be a group, such as a sporting team or class at school. If you recognize the presence, write the name(s) down beside the words and feelings.

The kinds of things you are likely to say/experience are: "I'm sorry! Please love me." (Mother!) "I'm not allowed to. I'm a bad boy/girl." "Nobody loves/likes/listens to me." "I'm not good enough." (My high school football team.) "They will laugh at me." "They will beat me/kill me." (Father.) "I'm scared. Please tell me I'm okay. I need you to love me." As you can see, this is the voice of the wounded child.

℮ Re-Parent

Having done this, you have before you the emotional energy that is causing you to give your power away to others. The first thing to do is simply acknowledge it, and love the energy. Imagine a loving stream of white light coming from your heart and shining down on to the page. Let it infuse the words with love and affection. Do this for a minute or so.

Then, using a soft toy or a mirror, speak to the wounded child and reassure him or her that everything is okay, that you will look after and protect him or her. If you feel any emotional energy, acknowledge it.

You may feel sad, ashamed, afraid, angry, and so on. If you feel the need, you can Connect with the Wounded Child by expressing those feelings.

Next, use Affirmations and Creative Imagination and Feeling to shift to a more empowered energy in your life. Some suitable Affirmations might include: "I now allow myself to live my bliss, regardless of the thoughts and opinions of others" and "I am now willing to stand in my power. I release the need to seek approval from others." Say these while standing straight and tall, just as an empowered person would.

Then imagine yourself in situations where you previously gave your power away by seeking approval from others. See, feel, and hear yourself in that situation being your empowered self, being the Sage.

☉ Apply

Finally, take note of your energy and feelings as you go about your life. When you see yourself giving your power away to others by seeking their approval, acknowledge what is happening. In addition to using the Quick Check to measure your need for approval in general, you can also use it to assess your need for approval from specific individuals or in specific situations. After measuring your need for approval, connect with the ego states behind it, and complete whatever steps in the process that you feel you need.

Use Affirmations and Creative Imagination to help you shift the energy and change your behavior. What this process does is move the shadow into the light, making the unconscious conscious.

This in turn allows your consciousness field to resonate at a higher vibration, making empowered decision-making more likely.

MORE STUFF IS NOT ENOUGH

We need to acknowledge the essence of truth that the New Age movement and a "can-do" attitude contain. However, we also have to examine the dangers inherent within these approaches.

> *The current world crisis is a wakeup call. More money and machines are not enough. Spirit needs the integration of self and soul, in the simplicity of your presence, here and now, fully extant within your body. It is this that will allow your love to shine through into this world.*

The materialism of the modern world has created the delusion—the distraction—that what we need is more stuff. This is not just an American problem. It is a global issue, and developing countries like

China and India are buying into the mind-set. We have slowly fallen into a collective drowsy numbness where consuming products and amusing ourselves with gadgets is the central meaning of life. The current world crisis is a wakeup call, telling us that money and machines do not free the soul.

The truth is that we don't need all that much stuff. What Spirit genuinely calls for and needs is love: the integration of self and soul, and to express that love in creative ways that allow Spirit to shine through into the world. When this happens, your life will automatically be in alignment with the evolution of the human oversoul template.

What I see in some self-help and New Age philosophies is a worldview that provides tools and techniques for manifestation, but often with no concurrent tools for introspection, for integration of self and soul. The truth is that all the cars, houses, and stuff in the world will leave you empty if you do not make the spiritual journey within.

Make no mistake. When you stand in your power as a man or woman, you will have a far greater degree of love and power than you can possibly imagine. That love and power, though, is born of Spirit, not the desire of the ego for more stuff, more attention, and more status.

An empowered human being is a wise human being, one with depth. Despite superficial appearances, a human being expressing an unbalanced control and power consciousness is not empowered at all. Fundamentally, he is weak, and remains trapped in fear and separation. This is true, regardless of how much he gets what he wants. The total misuse of power by Hitler stemmed from his weakness, the complete absence of wisdom within his personality.

Recently I read an article about a certain pop culture figure who has the kind of fame, attention, power, and money most people can only dream of. She has a certain spiritual philosophy herself, although it is heavily centered within the ego. Yet, if you allow yourself to look at her through the eyes of Spirit, a great deal of her energy takes the form of fear. She lives on a refined diet from which she has eliminated all food products that are known to have connections with aging, such as sugar. Her poor partner was forbidden from bringing such things into the house! The writer of the article referred to the woman with the typical judgmental scorn of the popular media. The truth is that this star's behavior is not particularly surprising. The fears of the decay of physical form, and of death itself, are universal.

In part such fears are biologically wired into us, but the fear is also an expression of the ego. If you are honest, you will also recognize this fear within yourself. The ego inevitably identifies with the body and the personality state. The star's behavior was a typical attempt to establish control and power—over the body, and also over mortality itself.

Looking after the body is part of being a responsible human being. It is the intention underlying the behavior that establishes whether the behavior is empowering or not. In this case, the star's behavior was underpinned by an attempt to preserve the body because of the ego's identification with it. No attempt to perpetuate an ego state is empowering, as all ego states are born of fear and are impermanent. Empowering behavior is underpinned by the wisdom of Spirit, and part of that wisdom is being aware that fear of death and impermanence can strangle the soul.

LOVING THE EGO

Now, just before you take your ego out the back and beat it with a large stick, hold on. For the genuinely empowered person, the ego is not erased—it is fully acknowledged and incorporated into the psyche. All of us have a personality and an ego. Pretending it is not there or giving it a daily thrashing is self-abuse and a recipe for self-delusion. It is at this point that some spiritual philosophies get into trouble. Denial of what lies within creates a separation between the conscious mind and the psyche. In that space of denial a shadow is created. That shadow, in turn, makes it impossible for the light of Spirit to fully shine through you. The light can only penetrate to those parts of you that you are willing to own, to love.

The act of rejection of the ego is the act of rejection of you.

With a little diligence you can reclaim the ego and feel good about being human again. There is no more freeing affirmation for the guilt-ridden than the following: "I am now willing to release the need to be perfect. I now allow myself to be fully human."

This was taught to me by my spiritual teachers at a time when I enjoyed the misery of a good self-thrashing on a daily basis. Self-abuse is one of my soul issues. It was hard, but I decided to give it up.

In Practice 4.2

℗ Checking Your Intention

Every action and every thought has an intention behind it. The intention might be pure or it might be something emerging from the ego. The ego is a trickster, but a little introspection will bring it out from the shadows. To identify the intention behind a decision or intended action, use the INI tool, Connecting with the Ego. Let's take a hypothetical example, involving a decision about asking for a pay raise.

℗ Connect with the Ego

Bring the idea and intended action to mind and see yourself in the situation. Then just let go and allow the ego to speak what it really thinks and feels about the situation. Don't try to censor it in any way. Typically, the ego will be trying to seek attention and sympathy, gain power over something, hide or deny something.

Let's imagine that in this case, after the connecting phase, you discover that your real intention is to express anger at previously having been passed over for promotions. (If you get no ego involvement, you can stop the exercise—but check yourself carefully.) This should take about a minute or two.

℗ Parent the Ego

After completing the connecting phase, set up a dialogue and parent the ego. Use a soft toy to represent the ego if you like. It might go something like this:

Ego: I deserve more money. Nobody respects me around here. I'm going to show them! If they turn me down, they will be sorry!

Parent: Getting angry and seeking revenge isn't going to help.

Ego: I don't care! I'm the smartest person in the office. I don't give a shit what anyone thinks! I'll let them know about me.

Parent: So, I see you don't want a raise, you want attention.

Ego: (*embarrassed*) Well, how else am I supposed to get noticed around here? They should say sorry for the way they treat me.

Parent: There's a better way to be acknowledged than getting pissed off and creating dramas. It will just cause more pain and suffering. So I'm not going to let you do it.

Ego: I want some attention! Nobody loves me!

Parent: That's not true. I love you, and (person) loves you. And we can change the way we do things. We need to get off the computer and start talking to people in the office.

Ego: (*sulking*) It's not fair!

Parent: Things aren't always fair. But we are going to take some positive action to help our cause.

Ego: What if it doesn't work?

Parent: Then we'll try another way. Remember, Spirit is with us, and that's more important than any promotion.

Ego: Yes. I feel ashamed. What's wrong with me?

Parent: There's nothing wrong with you. I love you. You just didn't get what you wanted a long time ago.

Here we have spotted a drama. The ego is setting the situation up for a conflict, so that it can confirm its belief that it has been wronged, that the world is unfair, and that it is not loved. Typically, the drama the ego is creating will simply perpetuate the problem, so you as the parent have to be forceful in correcting the ego.

℮ Affirm Positive Changes
of Attitude and Intent

In the second step, create positive Affirmations and repeat them, preferably out loud. In the case at hand, they might be:

> "I am now willing to release the need to get attention. I
> affirm my value."
> "I am loved."
> "I am willing to begin to conceive of the possibility that
> I am truly worthy of love" (where the ego is really
> hurt).

Later, whenever you feel the ego acting up (such as in the workplace) you can repeat these Affirmations to yourself. You can also dialogue with the ego—but in your head!

℮ Declare Positive Actions
That Address the Real Issue

Identify the actions that will empower you in the current situation and keep you aligned with Spirit. You can use the Quick Check to measure the energy on the actions. Some examples might be:

> "I am speaking to at least three colleagues a day, and
> delighting in the work we are doing."
> "I now smile and say hello to the boss at least twice a
> day. I stop and talk to her at least once a day."
> "I am now creating wonderful and innovative work, and
> subtly promoting it around the office."

The obvious thing to check energetically is whether there is energy for the original goal: in this case whether continuing to seek a promotion will take you forward on your spiritual journey. It may be that once you check your ego, the energy becomes positive again. If there is little or no energy on continuing, release the goal.

THE NEED FOR DRAMA

I have mentioned that if you are unaware of the soul template, and especially your soul issues, you will probably end up wasting time going the wrong way.

Engaging in "drama" is another major waste of the life force. Olympic one-hundred meter champion Usain Bolt might be a superbly gifted athlete and the fastest guy on the planet, but if he had run off the track in Beijing at the fifty meter mark to beat up his old man because of some childhood grievance, he would not be the world champion today. Drama takes you away from your vision, from what you really want and need. It is disempowering.

Dramas are the situations or personal emotional conflicts with others that we unconsciously create. They stem from a need for control.

Dramas are the unconscious, personal, and emotional conflicts that we create with others, or with life situations. They emerge from a need for control. The need for drama varies from person to person, and from time to time. It can be measured as an "index," which indicates your tendency to engage in actions that are projections of unacknowledged emotions. Generally speaking, your need for drama is inversely related to your intention to take responsibility for your life and especially your soul issues. When you are assuming responsibility for your emotional energy, your need for drama will be minimal. When you are not taking responsibility for your energy, then drama will develop, probably sooner rather than later.

Many human beings spend much time or even their entire lives engaging in drama, for in their disempowered alienation from Spirit they know of no other way. At this time in our spiritual evolution, human beings aren't too good at accepting responsibility for themselves. As we saw in chapter 2, this problem is the key issue of the human oversoul. All you have to do is go to a major online chat forum and see how many people are spreading hate, blame, and shame. At the time of this writing the average level of responsibility of human beings on this planet is about 5 percent. Another way of looking at this is to say that we give 95 percent of our power away. Simply wimpy.

As a Sage, you will naturally take more responsibility for yourself and for your life, and in doing so you will be assisting the evolution of our species.

THE SAGE AND THE WIMPY ONE

Standing in your power is easier said than done. You cannot stand in your power if you are not assuming a high level of responsibility for your energy. Of course, drama is not all your doing. When you engage in drama with others, they also have a role in the proceedings. For the average human being, the vast majority of her psyche exists in shadow, and so the energy of others has multiple doorways in which to enter her mind and manipulate her. She will be all too easily dragged into drama. That manipulative energy will come from friends, family, society, and the human collective.

The average level of responsibility of human beings is 5 percent. This means we give 95 percent of our power away.

Wimps give their power away all too easily to others. They are scared of abandonment, failure, and judgment. The energies and opinions of others are more powerful than their self-belief. When I was eighteen years old, I was pretty wimpy. At that time, I had enrolled in the Bachelor of Arts program at the University of Newcastle, and I went to the school before the term began to choose my courses for the upcoming semester. I wanted to study psychology and philosophy because I was interested in those subjects. When I went up to the chap in the psychology department to enquire about the program, he told me that psychology required quite a bit of math. Doubt immediately entered my mind. I wasn't sure whether I could do the math. I blinked, and scrubbed that one off my list. If I had been a boxer I would have been flattened in the first three seconds of the fight. I simply did not have enough belief in myself at that age to consider the possibility that I could find the way to overcome whatever challenges came forward. I stood there and let life flatten me.

Of course, you can't really blame a shy eighteen-year-old for lacking personal power. Yet many people remain this wimpy all their lives. As soon as life throws up an obstacle, as soon as someone pushes them, doubt and fear emerge from the psyche, and they fall over.

The universe is on your side. Integrated Intelligence and guidance are always at your disposal. But you have to understand that at a psychic level, humanity is often against you. People don't like change, and they don't like risk. Strangely, wimpy people and bullies don't like others showing them up either. So as you shift gears and move forward, some people will set up psychic roadblocks for you—and a few physical ones too. This is why you have to be conscious of your shadow. The Sage sees the roadblock, and just drives around it. No drama. The wimp doesn't even know the roadblock is there, and just gives up. Or he revs the wheels, kicking and screaming, blaming the universe and plotting revenge, going nowhere.

After being discouraged about psychology, I studied English and history as an undergraduate, and deviated from my soul purpose. Temporarily. Yet a deviation is not a denial. If you're on the Sage's path, you will forgive yourself for your limitations and errors of judgment, and gently return again and again to your bliss, even as the universe calls you home. As the years pass, your wisdom will grow. The universe will not deny a spirit with courage and conviction.

Society also will tell you what you should and should not do, and what you should and shouldn't feel. It will tell you to sit down and shut up when you could be taking concrete actions that move you closer to your dream, and it will tell you to do lots of stuff that serves no useful purpose: "Here, type up the minutes of this meeting, and put them on the website. That'll keep you busy for thirty minutes." "Why?" "No why. Just shut up and do it." "And the swine flu is coming. Feel free to panic for several weeks while we sell these newspapers."

The Sage can feel what is and isn't necessary. She knows what is and isn't real. She is empowered by her deep knowing. She doesn't waste time in drama, whether her own, or that of society and humanity. The Sage's power emerges not merely from the accumulated wisdom of her life experience, but from her Integrated Intelligence. It is the power to keep the mind and heart centered upon her bliss, in the peace of the present moment, and free from the distractions of the ego. A recent example from my own life will demonstrate how this kind of power is supported by the INI tools.

Three Dramas

I was taught about responsibility levels many years ago by my spiritual teachers, but at times I fall back into old patterns. The term *responsibility levels* refers to how much personal responsibility you are taking for your life, and for the psychic energy you are sending out into the world. Recently I had a bad day where my responsibility level dropped to a very low level—way too low for one on a spiritual path. This bad day snuck up on me because I wasn't paying attention. By the end of the day I had at least three major dramas going down simultaneously. The first was with my wife, where a small issue during a phone conversation was blown out of proportion. Instead of dealing with the issue with a simple acknowledgment of the problem, and asking for what I wanted, I implemented the "closed door" policy, and hung up. Stupid.

The second involved an interaction with an anonymous person on an Internet chat room. I invested about thirty minutes pointing out the errors of an individual's thoughts regarding a certain issue. Then it escalated into a series of exchanges. I used polite language but my energy was involved in blame and anger. Stupid.

When you engage in blame or anger,
you are not assuming responsibility for your energy,
and drama will follow.

Yet the biggest drama occurred psychically; it involved an e-mail I had received from a close relative a few days earlier. While this e-mail was superficially "loving," the intention behind it was manipulative. A large batch of negative psychic energy accompanied the e-mail. This had been a recurring theme with this person, and it pushed my buttons.

I went into blame and anger. Of course this added fuel to the psychic fire, and soon our energies were locked in battle. I did a bit of inner work on it, Connecting with my Ego. However, in the day or two that followed, I got busy on other things, and failed to keep my ego in check. Before I knew it my responsibility levels were down to 15 percent, and soon I was throwing punches at passersby, so to speak. Stupid.

This drama with my relative was actually the foundation of the other two, as the unresolved energy became transferred to the other scenarios. This is typical of human behavior. The boss yells at you and you go home and kick the dog. Poor Fido.

The morning after these dramas broke out, I awoke exhausted and with a cracking headache—common indicators of failing to take responsibility for your energy. I knew that I was out to sea without a paddle. I had to do something, and fast, or I'd be in for a crappy week or two.

> *What the wounded child needs is love and attention,*
> *including discipline. Discipline is a very necessary form of*
> *love. Love is doing that which promotes the highest good*
> *for the spirit of the person.*

The first thing I did was acknowledge that I'd gone into drama big time, and that it was largely my own doing. I then sat down and immediately did a session of Connecting with the Ego. My ego spoke to me straightaway. In a nutshell, my ego wailed: "The world is cruel and unfair! Everybody is out to get me! They all pick on me! Nobody loves me! It's so hard. Poor me! So screw you! I hate you all!"

This is not a great set of attitudes to be taking into your day. You can imagine the potential for relationships blowing up in your face when this kind of energy is sitting just below the surface of the mind.

The energy I channeled reflected my soul issues. You can see they are very much the voice of the victim. I've integrated it pretty well in recent years, but every now and again it returns. Working with soul issues is typically an ongoing process of assuming responsibility for certain tendencies and energy, not a one-off "Aha, now I'm free of it!" situation.

The next thing I did was the Connecting with the Wounded Child technique. I allowed that part of me to open up. After Connecting with the Ego, this was pretty easy, as once the ego is given voice we are brought a step closer to the deeper psyche. In a sense, the wounded child is the next step below the ego. I was immediately taken back into a childlike state, expressing enormous rage, particularly at my mother, but also at my father and older brother.

There was a huge amount of blame for not getting what I wanted and feeling neglected. I permitted this part of me expression for about five minutes. However, I could see that this child wanted to spend all day screaming at the world, and that this would lead nowhere. So after allowing it its few moments of "party time"—screaming, hating, and crying—I dialogued with it. I had to be a very strong parent, as this part of me is particularly stubborn and very deeply hurt. Imagine dealing with an enraged child who is out of control, and you get the idea.

After my Connecting session, I reminded myself of what was important and what I was working toward, and felt myself within those positive situations, with peace and love. My responsibility levels went up considerably after all that. But, most importantly, I took immediate action. I went back to that website and wrote a short entry for my virtual rival, saying it was fine if we saw the situation differently, and wishing him well. Later I called my wife and initiated a positive conversation that brought us back on track. And with continued patience and discipline, the psychic drama with my relative melted away. Within a day or so my energy was back on track.

REDUCING DRAMA WITH LOVE, POSITIVE FOCUS, AND PRESENCE

One of the important dynamics in my working my way out of my recent bad day involves the recognition that what the wounded child needs above all is love and attention, and this includes discipline. Discipline is a form of love, and a very necessary form. Love is the act of doing what promotes the highest good for the spirit of the person. Giving the candy to the screaming kid might make you both feel good at the level of ego, but it may be unloving in the bigger picture. Once you begin to stop thinking of love as a feeling, and begin to see it as an act of true generosity, you can cut out much confusion surrounding what is and isn't love. The key then becomes determining whether the action is for the highest good of the person involved.

When drama escalates, you have to keep working at it, even after you have completed your Connecting sessions. You have to maintain self-discipline and a high level of responsibility for your words, actions, behaviors, and psychic projections onto the other people involved. There is no use saying nice things to the boss if you are beating him up with your energy. Telling the boss, "Okay, all is forgiven, let's move on, okay?" is not going to work if your deeper mind is saying, "I hope you get hit by a cement truck, you old fart."

The Sage has to be on the ball. Higher levels of responsibility and discipline are required to really live an empowered life. For some ongoing dramas you may have to keep doing the Connecting exercises daily for a while. This is just one reason why it is important to set aside some regular time every day for self-work. Even when I am busy, I devote around one hour per day to it. You can use this time for any inner work you like: meditation, mindfulness, writing in your Intuitive Diary, reading uplifting books, inner child work, and so on.

The universe is on your side. Integrated Intelligence and guidance are always at your disposal. But you

have to understand that at a psychic level,
humanity is often against you.

After doing your inner work, and in particular work with the ego and the wounded child, remember to gently return your attention to your bliss. What you focus upon expands, so your inner work needs to retain a positive focus, even as you integrate the shadow. This is something of a balancing act. If you focus too much on the shadow, pain and suffering will tend to expand. But if you deny legitimate suffering, the shadow will control you, and take you away from your soul purpose. So, even as you dance through life, you need to keep the wounded child at your side, and pay attention to its needs. You can use Deliberate Feeling, positive Affirmations, and the Creative Imagination and Feeling tools to help you keep correct focus.

What will help reduce drama in your life more than anything else is to bring your mind into presence. Remember, drama emerges from unresolved energy that is not real, in a physical sense. This energy is trapped in your psyche as a part of a past that no longer exists. It only becomes a drama when you fail to acknowledge and take responsibility for it—and so end up kicking the dog. Presence techniques can help bring your mind into the present moment, and out of the creative fictions of the mind. We will take a closer look at what they have to offer in the next chapter.

five

Moment to Moment

Finding Spirit in Presence

If you could have any one thing you wanted right now to express ultimate abundance, what would it be? This is not the Miss California contest, so just be selfish for a moment and forget about world peace and an end to all poverty. What is the most important goal you could possibly materialize right now? Take a moment or two to consider this question before moving on to the next paragraph.

What did you go for? There's a good chance you went for something to do with career, a physical object, travel, or a special experience. When you think of empowerment and abundance, though, there is something that has to come before any of this, if those other things are to have any real capacity to transform your life and bring a greater degree of spiritual development. That thing is *presence*.

> *With presence comes the realization that*
> *nothing that the mind thinks of is actually real.*

Presence occurs when the mind is fully in the now, in silence. With presence comes the realization that nothing that the mind *thinks* of is actually real. Almost any thought that you have involves an imagined past or future.

Presence is the most powerful and transformative actualization of all. This truth becomes readily apparent when you see the lost look in the faces of certain celebrities and other powerful and famous people on the planet. In many cases, they have gained no greater sense of happiness or well-being than the average person, despite having achieved all the trappings of ego—fame, money, power, a pet psychiatrist, and so on. In many cases, their state of well-being regresses.

I used to live in a very nice area of Hong Kong called Tiu Keng Leng, which means "pretty crest" in Chinese. In decades past it was called Rennie's Mill Village, after A. H. Rennie, the English flour salesman who originally developed the area. In a rather sad story, Rennie committed suicide in 1908, when his Hong Kong Milling Company went bankrupt. When the area was later redeveloped, the name was changed to Tiu Keng Leng because the locals thought it would bring very bad luck to live in a village named after someone who had hung himself.

> *Judgment should not be confused with discernment.*
> *Judgment has an emotional energy. Discernment is a*
> *nonjudgmental, nonemotional awareness.*

Rennie is not the only man to have taken his life when he lost his fortune. I don't mean to be disrespectful, but I feel people who make these types of fatal decisions have bought the story of the ego, which is that status and financial wealth are worth more than the infinite beauty of presence. Many wealthy folks lose presence in the pursuit of money, and when the cash cow keels over, they feel they have nothing left to live for.

In fact, the bankrupt still have something far more valuable than money: the capacity for presence, and the knowledge of Spirit. Not without its price, it is nonetheless completely free in fiscal terms. No market conditions can ever take away the wisdom of the Sage, for he would never give his power away to the immaterial rise and fall of economic graphs. When the economic tsunami hits, you'll find the Sage changing into his Speedos and grabbing his surfboard. He can afford to party because in the silence of presence he has detached from the fear of the collective. He knows who he is, and Integrated Intelligence permits him to surf to safety.

JUDGMENT AND PRESENCE

Presence is an expression of love. In presence the mind becomes quiet and judgment ceases. As soon as you judge, presence is lost. This is good news, because it means that if you choose presence you can finally stop wasting valuable life energy judging everyone and everything around you.

Judgment is also a key component in the development of drama. Judgment often emerges from your soul issues. As soon as you judge another person, they feel it at a subtle level, and their soul issues may be triggered. Before you know it, you are scratching each other's eyes out, energetically if not actually.

There are no two ways about it. You cannot judge and be present at the same time. They are mutually exclusive. If you want to experience your bliss, you need to allow presence in your life. And to allow presence you need to discipline the mind's tendency to judge.

Realistically, the modern Sage cannot live in a cabin in the woods, at least not if he wants to participate in the modern world. This fact makes our task a little more difficult than for Lao Tsu living in his little hut in rural ancient China.

As soon as we set a goal or think about what we are going to eat for lunch, it has the potential to take us into the mind, and away from presence. The key then is to be able to gain enough self-awareness and control of our thoughts to move between presence and mind whenever we want. We have to learn how to strike a balance between the two.

Now just as you start complaining about how important your judgmental opinions are to the world, I'm going to stop you cold. Most of your opinions aren't really all that important in the greater scheme of things. Sorry to deflate you a bit, but it's good for you. Sure, you may have many valuable insights and you might even be an invaluable source of knowledge and even inspiration to others. But all the rest of it is rubbish. Just go to the Internet and you'll see people mouthing off at the world, telling everyone the way it really is. And it makes not one bit of difference to anything. It just keeps them stuck in the mind and its illusions. And that's not even counting the online dramas.

Ultimately, it is all about love. Love is, in part, acceptance and alignment with what is. Judgment is the opposite of love. As soon as you judge something as being wrong or bad, you create disharmony, and your energy field moves into a lower vibration.

Now, here is the key point. Judgment should not be confused with discernment. Judgment has an emotional energy. "This president is a moron;" "I hate Mondays!" and "That guy is so aloof. He thinks he's better than everyone else." And so on. Discernment, on the other hand, is a nonjudgmental, nonemotional awareness. It may indeed involve the perception that something is not as you would prefer. Discernment brings to your attention that the president isn't so bright, that your working environment is not one that nourishes your soul, and that your workmate does not connect well with people.

Presence is simple.
You simply bring your attention to what is.

Finally, judgment creates suffering, and discernment does not. As we have seen, much of the suffering that people experience in daily life comes not from what actually happens, but from their refusal to align with what happens. They judge things and people as bad or wrong, and the ego makes a big song and dance about the whole thing. So, they don't learn. They lose presence. They don't get it.

HOW CAN WE ALLOW PRESENCE?

Presence is simple. You simply bring your attention to what is. Your mind will try to figure out a whole heap of reasons why you have to achieve presence, or argue that it is complicated, or that it has to be put off until tomorrow. But the truth is that presence is right here, right now, and nowhere else. How much more simple can that possibly be? We are aided in that by the two presence techniques I described in chapter 3, which can be done anywhere, any time. (There are obvious exceptions, such as potentially dangerous situations, which require you to keep focused on that one thing. So don't do them while driving a steamroller.)

The first and simplest way to become present is the Five Breaths method. Whatever you are doing, stop, and allow your attention to focus upon the breath as it moves in and out of your nose. Close your eyes if you like. After as few as five focused breaths your mind will become silent, and you are in presence. Like I said—simple.

The second method is the Oneness Technique of becoming present by silently connecting with a flower, a tree, a baby, a cup, or some other object that is already present. Simply bring your mind into relaxed focus on the thing you have chosen. If thoughts or judgments come into your mind, just observe them and let them go.

After presence has been permitted (you can't force it), the mind will tend to cut back in by creating a distraction. It will smack you in the face with another illusion of an imagined past or present, and the inner dialogue will return. This is when you have to decide between the two worlds: the world of the mind, or the world of presence. Again, it is really simple. Which one do you prefer? It might pay to remember at that moment of choice that the 90 percent of human suffering that is unnecessary exists when people are within the mind, and thus out of presence. This suffering consists of imagined pasts and futures, and the fear and drama that arise out of them.

> *Even the most calamitous events can be experienced in presence, or, for that matter, the most mundane in the chaos of the mind.*

The mind will kick in and start making excuses: "I cannot be present. I have a job to do. I have a kid with attention deficit disorder. I am studying toward my master's degree right now, so I will have to wait two

years. The economy sucks. The team lost the game, and we were robbed!"
(That's got to be worth half a day of sulking, at least.) These are all just
excuses. No matter what your circumstances, you have a choice to experience them directly in presence, or through the huffing and puffing of
the mind. Presence is a riverbed permitting water to flow gently down-
hill. The mind is the team of squabbling engineers trying to divert the
water uphill while taking legal action against the law of gravity.

With just a little discipline and presence, the mind can be balanced.
You might be studying in your spare time, but you can still bring presence to that study. You can do this by checking on your breath every
few minutes, and making sure that your energy is fully in your body, in
the here and now. When we are not present, a subtle dissociation process often occurs where bits of our consciousness leave the body. Parts
of our energy are off fighting our enemies, struggling with the finances,
or bopping that damn referee on the nose.

Who knows? Maybe you will go bust and be out on the street
tomorrow. I am not suggesting you ignore that possibility. There are
times when focused action is required. The Sage's actions, however,
are empowered by the knowing of Spirit. The alienated mind, having
no connection to deep knowing, has a tendency to run around like a
chicken with its head cut off.

The ideas of poverty and loss are, in a sense, a creation of the mind.
Like all events, they may be created because that is what you are putting
forward as the experience that reflects your mind's belief structures.
The alienated mind is unlikely to have the awareness to really understand this. It is in presence that you are most likely to perceive this level
of reality. That presence can then act as a platform from which you
employ Integrated Intelligence. You can sense the best way forward and
then create something different.

Nothing shuts down Integrated Intelligence and the wisdom of
the higher mind faster than fear. By choosing fear you shut yourself off
from the very knowledge that can help solve your problem most quickly
and readily.

Even the most seemingly calamitous events can be experienced in presence, or, for that matter, the most mundane in the chaos of the mind. As a young man, Mahatma Gandhi was a stretcher-bearer during the Boer War in South Africa. Reports indicate that he seemed completely impervious to his mortality. He ran about carrying wounded from the battlefields as if it were a football game. Gandhi always had something of the Sage within him.

RIDING THE RIGHT WAVES

Every surfer knows that you have to choose the right wave to catch if you want a good ride. A surfer will waste a lot of time and energy if he just jumps onto a wimpy wave. No matter how furiously he paddles, and regardless of the timing of his standing up on the board, if the wave is a dud he's going nowhere.

Consciousness is in many ways wave-like, with some waves having high vibration, and others having low vibration. You need to know how to catch the right waves. But getting on the right wave to your destination is not as easy as it might sound. The ego has a self-sabotaging function. When you begin to shift energy to higher states of being, the ego will jump in and tell you that it can't be done. Limiting belief structures about worthiness, abundance, human nature, society, God, and the universe will emerge. This is almost inevitable.

A dream I had some time ago metaphorically illustrated this point perfectly. At the time I had made a few significant breakthroughs in my life. I dreamed that I was bodysurfing a tall, elegant wave. I surfed high into the air, atop the arc of the huge, strangely low-density wave. It was quite unlike any wave really should be (given the laws of gravity). The entire thing seemed too high and too vaporous to support a human body. Initially it was exhilarating, as I surfed the wave high above the ocean. Then I started to panic, thinking I would fall and be crushed when the huge wave broke. So I descended to sea level. There was another dark, choppy, high-density wave coming in the opposite direction. The water was turgid and looked rather cold. That was where the little dream ended, with my jumping off the high wave and waiting to be swamped by the lower wave coming the other way.

Can you sense the meaning of the dream? I often use the Feeling Sense to understand my dreams, for it is often the emotional content of dreams that provides the key to deciphering their meanings, just as much as the symbols. This dream was not too difficult to figure out. Metaphorically speaking, the mind rides waves of energy, or fields of consciousness. The mind tends to be comfortable with a certain kind of energy, regardless of how dark or murky it is. In this dream, I was emerging from a lower level of vibration into a higher level. However, my ego panicked and "jumped off."

Note that the wave that I decided to jump on was heading in the opposite direction. In other words, the ego was taking me in the precise opposite direction from where I should have been going to create more empowerment and abundance.

WHEN DOUBT AND FEAR COME KNOCKING

There are times when doubt, fear, and drama start to get the better of us. When this happens, you can deal with it at the immediate level, or in depth.

In Practice 5.1

℮ The Immediate Level: Connect with the Ego

Here your goal is to gain control of the fear, return your focus to your vision, and restore your energy to a higher vibration.

Acknowledge the drama or ego projections. If you are involved in a conflict with another, or you sense drama, assume responsibility. Here the ego might wail, "Look at what he always does to me! I hate that so-and-so!" You might find an ego agenda: "I'm gonna get that woman! She will pay!"

Affirm your willingness to step out of the drama with an affirmation to the universe, such as "I am now willing to assume full responsibility for my part in this situation, and pull out of the drama."

If there is a drama, begin by channeling your ego states toward others in the drama. In the unlikely event that there is no drama, simply connect with the ego and let it speak.

Let your ego express all of its doubt, fear, anger, hopelessness, and so on. The key here is not to hold back, but to let it all out. You might find the ego shouting, "There's no way out! It's hopeless!" Or it might go into a victim mode, as ego often does. "The world is against me, Poor me. Nobody cares about what I want!" Don't spend too long on this—five to ten minutes should generally be sufficient. Any longer and you may reinforce the drama. Your goal is to expose the ego, not to let it run the shop.

℮ Re-Parent

Begin to dialogue with the ego.

You can do this in front of a mirror or grab a soft toy and let it talk to you. After each ego statement, address that voice as a parent would a child. Remember, the parent needs to be strict.

> **Ego:** They all hate me. Nobody cares about me!
>
> **Parent:** That's not true. I care about you. I love you, and look at all the people who care about you (name them if you like).
>
> **Ego:** I don't care! It's not fair! Nothing ever changes! It's totally hopeless. I'll never have what I want!
>
> **Parent:** That's just what you believe. Now I am not going to put up with that silliness. Remember how many great things we have in our life! And we are going to focus upon our bliss. See how wonderful that is!

Again, don't spend more than five minutes here. You just need to see what the ego is up to, and be determined not to let it continue to "play up."

℮ Affirmation

Here you express statements of willingness to move forward and focus upon the positive present and desired future. The Affirmations should be directly related to the issues you uncover with Connecting with the Ego or Connecting with the Wounded Child.

Repeat to yourself an Affirmation such as: "I am now willing to begin to truly believe that I can have what I want and need. I am now willing to believe that (insert your bliss) is already right here, right now."

℮ Creative Imagination and Feeling

The goal here is to allow the positive feelings associated with your preferred futures to fill your mind and your body.

Next, imagine your preferred futures, as if you are experiencing them here and now. Just imagine yourself confidently within those situations in the present moment. Tune in to the positive feelings they evoke, such as joy, love, hopefulness, success, and celebration.

I highly recommend that you play some positive and uplifting music. This will depend upon your personal choice. Some of my personal favorites include "I Believe I Can Fly" and "The Power of Love" (good versions have been done by Frankie Goes to Hollywood, Celine Dion, and Huey Lewis), and for a bit of mischievous fun, "My Future's So Bright, I Gotta Wear Shades."

In Practice 5.2

℮ *In Depth: Connect with the Wounded Child/Karmic Child*

If you find your progress is slow, it may be that you need to connect with the deeper psyche. While you are doing Connecting with the Ego, if you find strong emotions coming up, such as deep anger, blame, hurt, or sadness, it may be necessary to allow those parts of yourself to speak. This should be done immediately after Connecting with the Ego.

For certain in-depth issues or difficult periods of your life, the ego can pour forth a torrent of emotional energy. If you are in a private setting where you feel safe to express strong emotions, permit those feelings to rise within you and be expressed (as described in detail in Tool 14 in chapter 3).

Then set up a dialogue in which you allow the wounded child within to speak and be answered by the parent, with reassurance that it is okay to feel angry, sad, afraid, and so on.

Make sure you follow through with the last steps of the process: Affirmation and Creative Imagination and Feeling.

At times like this you may need to repeat these sessions daily until you feel you are beyond the problem. Ideally, the sessions should become shorter and easier as time goes on, as you establish the link with the shadow more easily, and gain the trust of the lost child. This is crucial.

Hearing the voice of the Sage is difficult at such times, because your mind is being swamped by fear and doubt. The way out of such situations is to bring the mind fully back to the present moment with one of the presence techniques. Remember, the story that the ego is selling you is not real—it's an illusion, so don't buy it. Listen to your Sage instead.

Sometimes, though, the situation will trigger your soul issues, and you may need to go deeper to the root of the problem. As I suggested in chapter 3, if you want to explore the psychic depths of your emotions, I highly recommend that you seek the guidance of someone experienced with regression therapy or an alternative healing process such as rebirthing.

Every moment you stay in the victim state you are dangling another ball and chain from your ankle, strapping yourself down to a lower level of consciousness.

THE VICTIM'S SOCIETY

Whenever you find yourself in conversation with others, grumbling about how unfair it all is and how he/she/they are to blame, you are in the grip of ego. Every moment you stay in that state, you are dangling another ball and chain from your ankle, strapping yourself down to a lower level of consciousness. It may feel good to complain about whatever it is you find fault with, but the cost is way higher than the benefits. You are also choosing the victim state over empowerment.

This is the "Victim's Society." It is not a very exclusive club. They'll let any old ruffian in. People will often try to drag you down into the world of the ego. Misery loves company, after all.

I suggest you politely excuse yourself from the Victim's Society. Tell them you have another appointment across the other side of town with the Sage's Society. They are a lot more prosperous over there anyway. It's tough when friends get too deep into victim talk, as you may well love them and treasure their friendship. Give them a break. All people go into victim mode from time to time. But don't sign up for the club. Politely change the subject. They will get the idea sooner or later that you won't play along with them.

In some cases, people may be so negative that you have to make a choice about whether you want to continue to hang out with them. One time I let a friend go because he was such a drama queen that he created conflict everywhere he went. You could never have a conversation with the guy without him saying how John or Martha was trying to run him down, and how he had to put Martha in her place because she was dissing him. His was a world of persecution and fear, where everyone was out to get him. The last time I saw him was when I bumped into him in a bookshop. I immediately sensed a cool tension in the air. Sure enough, after a few minutes he blurted out, "I remember what you called me last week. You probably thought I forgot, didn't you?"

Ironically, all sense of moral superiority is testament to the fact that you are stuck in ego, and at the lower end of the consciousness pile.

I was mystified, until he mentioned a conversation where I had jokingly referred to him as "you old bastard!" This is quite a common expression in Australia (and other countries), and is in no way a put-down. I had completely forgotten it. Yet he had been stewing over it all week. I realized then and there that it was time for us to part ways. With this kind of drama queen, nothing you do or say will ever be right. Sooner or later they will find evidence of betrayal or insult, and the drama beings again. My friend believed that the world was out to bop him on the nose. His belief structure made that a self-fulfilling reality. Lord knows I was tempted to bop his nose myself once or twice just to affirm his worldview!

It is in presence that the true beauty of synchronicity
can be sensed and appreciated.

Regardless of how frustrating people can be when they go into victim mode, do your best not to judge them. Judgment of ego is still ego, so your opinion will resonate with your friend's ego state. Ironically, all sense of moral superiority is a testament to the fact that you are stuck in ego, and at the lower end of the consciousness pile.

Judgment tends to create drama, because judgment is a rejection of the other. It is actually an unconscious attempt to invalidate and ultimately destroy another person. Naturally, the ego of the other will tend to react with fear and hostility when you judge them. The key then is to acknowledge your judgments of others, along with the ego states of the other person. Recognize the simple truth that we all have egos that tend toward pomposity, superiority, and judgment.

Once you have acknowledged ego, discipline it. Keep your attention in the present moment where your Sage will come forth. It is in presence that you will find true prosperity, joy, and empowerment.

SYNCHRONICITY NOW

When I began to write this book, I was living on the fiftieth floor of a high-rise building in Hong Kong. The first weekend I started to write, two kites continuously circled around outside my window. Kites are very large birds that glide about in great circles, effortlessly sailing upon the waves of the air. Time and time again they glided within a few yards of my window. It was as if nature was sending me a message that it was time to fly, to just allow the grace and beauty of Spirit to flow.

It is in presence that the true beauty of synchronicity can be sensed and appreciated. In presence, the mind resonates at a higher frequency. When the mind is not present it gravitates toward the lower vibrations of hurt pasts and fearful futures.

If I had not been fully present, I may have missed the significance of those kites outside my window. In modern science all meaning has been stripped from nature. The idea of the random dominates. At a certain level of consciousness—the alienated mind—it certainly looks that way. The links between events cannot be perceived.

Higher mind, with its Integrated Intelligence, is a little like the idea of hyperspace. In sci-fi movies, a spacecraft can move from one point in the cosmos to another by collapsing the space/time between them. It is as if two points in space are folded together within a moment, and the idea of "far" and "near" collapses. Then the spacecraft reappears in the second location. In three-dimensional space/time, we cannot perceive the link between things in different locations, but we can learn to feel it.

How do you determine the "meaning" of a synchronicity? Allow the silence of presence. Simply let go and allow the moment to speak to you. Permit the way of knowing to unfold—via a voice from within, inner images, and especially the Feeling Sense.

If nothing comes, that is fine. The ego may try to impose meaning upon an event, typically one that fits its agenda. If there is no information, no feeling, no meaning, then that is okay. Just let it go. When you begin to trouble yourself about the meaning of an event, you immediately go into the mind and lose presence.

Blunt Synchronicity

Synchronicity weaves together your vision, your psyche, and the universe. The messages are often profound. However, sometimes they are a bit blunt, and the meaning may not be what you'd prefer to acknowledge!

One day more than a decade ago, I had a dream early in the morning. I dreamed that the police were on the lookout for Jack the Ripper. He was lurking about, but he was being rather stealthy in his ways—not unlike you'd expect from a serial killer and rapist. I awoke with the dream fresh in my mind. It wasn't the kind of storyline that makes for a good start to your day. Still, it seemed to fit in with some of the inner work I'd been doing on myself, related to my issues with women. Was there a part of me that contained the rapacious rage of Jack the Ripper? It wasn't something I cared to dwell on. I shuddered and pushed the dream aside.

Later, I drove to the international boys' school where I was working. As I was on the road I pulled up behind another vehicle. My eyes were suddenly drawn to a sticker on the bumper of the car. It read "Jack's Back!" (an advertisement for whiskey). A shiver went down my spine. It seemed that the universe was just not going to let me rest on this one.

At school I entered my first class, a vibrant form two English group, containing boys aged around fourteen years old. The previous night, I had asked them to write the opening line of a mystery story. The first thing I was going to do that morning was to get some students to read that first sentence aloud to the rest of the class. The boys shuffled in and I readied myself for the first task of the day. For me, this was in part intuitive. I brought my mind fully into presence by concentrating on my breath, allowing myself to simply "be" with the boys. I stood before them, looked around the classroom and sensed where the energy was coming from (a process I had learned from my spiritual teachers). The decision was made via the Feeling Sense, which is attuned by presence. When my eyes came to rest on James, a jovial, freckle-faced fellow, I got the deep knowing that I was looking for.

"James, can you read us what you have written?"

James stood up happily. However, he had done much more than what I had asked. He had not only written the opening sentence, but also gone on and completed the entire story. What is more, he had also misunderstood my instruction. I had told him to read only the first sentence, but he continued on. I had not expected this, but decided to go with the flow and allowed him to continue.

James began to read his story of a woman who was brutally raped and murdered. My ears picked up. The police went on a hunt for the man responsible. They found him and tried to arrest him, but he fought back.

"The man turned and faced them like a wild animal," James read. "The policeman fired, and the man fell to the ground screaming. As he fell silent and death overtook him, a dark and horrible shadow rose out of the dead man's body. It was the spirit of Jack the Ripper!"

The universe only gives us as much knowledge
as we can handle at any given time.

I gulped. "Ok, thanks for that, James," I said. "That was great." But I could not help myself. "James, where did you get the idea for that story?"

"I dunno," he chirped back with typical teenage nonchalance. Now skeptical readers might think I am not telling the truth in what I just wrote. Maybe I collapsed some things that happened at different times into one anecdote. But I have not. Those synchronous events—the Jack the Ripper dream, the "Jack's Back" sticker, and James's Jack the Ripper story all happened within the space of a couple of hours.

Note, though, that the final part emerged from my allowing the process to unfold in a way I had not expected, by releasing control and allowing Integrated Intelligence to take over. If I had not read the energy in the room and picked out James, and if I had told James to stop reading after the first sentence, the synchronicity would not have reached its crescendo.

That synchronicity invited me to face something within myself: the part that had been deeply hurt by certain female figures from my child-hood. It was related to sexual energy and what it means to be male. The universe spoke. It had something unpleasant to tell me, but I put aside my ego, the fear of my shadow side. I listened and took the necessary action I was being "asked" to take.

This synchronicity was part of the evolution of my soul. At the beginning of my spiritual journey, I had asked Spirit that I might learn to love. At the time I put out that prayer, I did not realize that it would require years of inner work. In that classroom in New Zealand, years later, Spirit was continuing to answer the call through the medium of a freckle-faced schoolboy. James did not say it, but his words contained the energy of a hidden meaning. Love requires that we allow the light to penetrate our darkness—right to the core.

If I had known what was required for a guy like me to learn about love, I would have changed the order and put in a request for pizza instead. Spirit is a bit sneaky at times. It only gives us as much knowledge as we can handle at any given time.

PSYCHIC SEDUCTION

In my way of thinking, Integrated Intelligence is a great advantage for the spiritual journey. It can help us unite with the inner Sage. However, you can overdo it. You overdo it when the psychic realm becomes an end in itself, or when the quest for the psychic takes you away from presence.

It is well understood in the Buddhist tradition that psychic phenomena are not very important in themselves, and can distract the student on the spiritual pilgrimage.

This is a real problem with some New Age thinking. Psychic development is not spiritual development. There may be some connection, but they are different. The goal of spiritual development is the transformation of soul, humanity, and cosmos. It involves the integration of the spirit and personality, where the mind is brought fully into the real world of the present and out of the illusions of the mind. Conversely, the goal of much psychic development is to see more paranormal stuff: more woo-woo. Woo-woo can be fascinating. But mosquitoes also find mosquito coils fascinating. Until they get zapped, that is.

The psychic mind can be employed on your way to finding your soul purpose, but don't let it seduce you. There is an oft-told story from Buddhist lore. A student was sitting in meditation one day, when he suddenly saw an image of the Buddha appear in his mind's eye. Excited, he jumped up and ran to his master, who was cleaning bowls.

"Master! Master!" shouted the student in excitement. "I was meditating just now and I saw the Buddha!"

The master barely looked up from his cleaning, and said, "That's okay. If you concentrate more, he will go away."

It is well understood in the Buddhist tradition that psychic phenomena are not very important in themselves, and can distract the student on the spiritual pilgrimage. Contemporary spiritual teacher Leonard Jacobson makes exactly the same point. He once mentioned the case of a practicing clairvoyant, a woman who came to him and started talking about a problem with some psychic phenomena she was experiencing. He told her that she had a choice to make: between the gift of presence, or the mire of the mind, including the world of psychic phenomena.

This is another reason why I do not recommend that psychotropic drugs be taken on a regular basis by spiritual seekers. I do appreciate that they may facilitate awareness and understanding of higher spiritual states and knowledge, but the problem is that once the drug wears off, you are left once again in your ordinary state of consciousness. Further, although the drugs may bring to awareness the traumas of the wounded child and the karmic children, they do nothing to heal them. They also do nothing to teach you how to come into presence. In fact, the longing for the next trip may destroy whatever presence you have.

It is better to learn to raise your consciousness yourself, rather than rely on drugs. I have never used drugs, but understand that they can provide great insight at times. Still, I'm convinced that natural methods can supply many of the same insights. I first came to this conviction many years ago, not long after I'd first begun to meditate. A good friend of mine said that he had smoked marijuana (he was not a regular smoker), and during the altered state of consciousness was suddenly struck by how absurd his fear of his receding hairline was.

For a few moments, he became detached from his ego's neurotic fear, and saw his anxiety for the silly thing that it was.

What struck me about my friend's tale was that the same kinds of insights are a standard "benefit" of meditative practice. In meditation, you allow the mutterings, ideas, and fears of the ego to pass through the mind without judgment. This automatically grants the kind of insight that my friend was referring to. The best thing is that it is free for the meditator, and you don't have to get a lungful of soot nor experience the drug-related brain dysfunction that THC causes (they don't call it "dope" for nothing).

PRESENCE AND
THE WOO-WOO MASTERS

There is a certain spiritual teacher I know (let's call him Robert) whom I have greatly admired for a long time. Nowadays Robert has moved down a track that no longer resonates with me. Nonetheless, he greatly influenced me in my early days. The problem for me is that in recent years he has gotten into drug-inspired visions. As a result, his teachings have moved further away from the simplicity of presence that I feel should remain the essence of the spiritual journey. How can you be present when you are busy tripping out all over the place, communing with angels and fighting demons?

Robert believes that there is a realm of perfect knowledge that reveals to us all the truth we need. In fact I have never heard him question one of his visions, or admit that he was wrong. I think this is a little naive, or a little dishonest.

There may be some truth to the assertion that realms of pure knowledge exist, but the problem is that when we use the alienated mind to try to understand pure knowledge, the knowledge gained is still processed in a state of separation—where the ego tends to reside. That separated mind still has to "read" the visions and revelations and interpret them. Half the time a bunch of witnesses cannot even agree on how many masked men there were at the bank hold-up. How can we possibly report visions as if we are in possession of perfect truth?

In the first chapter, I told you of all the kinds of psychic energies that interfere with pure perception. It's a bit of a minefield out there, and you should be aware of this. To be fair to Robert, he does often talk about such interfering energies, and it is clear he knows how easily negative energies can distort visions. Still, he does oversell the idea of pure knowledge, and the essence of his teachings is now misleading and harmful, in my estimation.

You will have to decide for yourself what is the correct balance of the mental, the psychic, and simple presence. This balance may change at different times in your life. My view is now more in line with Leonard Jacobson's and has moved well away from Robert's. One of the reasons why I was also not able to embrace Leonard's teachings completely in years gone by was that I had an enormous amount of healing work to do on myself. I think Leonard did not have so much to do, which he has acknowledged. When part of the mind is locked into the pain of the past, it is impossible to be fully present, so I had to spend a great deal of time using the psychic—dreams, visions, and so on—to help me bring forth the contents of the psyche and take responsibility for my wounded child.

A very good indicator of whether a teacher is on a genuine spiritual path is to simply observe whether he or she can sit easily in presence and can assume responsibility for the ego. If a teacher needs to reach for a cigarette or a beer every short while, or is chasing skirt around, then it is a pretty sure bet that he is not fully present, and thus has not integrated his psyche fully.

You have to be careful with spiritual teachers. They can really help you on your path. I have been privileged to have some wonderful ones in my time. But an unconscious teacher working with dark energy can enchain you. The key is knowing why you are working with the teacher. No human being, and no spiritual teacher, is perfect. Least of all me.

Of course women can get in on the act too. In fact, the darkest energy I ever encountered on my journey was that of a female spiritual teacher. She was a spiritual fraudster without par, and fooled many, many people. This is not to say that she did no good. She actually helped a lot of people. But for those who got too close to her, there was trouble. There was a part of her that was the archetypal Dark Queen, and her goal was to enslave a circle of disciples, not only in this life but beyond. She wielded extraordinary metaphysical power. I was one of the many who gave my power away to her. She gave me a real spiritual thrashing that made me sit up and take notice, I can assure you. I became hopelessly possessed. My energy field was completely subsumed by hers, and it took me two years of excruciating self-work to disentangle myself from her energy. But, boy, did I learn a powerful lesson! You can be certain that it will be awhile before I give my power away like that again!

In the end, who is to say whether a failure is not a success turned inside out, as the success gurus like to say? If you learn from it, then it can be a catalyst that empowers your way forward. Still, a little foresight can save a lot of pain. Don't give yourself away to spiritual teachers.

Nowadays I am grateful for all moments of peace. In the end, I place a higher value upon being able to rest in simple presence than being entertained by woo-woo. Simple presence, and the love and peace that it brings, is worth all the woo-woo on earth and beyond. And I say that as someone who has seen quite a bit of woo-woo in his time.

Presence, though, has another obstacle in its path: the hurt that lies within. It is this pain that binds us to the past, and to the control of the ego. If we want to go the whole nine yards to our bliss, we are going to have to go looking for—and reclaim—the wounded child.

six

The Real Secret

What They Won't Tell You on the New Age Show

In the video and book *The Secret,* we are told that we can manifest whatever we want, as long as we put out the right signal to the universe. This secret has been suppressed. We are shown a scene from a cigarette-filled room full of gray-haired men, presumably plotting to keep the secret out of the hands of the filthy masses.

I hope those old fogies were fired, because they did a lousy job. The idea that you can manifest your dreams has been the central motif of Californian New Ageism for the past thirty years. It is also the central theme of the first book I ever read on alternative spirituality, some twenty years ago: Wayne Dyer's *You'll See It When You Believe It.* Wayne Dyer went on to become perhaps the most successful of all the law-of-attraction gurus, building a career on the premise that we can create any life we want, just so long as we believe it enough. "Your desires," he often wrote, "are sacred." However in recent years Dyer has had to change his tune somewhat, after life dealt him a series of ego falls, as we shall discover a little later on in this chapter.

The big problem, besides the obvious fact that the "secret" isn't a secret, is that it is observably wrong. The richest and most powerful people on the planet are not into Californian woo-woo. And, just as quietly, California is now in massive debt. What is more, a lot of

New Agers and hippies are not exactly living the good life.

Yet there is truth to the idea of manifestation. You *can* create your bliss—you just have to do it according to the laws of Spirit. Things are a little more complex than what we have been told. I therefore use the term *naive manifestation* to refer to the simplistic version of the idea. I once bought the naive manifestation idea myself. In 1998 I got myself into a rut, and decided that manifestation was the way to get myself out of it. The mistake I'd made was to spend too much time and energy on inner worlds. Sure, I learned an awful lot about the mind and consciousness, but unfortunately, I forgot there was a real world out there to attend to. I had casual work as a relief teacher, but the work dried up, as it often does near the end of the school year. So, just at the time I was supposed to be reaping the rewards of my exhaustive self-work, everything fell apart.

Still, being the stubborn type, I didn't give up. I knew that the only reason that I hadn't landed a position as CEO of a Fortune 500 company was because I didn't believe it enough. Every morning, on top of my other inner work, I meditated to a manifestation CD by a certain New Age guru. I imagined the money and job offers pouring in, and my life going from strength to strength. Strangely, nothing happened. I applied for jobs and got turned down. Suddenly, I had no money.

The landlord was nice about it. Too nice, in fact, and one day I found myself five weeks behind in rent. I refused to go on social security, because that would admit my failure to believe enough. Then, one day, I looked up after my morning manifestation visualization and saw the brand name of a tinned apple manufacturer written on the side of a cardboard box: "Dole." I knew then and there that I was going to have to put aside my pride. I hightailed it down to the social security office, crawled in, and applied for the dole.

Now, I have said that I believe that there is some truth to the idea of manifestation, and that it is just more complex than what we are often told. There were good reasons why I was unable to manifest what I wanted. By the end of this chapter, I will make clear what those reasons are. This should be of practical benefit to you, to help you avoid the mistakes I made, as well as learn a little about how the universe really ticks.

The truth is that we attract to us not so much what we want, but what we are.

I WANT IT ALL, AND I WANT IT NOW

It is time to come clean on the truth about what I call "New Age magical thinking." Some may not welcome the things I say, as we would all like to think we can have what we want, whenever we want. That's the inner two-year-old speaking. He goes by the name of "Gimme Gimme."

There are many levels of consciousness beyond the conscious mind, and this is why it is difficult to maintain a positive focus on what you are trying to create. Putting out a constant positive signal to the cosmos is not as easy as it first appears. Even while you are deliberately "imagining your bliss," the deeper layers of your psyche may be putting out a stronger contradictory signal.

Your personality might have the romantic comedy channel on, while your psyche is busy playing horror movies. There you are imagining yourself on the set of *Friends* when suddenly an ax slices through the front door and Jack Nicholson's character from *The Shining* pops his head through the crack and grins evilly: "Daddy's home!" Having Daddy issues tends to disturb the best intentions for romantic interludes with Mr. Right.

> *It is difficult to project a constant positive signal to the cosmos. Even as you are deliberately "imagining your bliss," your deeper psyche may be putting out a contradictory signal.*

Therefore, what you need to do is bring the psyche back into alignment with the intention of your conscious mind. In turn, your ego has to surrender to the call of Spirit. Finally, the right actions have to be taken, and at the right time.

At the time of my bum ride in New Zealand, I was full of doubt and fear. My vision was way ahead of what I was capable of manifesting. I took few actions toward creating what I imagined because I could not figure out the right actions to take. The truth is there were no actions that could get me to a destination that I was incapable of reaching. My ego was not aligned with the truth of Spirit.

For many alternative culture folks, the personality is prompted by the wanton lust of ego, dissociated from Spirit and the higher self, and all the while sitting in the goo of an emotionally damaged psyche. There's not much chance of manifesting your bliss in this situation. *Discover Your Soul Template* is an attempt to bring a greater depth to the idea of the manifestation of dreams, to understand that there are limits to what you can have and do, and that any old goal is not good enough. Spirit is calling you toward futures that fit your soul. Your ego may be oblivious of this.

THE NEW AGE OF "LOVE 'N LIGHT"

I want to emphasize that my intention here is not to attack all New Age thinking. The New Age movement is incredibly diverse, and I know many wonderful people who would probably happily class themselves as "New Age." However, there are limitations to "love 'n light" New Ageism. Remember the concepts of *intention* and *levels of consciousness*? It is not only individuals who have intention and consciousness levels, but groups also. As an example, if you take the average consciousness of the New Age movement in California, incorporating the alternative consciousness movement in general, my reading is that it is about 7 percent. While that may seem low, it is several points higher than for humanity in general (3 percent).

The collective soul issues behind the Californian New Age movement can also be sensed energetically. They center upon narcissism, a sense of being superior to the rest of humanity, a focus upon surfaces (rather than depth), abuse of drugs, a tendency toward not being grounded within the body, a belief in entitlement, blame of the system (generating lower levels of self-responsibility), and certain issues related to sexual expression.

> *The recent financial crisis has shown us that unbridled desire, free of consideration of the whole, is a recipe for delusion and ultimately disaster.*

In New Age thinking in general, there is tendency to focus on the "nicer" parts of the spiritual journey: "let's swim with the dolphins, meditate with crystals, and save the rain forests, but let's not think too deep about what lies within." When we acknowledge only the nice parts of ourselves, the shadow does not get adequately acknowledged and integrated.

Some New Age thinking also makes no attempt to contextualize the individual's journey within a greater dynamic. This is the narcissistic streak. Certain books and videos do not adequately explain that life moves beyond the needs of "me." Thinking that you can have whatever you want if you just believe it enough is a potentially spiritually regressive philosophy. It grants unmitigated power to the human ego, for it makes no distinction between the voice of Spirit and the desire of ego, including the lust for power, fame, riches, sexual gratification, or whatever agenda the ego sets up.

If there is one thing that the recent financial crisis has shown us, it is that unbridled desire, free of consideration for the greater good, is a recipe for delusion and is potentially disastrous. Whether it is within the New Age movement, or in the financial sector, or society in general, narcissism and greed are the inevitable result of such a philosophy.

This statement is not meant to demonize the New Age movement. Reading the issues of any group or collective—charity groups, human rights groups, women's rights groups, religious groups, and so on—highlights the shadow, and this will always be "negative." What the New Age does is bring in spiritual elements to very materialistic Western societies. It is an important phase of human spiritual evolution. We do need to acknowledge its limitations, though, if for no other reason than that New Age naïveté can trip us up on the road toward a truly empowered life.

There is a lesson here for all of us to learn, whether we consider ourselves to be on a spiritual quest or not. If we fail to "get it," the results may be awful indeed. We have been perpetuating a mass delusion, which has now been exposed. Will the collective ego listen, or continue on the path of self-deception?

The prime directive of Spirit is toward the integration of self and soul. Becoming a star, getting a Porsche, and pulling babes may not be part of the deal, sorry to say. Spirit wants you to experience divine love above all else, and for that to happen, you have to heal. You need to bring in the wounded child from the cold, and to do that you have to go into the land of the shadow. You have to get real.

This is where free will comes in. Your freedom to choose is both God's greatest gift and the most frightening responsibility you have been given. You are free to live life dictated by the whims of ego, out of alignment with your higher self, and to abuse your power. Or you can move in presence, where the Sage can speak through you. Make no mistake. You will constantly become slightly unbalanced, and sometimes you will topple right off your true path. It is your intention to serve Spirit that will bring you back on track.

Spirit will guide you all the time. But if you choose not to listen, then Spirit will not force the issue. It will just whisper quietly and patiently in your ear. If you drift so far astray from the soul template that you fall off the map and flat on your butt, Spirit is more than happy to see you take a swan dive. Or even send the cement truck, just when you step out onto the road.

THE PSYCHE STRIKES BACK

It would be nice if the trick to life was simply finding what was aligned with your soul template, and then taking it: "Gimme some of that!" You would be a bit like a child in a candy shop with mother's credit card. But it is not quite that simple. Every time you reach for something, physically or within your imagination, there is also a psychospiritual movement in the depths of your mind. The very act of thinking about a desired future brings out beliefs and memories from within.

In other words, every time you try to create, there is a concurrent movement of resisting energy. As that energy emerges, it synchronistically attracts to you the people and events that reflect those self-limiting beliefs. This is a further distinction you must take into consideration as you come to understand the law of attraction.

Every time you reach for something there is a concurrent
psychospiritual movement within your mind.
Thinking about a desired future brings out beliefs,
memories, and pain from within.

Think of it this way. Imagine trying to fire a large cannon from a boat. The boat is your mind, the cannon your method of forging your desired future, and the firing of the cannonball is your goal. Any weakness in the boat's structure, or for that matter, in the cannon, will be made readily apparent when you try to load the cannon onto the boat and fire it. If the boat is too small and weak—say a little wooden rowboat—you won't even be able to get the cannon on board. If you did manage to haul it on, when you fired it, the boat would be greatly damaged, perhaps even destroyed. If the boat is larger and sturdier, but there is a weakness in the hull, the pressure of the firing may cause a perforation—and then you would be taking on water! Suddenly it would be an emergency. You would no longer be trying to fire the cannon, but dealing with the water gushing in everywhere.

Creation is like this. How many times have you tried to set yourself a goal, only to find your anxieties building up? The bigger the goal, the greater are the issues that tend to emerge. Perhaps a person is trying to get a business off the ground. She decides that she wants to open a little shop to sell imported Thai clothing. Then she starts thinking. "What about the money? How reliable are the people I want to work with? Am

I really worthy of the personal and financial rewards that might come my way? Can I trust myself and the universe? Am I good enough? This world is so damn rotten, and life is hard!"

It all comes back to three things. Beliefs, beliefs, beliefs.

> *You can be expending enormous amounts of energy*
> *on psychic drama without there being a visible conflict.*
> *The Sage can work directly with the energy,*
> *integrate and heal it.*

If our wannabe Thai clothes importer does not deal with her belief structures, they will spill over into her emotional life, creating dramas with lovers, family, friends, and workmates. She may find herself arguing with her husband over whether to buy turkey or chicken for Sunday roast. She screams, "You should know what I want!" He yells back, "Why do you always expect me to pick up the food?" Before you know it the china set is sailing across the room in hubby's direction.

What is really happening here is that the "pressure" exerted by the woman's goal has triggered issues related to her father, because her father has hurt her and damaged her self-belief. In order for the goal to manifest, she has to believe in herself, believe in the possibility that she can achieve it, and believe that she is worthy of achieving it. Standing in the way is the shadow of Daddy, who imprinted upon her psyche the idea that women are dirty, weak, untrustworthy, and devious (common male projections onto females). Instead of processing this energy, she projects it out onto her hubby. Soon she is beating him up, and he is wondering why. Suddenly his wife is looking an awful lot like Ma, and in turn his buttons are getting pushed big time. This is a classic drama.

> *If you fail to rein in your need for drama, you disempower*
> *yourself. Drama depletes your energy, distorts your focus,*
> *and takes your attention away from your dreams.*

As mentioned, drama can also occur in psychic space, invisible to the eye, but still capable of draining enormous amounts of energy. The Sage is able to work directly with the emotional and psychic energy as it surfaces, then integrate and heal it. In other words, he is able to assume responsibility for the energy.

DRAMA DISEMPOWERS

The failure to love yourself completely and assume a high level of responsibility for your emotional energy leaves you vulnerable to endless interpersonal and psychic battles. If you fail to rein in your need for drama, you disempower yourself. Drama depletes your energy, distorts your focus, and takes your attention away from what you want to create. It also robs you of any chance of being fully present. The higher your propensity for drama, the less creative energy you have left to manifest your dreams.

Some time ago, I was involved in a doozy of a drama. The situation involved a certain think tank and the development of a report for a powerful international organization. As a member of that group, I was invited to participate. The discussion was all electronic, involving e-mails and other web media. As it turned out, my contribution was minimal, as I was busy at the time, and much of it was beyond my expertise and interests. After several weeks, a final document was prepared.

Many of the contributions had been rambling and the whole discussion was quite disorganized, so one group member, Sean, bravely volunteered for the onerous task of putting all the ideas together into one intelligible document. This huge operation took him a month. When the document was ready, Sean asked for comments from other participants. Feeling guilty that I had not really contributed as much as I should have, I offered to proofread and edit the document. This is where the drama started.

The document I received was rather shoddy, with multiple problems. I felt numerous changes needed to be made. Yet time was running out because we had to submit the report in only a few days. So I went through it with a big red pen (so to speak), and made many recommendations for changes. I then sent it into the group leader, Harry, to see what he thought. Harry was aghast. He said that everyone was too busy to go through all my recommendations, so they would just have to leave it.

Here is where my ego checked into the hotel. I was annoyed that my voice had been ignored. Then another group member, Chang, came forward and stated that he also thought the document was well below professional standard. Harry reiterated that other members had looked at it, and hadn't noticed any real problems. Sean wrote that if Chang and I were not happy with the document, we could have our names removed from it. He then blurted out that in all of his professional career, with multiple publications as a writer and academic, he had never received the kind of criticisms that Chang and I had put forward. He was indignant. His ego had checked into the hotel too.

Things were now getting pushy at the hotel check-in desk. Chang marched in and started clanging the bell at the front desk, demanding service. He sent e-mails and made postings saying that he had published twice as many books and papers as Sean, and that Sean had no right to submit the paper without his consent, nor the right to erase his name from the paper.

I tried to be diplomatic, and posted several times apologizing for any misunderstandings. I got no responses, which again pushed my buttons. Ignored yet again! Now I was trying to wrestle my ego and stop it from grabbing an axe and running around the hotel foyer.

My part in the drama sprang from a childhood issue. My parents were particularly strict, believing that children should be seen and not heard. My father had little time for love and nurturing. Children were basically tools for fixing stuff around the house and a cheap source of labor for the family business. Anytime I complained or acted up, I was silenced with physical punishment or sent to my bedroom without dinner or TV. In my father's defense, sometimes I got water if I was really good.

Chang's soul issues soon became clear to me. He wrote me an e-mail.

Did he start off with an analysis of the situation, or telling me how to resolve the problem? That would have been the rational approach, after all. But no! He got straight into telling me about his childhood and how everyone at school beat him up because he was different.

There it was in black and white. Chang's investment in the drama sprung from his wounded child. Yet Chang had no intention of accepting responsibility for that hurt, and working toward healing and group harmony. No, he wanted attention and sympathy from me, and justice from the group for being wronged.

By that point I had worked on the issue, having completed several sessions of Connecting with the Ego and Wounded Child, so I had pulled my emotional energy out. I had taken responsibility. I worked on some deep issues with my father and elder brother, especially some anger and sadness that were lingering within me.

Because I have a commitment to honoring Spirit and a vision to focus upon, I didn't let Chang pull me back into the drama (which is what he wanted). I checked out of the hotel, which wasn't easy, as there were bully boys at the door trying to push me back inside. I wrote a polite e-mail to Chang telling him I was sorry for his childhood mistreatment, but suggesting that we should focus on resolving the issue. Before I sent the e-mail, I checked the intention behind it (by letting my ego speak, and correcting it), and acknowledged anything that was ego-based. The intention that underpins action is very important if you want to resolve dramas, for even as you are saying or doing one thing, energetically you may be doing the opposite.

Sean was eyeball-deep in the muck of drama too, reacting from his soul issues. My sense was that his father had punished him also, and the criticism had generated a fear reaction, followed by anger. Where there is anger, there is fear. Eventually it all died down. The blood was washed from the hotel carpet. In a final irony, I learned that Chang and I had been given the wrong document—an earlier draft, not the final copy.

Ego agendas are a substitute for love.

There was also a broader group dynamic at work. All of us in the drama had been seduced by the ego's desire for power and attention. We were looking for greater recognition. The paper was our passport to global-level power. It was about-face, status, and prestige. Entire cultures are built on such ego stuff. However, as soon as you buy into the collective ego narrative, you become a channel for darkness. Our group was generating a vortex of dark energy, which we were all being sucked into. Our egos were being used as a channel through which dark energy could pour.

The "higher" you go in circles of power, the darker the energy tends to get. Many powerful organizations and world leaders are magnets for dark energy. Some individuals are particularly prone to becoming ensnared within such consciousness fields if they have major unresolved issues of pain and abandonment. For it is through the ego—and in turn the wounded child—that dark energy manipulates us. This is one reason why the world is so screwed up—ego and dark energy run the show.

THE NEED FOR LOVE

What the ego (and the wounded child) really want is unconditional love and attention. If it cannot get it from "you" in the form of self-love and acceptance, it will seek it from outside. Ego agendas are thus a substitute for love. So why bother with the agenda at all? It is a distraction from what really matters to you, and will only lead you into darkness, because it will never light your heart from within.

The wounded child's need for love and attention will not be met, no matter how high you climb the ladder of status and power. You might become president of the most powerful nation on earth, but for your spirit that will have no value relative to the "achievement" of creating genuine love.

There was a lesson for me in the think-tank drama. My intention in contributing to the production of the document emerged from an ego agenda for attention, to be elevated in status and power. It was a trap. It is important when dealing with higher levels of societal power that you are clear about your intentions. Use the Connecting tools to check the ego. Otherwise you might just find your inner pompous twit has become your outer pompous twit, and you are in the muck up to your eyeballs.

Current education does little to teach people about consciousness. The other members of the think tank have MBAs and Ph.D.s, have sold hundreds of thousands of books, and written countless academic papers. Many hold positions of societal prestige and power. Yet many are no more conscious of Spirit than high school dropouts. In some cases, they are less aware, as their egos have completely taken control of the ship.

HUMAN POTENTIAL, EGO POTENTIAL

Some spiritual gurus may conveniently fail to tell you that healing is an essential component of the spiritual journey. They enjoy building up your ego and telling you that you are special and that you can have it all. Then they ask for the check.

> *Some gurus may not tell you that healing is an essential part of the spiritual journey. False teachers build up your ego, say that you are special, and that you can have it all. Then they ask for the check.*

This is also a problem with much of the human potential movement in general. Neuro-linguistic programming, for example, often bypasses the feeling bit. One supersuccessful NLP guru (let's call him Ned) actually goes out of his way to teach that "going within to feel" is dead wrong. According to him, the way to go is simply to reprogram yourself for success. Ned teaches plenty of good stuff, and is supersuccessful himself. He helps a lot of people too, through his teachings and by generously giving to charity. In the history of human beings walking this planet, Ned is one of the wiser and more powerful.

The problem is that there is a dark side to Ned. I have seen this soul issue in other NLP practitioners also. In their haste to move forward and leave the past behind, they can create a wake of shadow energy. There is often a failure to listen to Spirit, and a split occurs within the psyche as the shadow is neglected. This makes them an easy target for manipulation. They can become magnets for dark energy.

North American NLP has an overall level of consciousness of about 5 percent. Responsibility levels are only slightly higher than average. Looking at the collective energy of "NLP" in North America as a group consciousness field, some strong themes emerge from its shadow. Beyond the public persona of "success and happiness," there is an intention involving ego-centered agendas, a movement toward power and control. Narcissism is a central theme, with an overriding "look at me!" mentality. It is also strongly materialistic. There is a notable projection of "I can have it all," conversely superimposed upon a sense of frustration and confusion. The latter emerges from the unaddressed issues of the wounded child.

The collective consciousness field of NLP therefore reflects the ego-centered tendencies of contemporary humanity, and in particular American materialism.

The consciousness tools of NLP are not wrong or intrinsically evil. In fact some of the INI tools are borrowed from NLP: Creative Imagination and Affirmation, for example, are widely employed in NLP. But without the balancing input of Spirit, the tools tend to be hijacked by ego-centered intentions, pulling users back into low-density consciousness fields. There is the same possibility with the INI tools if misapplied. However, my approach incorporates a greater degree of transparency and vulnerability. The ego and the wounded child are allowed a voice, and this minimizes the problem of ego-hijacking. I also emphasize connecting with the Sage, and allowing yourself to be guided by Spirit.

If you want to do a spiritual journey, you must address your soul purpose. To do that, you have to examine your soul issues and bring the wounded child in from the cold and into your awareness. You have to give the little boy or girl inside you the love and attention that it needs to heal. Only then will you be part of the transformation of humanity.

Many people just embarking on the spiritual journey (and more than a few old timers) enjoy the fantasy of the "love 'n light" delusion. After all, what is the point of a delusion if you can't have a good old time with it? The idea is that you devote your life to Spirit, and then suddenly you are walking around in a state of enlightenment, nose high in the air, throwing flower petals about, and wafting incense all over the place. You might say that there's nothing wrong with that, other than annoying everyone with some smelly stuff. Unfortunately, the "love 'n light" story is way too nice for the likings of Spirit. The only way to heal is to feel, and that means getting down and dirty. You must honor your pain, or it controls you.

THE NEED FOR DELIBERATE PRACTICE

Deliberate practice is the intelligent application of repetition in order to improve performance. New Age "go with the flow" philosophies may delude some people into thinking that hard work and deliberate practice are not required to achieve success and excellence in a particular field of endeavor.

Let me assure you that intelligence, sustained commitment, and hard work will almost certainly be required if you are to live an empowered life. The truth is that this is a very competitive world, and that standards of performance and excellence have increased dramatically in many fields in recent years. Certainly, if your goal is to reach world-class status, then deliberate practice cannot be avoided.

I highly recommend Geoff Colvin's *Talent Is Overrated* (see Recommended Reading) as a good introduction to this topic. It shows that deliberate practice is what often separates genius from very good. Colvin outlines the following features of deliberate practice.

- Deliberate practice is hard work. It is not what we normally think of as practice, such as when you strum a guitar for a bit of fun.

You have to move out of your comfort zone to perform deliberate practice. This is where we need to be careful that we do not trip ourselves up with the idea of "bliss." "Living your bliss" does not preclude the possibility of discomfort and a certain degree of sacrifice.

- Deliberate practice is *designed* specifically to improve performance. This means intelligent thought is put into the practice session, so that deliberate and conscious goals for improving performance are met. This in turn requires you to carefully define the elements of your skill that require enhancement, and then go about working at those. Benjamin Franklin, for example, wanted to be a great writer, but realized that his vocabulary was lacking, so systematically set about improving it.

- Practicing something systematically and intelligently is highly demanding. It requires a great deal of focus and concentration. Studies have shown that excellent violinists practice a lot more than those of lesser skill. Generally speaking, there are limits to how long you can practice, however. Sessions of no more than ninety minutes at a time, and totaling four to five hours per day are ideal. Any more than that and you risk burnout. Mental visualization should not be underestimated here, as it can greatly enhance performance, as long as the imagined practice is correct and conforms to the requirements of deliberate practice. That means that specific skills are identified, and the imagined scenario is as life-like as possible.

A lot of New Agers and dharma bums falsely believe that if it isn't fun and easy, then it is not spiritual. However, hard work and commitment are part of the journey. The Sage does this work in alignment with Spirit, keeping her mind present and mindful of intuitive prompts when deliberate practice is required. By drawing upon Integrated Intelligence during both practice and performance, the Sage will have the advantage over many others.

TELLING EGO AND SPIRIT APART

From what I have written above, it should be clear that there are intentions and dreams that are born of ego, not Spirit. That is something important to remember, because not every intuitive prompt from within is the voice of God. Your ego tends to feed you a long list of demands that it wants fulfilled at short notice. Dark energies will build up your ego. They will try to sell you the lie that you are special, that you are the Great One. Don't buy! If you do, your soul will be drawn into some very nasty energy fields.

Ego is part of being human, and deserves all the love
that every expression of the human personality requires.
Ego goes with you all the way to God.

To distinguish the voice of Spirit from the voice of ego, look for the tell-tale signs outlined in table 1.1, in chapter 1. Ego's pull is toward separation, specialness, and greatness. It is afraid of the ordinary, of simple presence, and of deep connection. It refuses to listen. It is stubborn and bloody-minded. It will not let go, for letting go represents the annihilation of ego. Your resistance to what is written in this paragraph is the pull of your ego, struggling to maintain its grip on you.

Make no mistake. Ego is not something to be feared, and it needn't be erased. It is part of being human, and deserves all the love and attention that any expression of the human personality requires. As one of my spiritual teachers Leonard Jacobson likes to say, "ego goes with you all the way to God."

The key, then, is to develop the right relationship with ego. The right relationship is one of honesty, of transparency. You have to be completely honest with yourself. The nature of ego is deception, so it will play hide-and-seek with you. That is perfectly normal. It is not a sin, and you do not have to partake in thirty days of penance every time you spot an ego state within. A gentle correction is often all that is required. Rejection of ego only builds its defenses higher, because so much of ego is the voice of the wounded child crying for attention, for acceptance, for love. So, just love it!

OF DREAMS AND ACTIONS

Limiting beliefs tend to make themselves known with one overriding emotion: fear. Yet it is not fear that is the problem. It is the running away from fear. Unless you turn and face the fear, your dream may falter.

Dreaming, planning, and then following through with concrete actions provide you with the opportunity to face the energy within your mind and soul. They bring you into a closer relationship with the soul template. The actions you take are intrinsically challenging, confronting, and, best of all, potentially healing and liberating. So, in a sense, the universe is playing a little trick on us. We think we are reaching for the dream, but we are really entering the shadow. If we bring the light with us (love and acceptance), the shadow begins to dissolve. This is our bliss.

This is not to say that a dream does not have value in itself. It absolutely does. But the greater goal of the universe is the integration of mind and Spirit, which involves the healing of the emotional energies that keep your mind locked in ego and away from the embrace of love. As you express your soul purpose, you articulate the integration of mind and soul.

Your excitement is the sound of the cosmos calling you home.

THE SOUND OF ONE EGO FALLING

At the beginning of this chapter I referred to bestselling New Age author Wayne Dyer, who has been teaching about the law of attraction for decades. However in recent years Dyer has suffered several rather large ego falls. Ego falls occur when the ego builds a delusion about who or what it is, and then life offers a "correction." Ego falls are actually a blessing in disguise. If you allow the consciousness of the event to be fully received, the lesson can be learned. The fall may actually lead to a deepening into Spirit—if you pass the "test."

Wayne Dyer's late-life tests have been difficult. First his wife, and the mother of his seven children, left him for another man. Not long after, he suffered a heart attack, and the one-time fitness fanatic ended up strapped into a hospital bed. Then, in 2009, he was diagnosed with leukemia. According to Dyer, his is not a life-threatening form of the disease, yet it surely must be a test of his courage and belief structures. Interviews that Wayne Dyer has given after these events indicate that he has encountered his problems with courage, honesty, and humility, and this shows him to be a man who walks his talk. He has openly discussed the way the ego creates illusions, and the way that ego falls can assist us on our spiritual journeys.

Wayne Dyer was once an advocate of the naive version of the law of attraction, but has deepened his understanding of the principle. He now says that we do not attract what we *want*, but what we *are*. And "what we are" includes the totality of our consciousness, including the shadow and our soul issues. This is why true consciousness work is not merely about "manifestation," but about deep soul reflection. It requires humility and an acknowledgement of our physical and emotional vulnerability.

From what I have written in this chapter it should be obvious why I was unable to manifest my vision during that rather difficult time in New Zealand. My dream was built upon a naive understanding of manifestation. Manifestation and true bliss are founded upon the guidance of Spirit, with love as the central theme. They require that we develop an unshakable belief in our self, grounded in an honest acceptance of our soul issues. From that guidance, honesty, and self-belief, an appropriate vision can then be developed and the right actions and timing will follow.

When your vision falls too far out of alignment with where you really stand, you go into delusion. An ego fall is inevitable. I was lucky. Spirit didn't send the cement truck. It sent the pizza delivery car instead. Not long after begging the government for cash to kick-start my life again, I took a job delivering pizzas. That was perfect for me for a few months. Strangely, I hadn't ever sat down and tried to manifest myself as a thirty-three-year-old pizza boy. Yet what I really needed to do was go back to basics. My soul had been reduced to a rather raw and vulnerable state, and I had become too introspective. I needed to get out into the real world with real people and do real stuff. Spirit doesn't always give you what you want. Sometimes it just gives you what you really need.

We are now getting awfully close to the end of part one of *Discover Your Soul Template,* where I have outlined the foundations that are required to build a Sage life. Yet another aspect of awareness is required if your Sage is to emerge from behind your shadow. And it is the most challenging of all.

seven

Doorways to the Soul

Finding and Loving the Wounded Child

Some years ago, at a time when my spiritual journey was just about to unfold, I was walking through a magazine shop in the little town of Taree in New South Wales, when I saw something that caught my eye. I stopped and picked up a backpacker's magazine. I began to flip through the pages. The magazine said there were youth hostels all up and down Australia's east coast, places where people could stay for just a few bucks a night. Suddenly a whole new world opened up before me. It was as if a new tunnel suddenly forged its way through the mountain ahead, and I was asked whether I wanted to pass through it. I said "Yes," bought the magazine, and walked out.

There were phone numbers. It took me a while to work up the courage, but a few weeks later, when I had returned to work in another town in central New South Wales, I rang up. I got someone on the other end of the phone confirming that backpackers' hostels really did exist. I said I might be dropping by.

A few days later I went to a camping store, bought a backpack and a sleeping bag, threw them into the back of my car, and drove away. I had never traveled by myself before, so I was scared. Maybe I should have been a bit more scared, because about six hours into the drive while on a completely deserted stretch of country road in the black of night, I brushed some gravel on a bend and found that my steering wheel had strangely lost the ability to control the vehicle. The road went right, and I went straight ahead, plowing through the scrub and down into a dry creek bed with a great thud.

I cursed and peeled open the door. It was my first car accident, so I was kind of expecting the vehicle to explode like they do in the Hollywood movies. But it didn't happen. Clawing my way up the embankment, I made it to the road and waited in the blackness for someone to come along. I was eventually picked up by a woman. She drove me to the next tiny town along the road.

It was a bummer of a start to my backpacking adventure. The car was a write-off. But I was undeterred. I left the crumpled heap at the local wreckers, strapped on my backpack, and thumbed a lift outta there. Finally free of the vehicle, I could do the trip real backpacker's style.

Eventually, I made my way up to the small town of Byron Bay on the far north coast of New South Wales. Byron Bay is Hippie Haven, and I just happened to stay at Hippie Central, an eccentric but very cozy youth hostel called the Arts Factory Lodge. There I was given my first real introduction to alternative thinking. There were all kinds of holistic and New Age practitioners hanging round. While I had no experience with that kind of thing, I was not totally skeptical either. On the crowded notice board I saw a flyer by a guy called Mike, who claimed to do some kind of energy healing for emotional blocks.

I thought for a moment. Hmm, that sounded a bit like me. I felt pretty emotionally blocked. Fortified, even. So I gave him a ring. After speaking to Mike for a few minutes, I made the decision to give it a go. After all, it couldn't hurt, could it?

The next day I walked down the little main street of Byron Bay, past all the little tie dye shops and veggie restaurants until I stumbled across Mike's quaint but nondescript New Age shop. I walked in and found myself talking to a youngish man with a beard. He looked a bit like Jesus. The look in his eyes was more the deeply pained, post-

Judas-kiss Jesus than the beatific younger Jesus. But it was Jesus-like nonetheless. This was reassuring.

Mike asked me why I had come to see him. After beating round the bush for a while and trying to throw him off, I finally came clean and told him I was a basket case. He looked sympathetic. Then he did something terrifying. He reached out and put his hand over my solar plexus and told me to relax. This was a little more intimate than I had expected when I agreed to pay the forty bucks. I felt my breathing contract, and a feeling that was almost dread descended upon me. This guy was going to see me. I tried to relax and tell myself that it would be okay and that nothing would come of it.

Something came of it. Mike reached into my heart and felt the tears of the wounded child. He saw me, and I knew it. Mike looked at me, eyes now more pre-crucifixion Jesus than anything else, and told me he felt a lot of troubled energy. He told me I really needed to look within myself to find my pain. He explained that he could help me with this if I liked. I paid the forty bucks, bolted for the door, and ran for five years. I wasn't ready to face myself. I knew that Mike was right, but I didn't want to think about it, and I certainly didn't want to *feel* about it. In hindsight, I realize that my meeting with Mike was a case of like-knows-like. Mike was also a deeply hurt young man, and he spotted me right away, being a little further along his journey than I was. Spirit made the connection and invited me to go deeper, but I said no. I wasn't ready. That would come later.

The spiritual journey is a healing journey. To heal it you have to feel it. That is the price you have to pay.

The spiritual journey is a healing journey. To heal it you have to feel it. That is the price you have to pay. Working with the conscious mind with such tools as positive thinking and creative imagination is great. Engaging in spiritual practices such as meditation and prayer is wonderful. But unless you address your emotional body, you will never actualize your bliss. This chapter is about the emotional part of the journey.

INVISIBLE PLAYERS

In the last chapter I wrote that what the wounded child within you really wants is unconditional love and attention. I said that if it doesn't get it from you, it will seek it from outside. The most common method is to seek control over or attention from others—via drama. Because drama is disempowering, energy draining, and basically a huge distraction, we need to get control of it. To do this, we need to deal with the problem at its source—the pain and distorted beliefs of the wounded and karmic children.

Drama always contains a psychic element. Behind the physical drama—the worlds, actions, feelings, and thoughts—a lot of psychic energy is being thrashed around. Many dramas have little or no physical reality at all. These usually involve ongoing unresolved issues with family members, relatives, and friends, including childhood friends. Psychic dramas are the most problematic because they are unconscious. Evidence of them does creep through, though, in dreams and the stray thoughts we have during the day. If you check your regular thoughts toward people from your past whenever they come to mind, you will gain a glimpse of the dramas within which your psyche is enmeshed.

When I was seven years old my family moved from the tiny town of Uranquinty in southern New South Wales, to the not-much-bigger town of Taree, on the mid-north coast of the same state. This was distressing, but I made friends with a boy my own age named George. We were best friends all through primary school, and although we became more distant in high school, we remained friends. Then at age eighteen I moved away from Taree to go to university. The last time I saw him was over two decades ago. Yet George and I still hang out every month or two.

Our energy connects. I meet up with George whenever I neglect my inner child, and when I fail to meet my need to be with friends to be playful. If George has some equivalent issue going down, we can end up hanging out in psychic space. This in itself is harmless, but what happens much of the time is that we play out unresolved childhood issues with each other. Often we are beating each other up, getting jealous of each other, or trying to push each other around. In other words, sometimes we are in drama.

That means we are not present in the world, and that we are wasting a certain amount of our creative and psychic energy, when we could be using it more productively elsewhere. In some instances psychic dramas are not too much of a problem. Yet in other cases the drama may be highly destructive or even debilitating, such as when we unconsciously give our power away to some distant person or discarnate entity. My reading is that around 20 percent of chronic fatigue cases, for example, are a product of possession, where one individual's energy field is subsumed by another's. The soul issues of our parents affect our psyches: their beliefs, fears, unresolved pain, and shame imprint themselves into our subconscious during infancy.

For the vast majority of the human race, not much can be done about these kinds of psychic dramas, as people are unaware of them. Having worked in public education for many years, I am always filled with sadness and a sense of helplessness when I see a school kid who is possessed. There is simply nothing I can do about it, except say the odd prayer to Spirit that the child may find freedom according to his or her soul purpose. Many such kids are diagnosed with bipolar disorder, attention deficit disorder, or just plain depression. The scariest thing is that they are mostly possessed by members of their own families, particularly parents and grandparents.

Some psychic dramas are basically harmless. Others may be highly destructive or even debilitating, as when we unconsciously give our power away to a person or discarnate entity.

As the Sage develops her awareness and power, she is able to free herself from the psychic control of others, including the collective energy of society and humanity in general. As you develop your Integrated Intelligence, you will become more proficient at identifying psychic drama. Once you have "seen" the dramas, you can use the INI tools to resolve them as you would for normal dramas. The key is bringing the wounded child home.

USING DRAMA FOR GROWTH

Like the ego itself, drama is simply part of being human, and we need not think of it as something bad. For the Sage, drama is an opportunity for healing and growth. There is no need to pretend that your stuff isn't smelly. Just love it. When you acknowledge the ego and do the necessary work with your soul issues, you will gradually integrate the shadow with the conscious mind. You will reclaim your lost children.

As was the case with my think-tank drama in the previous chapter, the key is to take responsibility for your part in the drama, and pull out of it. We create drama because there is a payoff, and it always involves attention or control and power. A prime agenda of ego is to ensure that its map of reality, no matter how twisted or painful, is maintained. In the case of Chang in the think tank, the drama was an opportunity for him to re-assert his victim status.

None of us was raised in a sea of unconditional love. This creates a wounding within us, our original pain. Your soul issues emerge directly from such emotional hurt.

He badly needed a few people to beat him up just to confirm that the world was against him. The added bonus was the opportunity to get some sympathy (read "attention") as a substitute for love. While getting roughed up by the bully boys might not seem like power at first glance, the control lies in the ego's ability to remake the world as it sees it. Like Chang, I enjoyed a good face stomping in my heyday—on the receiving end.

We can see that Chang's intention was to perpetuate the narrative of his life. He had minimal intention to resolve the drama, and absolutely no intention to address his pain and do some healing work.

Like many human beings, he will most likely go to his grave having failed to address his soul issues, and perhaps having added a few more points to his karmic record.

ORIGINAL PAIN, ORIGINAL SHAME

The truth is that none of us was brought up in a sea of unconditional love, and this fact creates a wounding within us. We can call this our original pain, and our soul issues emerge directly from it. A child becomes frightened and angry when she does not get the love she feels she deserves. For the child, this nonacceptance is a betrayal of the soul's right to perfect love. It represents the threat of death, for a baby is helpless, and rejection brings forth the fear of abandonment by the mother (and to a lesser extent the father), and the death that would inevitably follow.

Another significant form of wounding occurs when, as a newborn, your parents and relatives unconsciously imprinted their unresolved issues onto your psyche. This occurs psychically and may have little relationship to the way they physically interacted with you (although there often is a correlation). They may have been really loving, yet still have dumped all their stuff on you. This is something that challenges many spiritual seekers as they become more aware of Integrated Intelligence. We'd prefer to think that our parents were loving. A more truthful way of looking at it is to understand that they were as loving as they knew how to be, given the fact that their awareness of these things was probably nonexistent. Remember, the average level of human consciousness rests at about 3 percent. Let's give the old folks a break.

KINDS OF PROJECTIONS

During your childhood, the soul issues of your parents and caregivers deeply affect your psyche. Virtually all their beliefs and fears, unresolved pain and shame will imprint themselves into your subconscious. These could involve many aspects of life as a human being: money and abundance, attitudes toward certain groups and races of people, alcohol use and abuse, human nature, and so on. Once of the most common and significant projections is sexual shaming. All of us carry sexual shame. It is a prime issue of the human oversoul, and a strongly repressive belief structure that humanity has chosen to explore. For the newborn, the sexual shame it receives includes the negative beliefs of the opposite-sex parent. A boy with a mother who holds strong negative beliefs about men's sexuality may receive the message that all men are bastards; that they are dirty, rapacious beasts who only think of one thing (sound familiar?). A baby girl with a deeply hurt father may receive his shadow projections about women being controlling, sexually manipulative, unfaithful, and so on.

Sometimes these projections can come in the form of intense psychic attacks. In my case, as an infant I suffered repeated negative sexual projections from an elderly female relative. She had experienced much sexual abuse herself, and the idea of a male baby growing up to be an empowered man was abhorrent to her psyche. She also had unmet sexual needs, which she projected onto me. But the universe wasn't content to see me physically abused by just one puny human. Seven generations ago on my father's side of the family, an ancestor of mine contracted a sexual disease. The intense shame of this got transferred onto his children, right down the line to my generation of the family. Though the gonorrhea has long gone, the shaming energy persists. To this day I have to maintain vigilant work on this energy, as my father's spirit still projects the shame of it on me and other family members.

This is an unconscious way to control the energy of the family consciousness field. I have repeatedly passed on the message to the old bastard that he is dead, and that he should start acting that way. Unfortunately, listening was never his strong point. It is not only consciousness that transcends the death of the body. "Unconsciousness" goes with you as well.

Such projections are a powerful rejection experience for the child.

They create a profound wound, a deep shame. All of us carry this wounding, to a greater or lesser degree. In particular, this energy of sexual shame becomes imprinted on the child's genital area. If you could read the energy of it in an auditory way, the message is always something like, "That thing is dirty. It makes me feel sick!"

Another common form of shaming that locates itself near the genital area of the body is toilet shame. This involves the belief that defecation and urination are dirty. In some societies this shaming is pronounced—especially in Western society—while in others there is relatively little—such as in Chinese society. Some health problems people experience in later life (including constipation, bowel irritation, cancers, and sexual dysfunction) are a result of the negative psychic energy imprinted upon these areas of the body. These energies can be healed. In connecting with the original pain, the energy of the time of imprinting can be brought forward (including the psychic interaction that surrounded the shaming) and the energy released.*

THE LOST CHILDREN

When these traumas occur in the child, parts of the psyche may split off from the energy field. These splits then come to exist in a state of dissociation from the conscious mind or personality. I call these the "lost children." As an adult you will probably not be consciously aware of them, as they remain obscured in a murky inner world. Nonetheless, they strongly influence your beliefs and behaviors, your ability to stand in your power as a man or woman, and ultimately your level of consciousness.

In chapter 5, I talked about the importance of presence. The distinction I wish to emphasize here is that you cannot come fully into presence while parts of your energy field are stuck in the past. This is important, because, as I have said, to find empowerment and abundance,

---

*This is more complex than can be detailed here. Perhaps in a later volume I will address this issue.

and to tap in to the wisdom of Integrated Intelligence, you must bring the mind fully into the present. As long as you have these lost parts of the psyche floating around in psychic space, it is effectively impossible to be responsible for the vibrational energy that you put out into the cosmos.

> *As a Sage you need to become aware of your psychic*
> *projections toward infants and children.*

As a Sage you need to become aware of your psychic projections toward infants and children. Being a Sage is about taking increasing responsibility for your life. That includes your energy. As you do your healing work, as more light comes into your consciousness, your projections on others (including children) will automatically reduce. Your intention to heal and be responsible for your energy is part of the transformation of the human race, one of the outcomes of Integrated Intelligence. And that is a wonderful thing.

Cat Fights and Lost Children

Your lost children will silently go about creating drama for you. The psychic space of humanity is full of billions of lost children, all deeply hurt and angry, engaging in psychic battles of power and control. The dramas your lost children create mirror your beliefs and worldview back to you. Such dramas exist within low-density consciousness fields. Drama therefore traps you at lower levels of consciousness. You can attend the latest workshops about creative visualization, abundance, or manifesting your dreams. You can get all pumped up. You can run around all day shouting that "I deserve all that I can imagine, because I am beautiful!" But if your psyche does not heal, you will still go home and kick the cat, and then be thinking "Why did I do that?"

In short, unless you develop an awareness of, and take responsibility for, your lost children and bring yourself into presence, your spiritual journey will be painfully slow. Or, more than likely, it will simply stagnate. In a practical sense it means that your capacity to live your dream will be greatly diminished.

Don't get me wrong. Without presence and unconditional love for yourself, you may well be able to manifest a great many of your material goals and dreams. Plenty of people do. History is scattered with tales of many an upstanding young twit who managed to pull it off despite having the spiritual maturity of a garden gnome. Certain politicians come to mind. Still, if you do not do your inner work, you make things more difficult for yourself. You not only disperse your creative energy, you also miss the boat as far as the greatest prize of all is concerned: unconditional love. For the soul, the Porsche is still the booby prize. Manifesting a nice car might be useful within the greater creative spirit of the soul, but it is just another prop on the stage of existence.

BEHIND THE WOUNDED CHILD: THE KARMIC CHILDREN

Feeling pain is not an end in itself. Only masochists enjoy their suffering. The focus of your journey is love and creation. However, embracing your pain is part of the reclamation of the wounded child—and the karmic children you have left behind. What you will find if you allow the wounded child to speak is that another voice, another pain, will often emerge from beyond it. If you permit yourself to fall into that voice and its emotional energy, you will "see" the karma—through feelings, images, sounds, and voices within your mind. For readers with an advanced awareness of such things, you can use the Connecting with the Wounded Child/Karmic Child tools to get to the bottom of the issue. For those less experienced in dealing with the emotional body, I recommend working with an inner child practitioner or a regression therapist. However, as always, choose wisely who you work with when probing such delicate parts of your self.

Recall that your soul issues and your karmic issues tend to mirror each other (reflecting soul habits), and this means your lost children and karmic energy can be very similar. They usually overlap. If you use the Connecting tools, you will often find that your emotional energy will shift between one and the other. Past life regression therapists know this link well, and will often ask clients in a hypnotic regression to move from connecting with their childhood pain, into connecting with painful experiences from past lives.

Love your fear, love your pain. It is the running away
that creates most of the suffering. Surrendering
will free your soul.

The way to integrate the wounded and karmic children is to own them, and to feel them. After this you can re-parent them, bringing them fully into your energy field/body in the present moment. You can tell them that they are loved, that they are safe, that you are not going to let anybody hurt them. This is a crucial part of the healing process. It is important that after using the Connecting tools, which involve bringing forward pain or "negative" emotional energy, you affirm a positive interpretation of events, and commit to a desirable future. This will help to pull the lost child toward something new, hopeful, and beautiful; and keeps your bliss in focus. The lost child is too stuck in its own pain and negative beliefs to be able to see your vision. You have to act as its surrogate parent, and give it the hope, love, and attention that it has never received. That's why it got lost in the first place, why it split from you. It's up to you to convince it that things are different now. At the end of a Connecting session, Affirmation and Creative Imagination will aid in doing this. Finally, bring yourself fully present and grounded in the body. Let go of whatever story the wounded child tells you. I like to give it to God.

One of the first things I was told by Spirit when I began my spiritual journey was to "love your fear." The same is true for your pain in general. Most of the suffering is created by the running away, and the cycle of fear and denial that this generates. In fact, surrendering to pain and fear can be blissfully freeing. This does not mean giving up (a subtle distinction). It means permitting a higher part of the mind to assume responsibility for the pain within.

LIFE'S A MOVIE, SO BE GROOVY

You are probably not so keen on getting into this pain thing right now. That's fine. My intention in writing this book is not to have the planet crying out in existential suffering. I am simply bringing the big picture to attention. Just keep it there in the back of your mind, and let it sit for the time being.

The good news is that there is a relatively simple way to identify your soul isues and karmic issues: take note of stories that really resonate with you, and push your buttons. These stories can be from novels, movies, TV shows, newspaper stories, gossip columns, something a friend shares with you, songs, or just about any other source. I became aware of this when I began to work with Spirit, and to open my emotional body. While watching movies, I allowed myself to open to the energy of scenes and situations that resonated with me. Some movie sequences that really affected me deeply were the beach landing opening scene of *Saving Private Ryan* and the scene from *Gladiator* where Maximus returns home to find his house burned to cinders and his wife and child dead. They reflect two of my soul issues: fighting in war and a sense of guilt at having failed others. In one of my past lives I felt responsible for the death of my brother on the battlefield (my brother again in this lifetime). It is for the same reason that the simple song "Two Little Boys" by Rolf Harris always brought out a strong reaction in me. The battle scene in that song is not far removed from that past life event.

One sequence in the movie *The English Patient* really traumatized me. It was the part where Ralph Fiennes leaves his lover (who has been badly injured in a plane crash) in a cave in northern Africa, to go and fetch help. She has no food or water, so he has a limited time to return to save her life. Unfortunately, he is detained by the Nazis and is unable to get back in time. When he finally does reach her, she is dead.

If you take note of them, you find that your dreams also contain themes and storylines that move you. For example, in a dream recently I found myself walking along a grassy cliff top above the ocean with my wife. She was walking ahead of me, and turned to say something. She did not look where she was going, and disappeared over the edge of the huge cliff. I was immediately filled with the greatest dread, as I tried to race down to find her. I had to go through some kind of military checkpoint to get to the base of the cliff. I woke up before I got to the dream's conclusion.

You can see a similar theme in the narratives of both the movie and the dream. The issues are feeling helpless to save a loved one, and racing against time to get to her, and (it seems) to no avail. The military is also involved in both. This dream told me that certain issues of mine involving personal guilt and fear of the loss of love were not fully integrated within me.

Stories can resonate with us in both a negative and a positive sense. As a little boy, I recall being deeply fascinated by the *Kung Fu* TV series starring David Carradine. Looking back I can see what it was that grabbed me: the idea of an incredible power, which sits invisibly within the body of a humble and quiet man. In many ways, the character in that series—Caine—was my first exposure to the idea of the Sage. If you look back at your own childhood you will see stories that really pulled you in. Look at them, and see what they tell you about your soul template.

In Practice 7.1

ꐘ The Stories That Move Me

Set some time aside to look more closely at the stories that have been significant to you. They will help you to know your soul purpose.

Do this exercise in your Intuitive Diary. Write down all the stories that have moved you deeply in your life.

In particular, what were the books, short stories, fairy tales, movies, songs, and poems that affected you the most? What kind of feelings do they arouse in you? What are the central themes and motifs? Which characters do you relate to, and why? What lessons do the main characters learn?

Finally, reflect upon how all this relates to your current life: your character, habits, problems, relationships, and your strengths, abilities, and gifts.

The stories that move you may have literal past life equivalents, or they may be a result of other collective energies that are contained within your psyche. The latter can be implanted in your energy field at around the time of your birth, by parents or relatives. The stories might also reflect themes contained within your soul group, or humanity itself. When this is the case, it is usually not necessary to feel the collective pain. You simply have to become aware of the story, and then speak to the karmic child to tell it that the story is not real anymore. The story will involve fear and constriction—they all do. You can tell the karmic child that it is not necessary to be afraid, and that the story is now at an end. You are not going to allow the story to repeat itself.

These first seven chapters of *Discover Your Soul Template* have made it clear that the Sage's journey is not quite as simple as putting in your order to the universal supermarket—an analogy used in some naive popular books on manifestation. You have to lay the groundwork. You have to eat your greens before you get your ice cream. You now know what is required to understand and successfully use Integrated Intelligence. You have the INI tools, and know about the soul template, allowing presence, and reclaiming your lost children. We are now ready to move on to an exciting part of the journey: using your soul's wisdom and the infinite intelligence of the cosmos to create your bliss.

PART 2

Living an Empowered Life

*If you follow your bliss, doors
will open for you that wouldn't
have opened for anyone else.*

JOSEPH CAMPBELL

eight

Answering the Call

Finding Your Dream

So now you have the tools you need to find your bliss and make your way toward it. Even better, you have an appreciation of the big picture, including the nature of your soul. Now's the time to actually discover what you really want to do, and start doing it.

"But wait," you may be saying. "How do I know what I really want to do? How do I tell the difference between my calling and an ego trip? And what if I make the wrong choice?"

Don't panic. This chapter will provide you with the answers to these questions. You will need your Intuitive Diary here and for the following chapters as well. You are going to commit words to paper, and then follow through with definite actions. In this chapter we will focus on discovering and building your dream: how to get the ball rolling. In the following chapter we will focus on the details: how to keep the ball in motion. And all of this will be grounded upon the wisdom of Integrated Intelligence.

THERE IS NO PLAN SET IN STONE

One thing that confuses many people when they set about finding their bliss is the belief that there is one right path, which God has set in stone for them. This idea can lead to a great deal of tension and confusion, as the person looks for "signs" from above to direct them to their destiny. But there is no destiny.

Let me repeat that. There is no destiny.

It is true that you have a soul template with certain issues to be resolved, and special aptitudes. However, you were not put here to be a butcher, baker, candlestick maker, or anything else. God is not going to say, "Here son, you are going to be the local butcher. Now get down there, shut up, and grab that chopper." If you were put here to be the local butcher, no ifs, ands, or buts, then how could you possibly learn anything about power? Or expressing your soul? Free will is absolutely fundamental to your journey here on earth. It is the central motif of the human oversoul template. The idea of destiny is a contradiction to free will. It is by exercising the power of choice that you learn about the appropriate expression of power. This includes power expressed with, over, or under others. It also incorporates power turned inward. For whenever you affirm yourself, you are standing in your God-given power. Conversely, you may invalidate yourself through negative belief structures. In both cases you are exercising power—and therefore, choice.

> *You were not put here for a specific calling. Your task is*
> *to bring your consciousness into presence, get to know*
> *your soul and develop a vision that fits it.*

There are paths that resonate powerfully with your soul, and paths that resonate less. Then there are paths where you miss the boat altogether, ones that are a violation of your soul, or the souls of others. You need to listen to your excitement, to your guides, and to the universe as you make decisions in your life. When you employ Integrated Intelligence successfully, you can tune in to your inner voice. You can listen to life's prompts and embrace synchronicity.

I said there is no destiny. However, some people are given special gifts, and they incarnate to fulfill a role or function for the evolution of their soul, or the evolution of humanity. In the latter case, these may include some leaders, politicians, artists, musicians, writers, and so on. Mozart came to compose, Mother Teresa to demonstrate compassion, and the Buddha to teach about Spirit. My sense is that Obama is here to assist in the healing a humanity, as just in the process of being president he has brought of lot of the shadow energy of America out into the open. Yet, even these greats have the free will to exercise their gifts in the way they see fit.

The bulk of humanity is hopelessly out of touch with Spirit. Most people do not progress much along the path of Spirit in a single lifetime. Many make absolutely no progress, and live and die at close to 0 percent consciousness. Many people whom we consider successful according to modern society's value structure have "achieved" almost nothing, spiritually speaking. Conversely, many great human beings have lived and died, advanced humanity enormously in a spiritual sense, but aren't even mentioned in the history books. Jessica, the woman who inspired the idea of Integrated Intelligence, and whose wisdom lies behind much of what appears in this book, can't even be found on a Google search.

The question then becomes, "Whom do I serve?" Would you be willing to be a societal nobody to be a spiritual somebody? Of course, the truth is that it is usually not an either/or choice. But much of what appears in the guise of "spirituality" in the modern age is actually ego stuff, and is there to boost human ego. It can get a bit confusing. The key is to listen to Spirit.

PLENTY OF JOBS, BUT NO VACANCY FOR SPIRIT

When young people are looking to choose a career and they don't know who they are, they might go to a career counselor and do a psychometric test. These tests name the aptitudes of an individual, and then identify the industries to which he is best suited. The counselor will look at the results and suggest what he should do and be. She might even give him a nudge this way or that, according to what the counselor sees as the prevailing market trends. A good guidance counselor will also use her intuition and experience.

*Why ask someone else who you are? A much more
empowering process is to commit to knowing yourself
from within, and allowing your soul to speak.*

But why ask someone else who you are? A much more empowering process is to commit to knowing yourself from within, and allowing your soul to speak to you. And you get to save the counseling fee. It is tragic that modern education systems have almost completely forgotten to teach the young how to get in touch with themselves. If anything, it has gotten worse in recent years, with the advent of IT-focused education. Learning how to use the inner mind should have an equal place in the modern world. In the end, self-knowledge is even more important than technical knowledge, as it helps the child develop a sense of self, creates intrinsic motivation, and ultimately generates a better society of self-aware and responsible human beings. Young people who have been pushed and prodded through the system like mice through a maze are all too likely to end up alienated, confused, lost, and angry.

*Knowing the soul does not necessarily precede finding
your bliss. Your soul issues and aptitudes will become
clearer as you live, work, and love in this world
and as you listen to your spirit.*

Your primary purpose here on earth is not to develop a successful career, nor to get rich or become famous. Your primary purpose is to bring your spirit into alignment with your soul purpose, and your soul purpose into alignment with the greater purpose of humanity and the cosmos. And to that end, career, money, and possessions may not be central to your "calling." Expressing your soul purpose through creation is very important. But even more important is to understand what your soul issues are, to integrate and heal them, and to bring your mind fully into presence. Only in that way can you express the love that lies at the heart of the purpose of cosmic creation.

WHICH FOOT FIRST?

Knowing the soul does not necessarily precede finding your bliss, however. Your soul issues and aptitudes will become clearer as you move through this world, and listen carefully to the guidance from within. Your relationships and your work will bring you in touch with your soul. Love and work trigger emotional reactions from the mind. They help reveal us.

The key is to appreciate that in modern society the relative importance of these aspects of life has been inverted. We are taught to put money and career ahead of inner work and healing. In some societies, family and relationships are thought to be more important, such as in China's traditional Confucian society. Relationships are indeed crucial, but self-awareness is even more vital, as relationships cannot flourish where self-ignorance is prevalent. The modern expression of Confucian society in China has placed family above self-awareness, with the result that families often unconsciously subvert the soul paths of the individuals within them. The same can happen in any society. This is a kind of codependence in which you give your power away to the family so that your needs for belonging are met.

Political organizations and governments try their best to take away our power too, by insisting that the collective is more important than the individual. While the self-aware individual will respect and honor the collective, she will not allow herself to be disempowered by it. Governments love to legislate and pontificate, to tell people what to think and do.

Hopefully that legislation is for the highest good of all. But often it is irresponsible, such as when governments deliberately manipulate the media to encourage hatred of an external group. When the going gets tough, blame Bin Laden (America), the Dalai Lama (China), or George Bush (everyone). This is not to suggest the object of blame is necessarily faultless, but the reality is that the hate directed at the enemy is always a manipulation designed to perpetuate the power of political groups.

Remember, all blame takes you away from presence, away from Spirit. The objective of a government in uniting its people through blame and hate thus takes the people further away from spiritual truth. This process usually takes us away from the purpose of the human oversoul.

FOLLOW YOUR EXCITEMENT

Okay, let's get straight to the point. Here is the secret formula for finding your bliss. Ready?

You find your calling by following your excitement.

This simple approach will take you directly to where you need to be to honor your soul template. It is your feelings that are the guide to your bliss. To find and live your bliss you need to do what you love. And what is love? As used here, *love* is not a thought, an intellectualization, nor a philosophical position. It's a feeling. The way to find your bliss is to take note of what excites you.

Follow your excitement. Build a dream. Then live it.

However, this is one of those cases of simple but not necessarily easy. The late mythologist Joseph Campbell is famous for advising people to "follow your bliss." What he didn't tell us too much about was how to do it, nor did he make it clear that the decision to commit to your calling doesn't automatically ensure a trouble-free ride to paradise.

What Is Excitement?

What exactly does it mean to say something is *your excitement*? Not everything that is exciting is your excitement. I remember being terribly excited when I watched the adventure documentary *Baseclimb* in the '90s. It is the story of two Aussie guys who climbed Trango Towers, a giant plateau in Pakistan, then jumped off with parachutes. Yes, it was exhilarating to watch. But never in the dozen or so years since I watched the video have I wanted to mountain climb or parachute. No thanks. I've done bungee jumping, and that's enough for me!

Lots of things in life are exciting. Maybe you think making love is exciting, but that doesn't mean you should be a porn star. Then there is excitement born of the ego, from a desire for attention, control, or power. I'm sure Hitler and his bully boys felt pretty excited during the

Munich beer hall putsch of 1923, when they tried to take control of the city after a few too many beers. This was pure ego in action.

It is not simply the literal event that represents your calling. The feelings and the processes involved are just as important as the event itself.

No, there's another special kind of excitement, which resonates with your soul. Nobody can teach you how to discern it from other forms of excitement. You just know. But there is often a physical, indeed spiritual sensation that many people report when they "know" something at a soul level. It tingles! Take note of that tingling sensation in your spine when you see or hear something wonderful, for it is your higher self communicating with you. When your eyes widen with wonder, stop and allow that moment to speak to you. It may be your spirit calling. At times you will get help. Tingling sensations on your arms, legs, or other body parts are sometimes a way that your spirit guides try to alert you to something.

You can also trace your excitement retrospectively. In Practice 8.1 below outlines the process of looking back at your life and recalling those things that really moved you in a positive way and genuinely excited you. These can include any life experiences, including inner experiences and dreams. I have mentioned a few of my own signpost experiences in this book: watching the TV series *Kung Fu* as a small child, the Ron Laura lecture, the wonder of seeing UFOs, my spirit guide dream informing me that I was using but 3 percent of my mind, and finding my spiritual teachers in New Zealand.

As the Mapping Your Excitement exercise indicates, it is not simply the literal event that represents your calling. If you feel a soul excitement while traveling in China, the significance of the event might be related to China itself, the idea of exploration, or a sense that you could be part of the opening of an entire civilization. The feelings and the processes involved are just as important as the event itself. Don't take it too literally.

Table 8.1 below is an example of using signpost events from my own life. You will note that as each thing happened, I allowed the energy to pull me forward toward my bliss. I recognized the events for what they were. And where there was doubt—such as with the spirit guide dream—I left a space open for possibility. Allowing yourself to be guided by the cosmos in this way is part of the alignment process. It is true that in certain cases I could have acted more definitively. But I wasn't ready. Unfortunately, I didn't have many role models, and much of the time I had to work things out myself.

I realized fairly early on that I wanted to be a writer, teacher, and speaker in this field, and that I wanted to be involved in the healing of the human race. However, I didn't realize quite so young just what would be required to do so. Healing has been an essential part of my story. Living my bliss as a writer and teacher in this field would be impossible without the healing work, and I was pretty badly damaged goods.

TABLE 8.1. MAPPING MY EXCITEMENT SIGNPOSTS

AGE	EVENT	FEELINGS	PROCESS	SIGNIFICANCE
6 y.o.	Watching Kung Fu.	Awe, excitement, wonder, new worlds.	Watching, listening, feeling.	A quiet, shy, and gentle man can carry immense invisible power and have enormous courage.
10 y.o.	My teacher, Mr. Vandenberg, encourages me to believe in myself.	Great surprise (me, smart?). Passion for learning new things. Gratitude for teacher.	Absorption in the moment. Love of learning. Self-belief.	Teachers can be great inspiration. I am smart too. I think I can do it!
10 y.o.	Writing my first short story.	Intense excitement, passion, a feeling of being able to create new worlds.	Flow, allowing excitement to take me away.	I love to write, to create new worlds!

TABLE 8.1. continued

AGE	EVENT	FEELINGS	PROCESS	SIGNIFICANCE
24 y.o.	The Ron Laura lecture.	A real buzz, intense intellectual stimulation.	Listening, feeling. A strong intellectual part. Listening with my ears and heart.	I can use my intellect to express these ideas! There's something more to life!
26 y.o.	Meeting Lesley. Spirit guide dream and UFO experience.	Wonder, awe, excitement, being strongly moved by something within and beyond me. Doubt (can this really be true?).	Experimenting with meditation and other ways of knowing.	My understanding of mind has been limited. I must learn more.
30 y.o.	Meeting my spiritual teachers and doing deep healing work.	Shock, confusion. Deep emotions/ vulnerability (and fear of them).	Connecting with greater knowing. Open to feelings.	There are people who live this stuff. Maybe I can live it too.
36 y.o.	Writing my Ph.D. thesis.	Passion for knowledge, feeling this is meant to be.	Flow, channeling.	This is so right. It's meant to be. I'm in sync with my soul purpose.

What are the overriding themes emerging from these events?
I love to be extended beyond my current self-concept. I love to learn and to write. I love to be inspired! There is something beyond the physical body and material life that drives all this. I must follow this voice. I can never simply follow the crowd.

How might I turn this excitement into a calling—a service for others that can be a source of income?
I feel that I am a writer, speaker, and teacher. I can use this knowledge I have to help others in this way. I can do this through books, videos, and Internet publishing. I can also counsel people directly, and assist organizations with tapping into intuitive intelligence to build responsible, sustainable, and spiritual business models.

One might argue that it is unfortunate that it took me so long to get the damn boat into the water. But that would be an ego judgment. My journey has been to explore the depths of the mind and soul in a profound way, a way not supported by the mainstream culture and education in which I have lived, worked, and studied. It has been tough and lonely at times. It has taken more time, courage, and commitment than most journeys. I chose a tough bliss, and one that has stretched me a long way. I have paid a big price, but the rewards have been great too.

Each journey is unique. You may require far less depth work, and may be able to launch your ship far earlier than me. Or you may need more. It is your story, your bliss.

In Practice 8.1

℮ *Mapping Your Excitement*

You will need your Intuitive Diary and a pen for this exercise, or alternatively you can use table 8.2 below. If you like you can play some quiet baroque music in the background, but do not use any music that will deliberately influence your mood (e.g., sad music, heavy metal, disco music, etc.). Key distinctions are between the activity, the process, the feelings, and the significance, as indicated in tables 8.1 and 8.2. You do not need to fill in every column for every significant event.

Take a few deep breaths and relax deeply. Now, look back over your life and begin to allow memories of things that really moved or excited you to come to your mind. Begin with your time as a child—your earliest memories—and work right through to the present day.

When you have completed the list, look for the common themes. What types of activities and experiences? What are the feelings? Is there some message there for you?

> *When you discover your bliss and set yourself a vision,*
> *you should consider the price that you will have to pay.*

Allow yourself to intuitively feel the answers. Finally, how might you turn this excitement into a calling—a service for others that can bring you income?

When you discover your bliss and set yourself a vision, you might like to consider the price that you will have to pay. If a man loves pigs and wants to be a millionaire pig farmer, he had better like pig poo, because he is going to step in a lot of it on the road to his bliss.

TABLE 8.2. MAPPING MY EXCITEMENT SIGNPOSTS

EVENT	FEELINGS	PROCESS	SIGNIFICANCE

What are the overriding themes emerging from these events?

How might I turn this excitement into a calling—a service for others that can be a source of income?

THE MULTIPLE BLISSES THEORY
OF THE COSMOS

In Practice 8.1 will give you some insight into your bliss, and your ongoing commitment to listen for and follow your excitement will help guide you. Still, you may not be clear about what you want to do with it. This is normal. There is no destiny. It's just a matter of aligning with your spirit, and choosing goals that reflect your soul purpose and your soul template.

Your precise goals may change. In fact, it is a good idea to regularly check in on the energy behind your goals. If the energy has dissipated, then you can focus upon something different. Often it will be something related, but in a slightly different direction. Or the timing will change. Often we overestimate how quickly we can manifest a goal. If you set up an unrealistic time frame you will only end up rushing, and thus lose presence and your connection with Spirit.

The key is to keep listening, taking actions based on your intuition, then listening for the feedback. This is part of the Wisdom Cycle, which you will learn more about in the next chapter.

A final point is that your soul purpose may not be a "job" in the traditional sense. I once had a friend who was a clairvoyant and spiritual teacher. Her dream was to attain financial security so she could do her readings for free. Maybe you too have a gift you want to share where the reward is not financial. That's fine. Just check your intention, though, as this vision could well hide certain restrictive beliefs about money.

Everyone's Bliss Is Different

Jason Wu is now one of the world's most famous fashion designers. He is the twenty-six-year-old man who shot to fame overnight, when it was revealed that he was the guy who designed the dress Michele Obama wore at her husband's presidential inauguration ceremony in early 2009.

He is a young man who never let the doubters get in the way of living his rather unusual bliss. Can you imagine the reaction he got when, as a teenager in technology-and-science-mad Taiwan, he said that he wanted to be a fashion designer? One who designs dresses, no less! Jason's version of accounts is telling. He says that as a Taiwanese man, he was supposed to be a doctor or a lawyer. "But," he continues, "my heart is painting and drawing. It was in my DNA to be fascinated with the way clothes are made."

Jason's soul aptitudes are clear enough, and they are not about finance and technology, very much the dominant thrust in many East Asian cultures today. His soul aptitudes are not highly valued by his society, but he stuck it out. Another difficult thing that Jason has had to deal with in his short life is that he is gay, a great challenge in the relatively conservative society of Taiwan.

Jason Wu is an inspiration to all those who want to follow their unconventional bliss in the face of a conventional world.

It takes all sorts. A man named Carlos Barrios worked as an accountant in Mexico City. Forty-five-year-old Carlos hated his office job, the same one that he had been doing for twenty-four years. He just had to get out. He quit and found his dream job—as a sewage diver in the bowels of Mexico City! That's right, each day he dons a diving suit and descends into a cesspool of stinking feces, urine, dead dogs, and sometimes even dead people, clearing blockages that might disrupt the free flow of sewage underneath the city.

Now, most people would probably call this a "shit" job, but Carlos loves it. It's certainly not my preferred way of making a living. But Carlos is doing a job that he knows contributes to the running of the city, and it pays well to boot.

So, never let anybody tell you that your dream is not worthy of accomplishment. That is none of their business. And if a loved one is dependent upon you for a source of income, just send them love, and tell them that "you gotta do what you gotta do." Hopefully, you won't have to say something like, "Sorry Hon, but I'm throwing in the job as a bean counter and heading for the sewers." But if you do, and if it is truly your calling, you will find a way to work through it. It pays to remember that while loved ones often resist major life changes that threaten the certainty of things, they tend to quiet down once the decision has been made.

In Practice 8.2
℮ The Dream Scheme

In Practice 8.1, Mapping Your Excitement, and tables 8.1 and 8.2 have given you the big picture. Now that you have the main goal, it is time to begin to get specific.

This means naming the goal and subgoals, and identifying specific actions you can take to achieve them.

For example, after listening to your excitement, you have decided that your bliss is to be a bestselling science fiction novelist, as indicated in table 8.3, below.

This requires specific subgoals, with dates and actions.

- One subgoal might be to produce a 100,000-word science fiction novel, *Beyond Worlds*.
- Further, to begin to develop a portfolio of writing and a name for yourself, you plan to submit a short story every two weeks to magazines, writing journals, and so on.
- Meanwhile you decide to produce a 500-word article on science and technology for various media outlets each month, related to your novel.
- A final subgoal is to set up a website showcasing your work.

The number of subgoals is up to you, but don't overdo it. It's best to be a little cautious to begin with.

TABLE 8.3. PUTTING MY BLISS INTO ACTION

MY BLISS: To be a full-time bestselling science fiction writer

SUBGOALS	ACTIONS	TIMING
A. Produce a 100,000-word science fiction novel, *Beyond Worlds*.	1. Write 500 words every morning, six days a week.	Mon.–Sat.
	2. Contact one literary agent each week with query letter, e-mail or hard copy.	Every Mon.
	3. Attend the writer's group every week for feedback on drafts.	Every Sat.
	4. Gain contract by end of June.	End June
	5. Publish *Beyond Worlds*.	Dec. next year
B. Submit short story every fortnight to magazines, journals, etc.	1. Use Free-Form Writing for first draft.	Week 1 work 9–10 p.m.
	2. Polish and submit final draft.	End week 2
	3. Use Free-Form Writing for final draft.	Week 3
	4. Polish and submit final draft.	End week 4
C. Write a 500-word article on science and tech for media outlets each month.	1. Choose theme.	First Mon./month
	2. Use Free-Form Writing for first draft.	By end week 1
	3. Research topic—max 3 hrs.	End week 3
	4. Write second draft.	Week 4
	5. Third draft and submit.	End/month
D. Set up a website showcasing my work.	1. Begin checking for inexpensive sites and blogs.	Tomorrow
	2. Choose the site and domain name.	End of month
	3. Start uploading stories to site.	Next month 3/week
	4. Complete uploading.	End next month
	5. Upload stories and articles, 3/month.	1st Sun./month

Using this example as a guide, fill in table 8.4 with your own sub-goals, actions, and timing.

Use the Quick Check to confirm whether the goal, subgoals, and timing are right. You can double check using the Feeling Sense, by placing your energy into the goals and actions and sensing if they feel right. You can do this within a Light Trance if you like.

But you are not finished yet. You have to start taking action NOW. Make a commitment to take at least three actions per day toward actualizing your bliss.

TABLE 8.4. PUTTING MY BLISS INTO ACTION

MY BLISS:

SUBGOALS	ACTIONS	TIMING
	1. 2. 3. 4. 5.	
	1. 2. 3. 4. 5.	
	1. 2. 3. 4. 5.	

TABLE 8.4 continued

SUBGOALS	ACTIONS	TIMING
	1. 2. 3. 4. 5.	
	1. 2. 3. 4. 5.	

DON'T QUIT YOUR DAY JOB

It takes time to shift your life focus. If your bliss involves a major change of profession or lifestyle, there may be a long period—maybe years—of work, reeducation, or retraining ahead of you. The shift will probably bring forth much latent negative energy within your psyche. The restrictive belief structures that stand between you and the manifestation of your dream will have to be addressed. That may be a simple matter of acknowledgement, or it may require a great deal of inner work. It depends upon how big the issue is.

I first decided that I wanted to move into the area of consciousness studies and spiritual awareness some seventeen years ago. I made the decision after I read Wayne Dyer's *You'll See It When You Believe It*. Dyer said exactly what the book's title suggests: just believe it and it will happen. Now, as I argued previously, the real situation is more complex than Dyer suggests. I wanted to be a writer and speaker. But at the age of twenty-six, I just did not have the power to pull it off. There was far too much baggage within my psyche. There was also the other small problem that I wanted to teach others about a subject that I knew relatively little about.

But I didn't let that simple truth stop me! Ignorance is bliss, or so they say. Blissfully, I didn't have a clue about my inner "issues" at that stage of my life. So I quit my job as a schoolteacher in a remote inland town, and went to live in Coffs Harbour, a nice country town on the mid-north coast of New South Wales. I wrote a great little book called *The Freedom of Dynamic Consciousness*. Well, I thought it was great! Then I waited for the offers of publication to pour in.

They never came.

Luckily, I didn't have any dependents, and there was no major hassle. I just got a longish holiday learning a few hard lessons. And a few fun ones as well, for in many ways that period was one of the most rewarding times of my life. I was pursuing my dream, and the universe was responding, pushing me along the path of least resistance. However, the path I had chosen was a difficult one, and there would be a few lengthy digressions along the way! The distance between what I wanted and where I stood was enormous. I did not realize it at the time. When the distance between your present reality and your vision is vast, there is a lot of territory to traverse before you arrive at the destination.

The human psyche can only handle so much change at any given time. Your guides know this, and it is why they only give you a little information at a time. You must respect this limitation of being human. If you push yourself too far, too soon, your psyche will be unable to cope. You will experience an ego fall, as the reality of where you really stand is brought home to you. As the gap between reality and your delusion collapses, a period of chaos and energetic instability will occur. This instability can manifest in various ways, but most likely it will involve considerable drama, and a lot of kicking and screaming from the ego because it can't get what it wants.

So, keep your day job, at least for the moment. Take small steps at first. After you develop an action plan, follow through with the actions.

Then, when the times come for the giant leaps, you will have the power and energy to pull them off. I followed my bliss, but didn't get what I wanted straightaway. But what I did do was initiate the process, one that would take the best part of a dozen years before the publication of my first book. I thought I was going to get there overnight, but it took travel through a dozen countries, several personal heartbreaks, the enormous self-discipline of doing a Ph.D. while working full-time, and quite a few knocks and bruises before it happened.

As they say, be careful what you ask for—because you just might get it. There is that damn "price" to pay. There will almost certainly be some degree of hardship or genuine suffering with any path you choose. You can avoid much of it by keeping an eye on the ego and using Integrated Intelligence to guide you. But the Earth School is not for sissies.

FINALLY

This chapter has been about naming your dream, but there is one last thing to keep in mind before you go any further: Your dream may inadvertently become your scourge. Longing after something in an indefinite future inevitably separates your mind from Spirit. This is the bliss trap: The constant craving for bliss ensures that you never find it. Don't let the search for the One Big Thing destroy the bliss of presence, which is already here. It really is the little things that make life worth living. The Buddha would say that the journey is more important than the destination.

Listening to your excitement, naming your dream, and identifying definite actions are just the beginning of your journey. Now you have to actually get off your bum and do something about it—but not just any old thing. You want to keep choosing actions that are aligned with Spirit, and that are both powerful and empowering. You want to keep on track. It is here that you have an enormous advantage over the vast bulk of humanity that lives within the alienated mind: your Integrated Intelligence.

nine

Keeping the Dream Alive

Living Your Soul Purpose, Now and Forever

Choosing a dream is not enough. In the universe of light and darkness, of yin and yang, you will be asked to choose again, and again, and again. The truth is that you choose in every waking moment, and strangely enough, even when not awake. For much of humanity the choices are unconscious. And they don't even know it.

You need to be able to stay focused on your dream, and to act. You need to distinguish between the voice of Spirit and the pull of ego. You need to know what actions are both powerful and empowering. You need to listen to your guidance, to the universe, and you need to be able to harness the synchronicities that come your way. You must know when to push and when to relax and let go.

And you must be able to tell the difference between legitimate and unnecessary suffering. Following your bliss is not always so blissful. Sometimes life can be tough, and you just have to ride it out. Meanwhile the ego and dark energy will try to pull you toward false dreams. They will lead you toward separation and alienation, away from Spirit. You need to be able to stay with your purpose.

This chapter is dedicated to helping you learn to be able to choose wisely and act powerfully. In doing so, you will keep your dream alive.

NOWHERE MAN MAKES HIS MOVE

In the year 2000, I was teaching English in a small city in southwestern Taiwan. One morning I woke up alone in my apartment and knew something was wrong. I looked around. The room felt strangely desolate and empty. I had everything I needed at that time: a nice place to live, an attractive Taiwanese girlfriend, and debt-free financial stability, if not quite security. The room was the same as it had been the day before, and the week before. What had changed was something within me. I felt empty. In fact, it was more than that. It was a sense of depression, a feeling that I was not accustomed to. Fortunately, I had spent years working with the inner worlds, including practicing meditation and doing emotional work on myself. I knew that there was a message for me in the feeling.

The following morning I awoke and the feeling was there again. But this time there was a song playing in my head. It was a song by the Beatles, "Nowhere Man"—"Doesn't have a point of view, Knows not where he's going to, Isn't he a bit like you and me?"

To quote Lennon and McCartney, I had become a real nowhere man, sitting in my nowhere land, making all my nowhere plans for nobody. In the random universe of the mechanistic worldview of modern society, synchronicities like a song playing in your head are merely coincidences, haphazard events that you can make of what you will. But I saw it as something deeply meaningful. I reflected upon things for a week or so, and then decided to take some action. I realized I'd become stuck within my own comfort zone. Life had become easy, yet meaningless. I was not challenging myself. Worse, there was a strong feeling that I was not doing what my soul was calling me to do.

Then, during a meditation just a few days later, three letters suddenly appeared before my inner eye: "Ph.D." About five years before that week in 2000, I had deferred my enrollment in a doctoral program, and headed for New Zealand. It appeared my guides were nudging me toward resuming my studies. Yet it was a huge decision. Writing a doctoral thesis would take several years, and there was no guarantee that I would be awarded the degree after submission. Doubt came in. Maybe I wasn't smart enough. I might fail. However, after some reflection, I decided to resume my research. But what would I study?

Just a few days later, while I was doing some yoga in the morning, a small but life-changing message came to me. I was in relaxed presence, my mind quiet, when a voice said, "bear," and I stopped. Straight away I remembered a book I had read a few years before, *Education for the 21st Century*. It was written by two Australian academics, Hedley Beare (pronounced "bear") and Richard Slaughter. I grabbed the book from my bookshelf, and leafed through it. The book holds a spiritual view of education, and the ideas resonated deeply with me. I contacted both the authors by e-mail. They put me on to a futurist and academic named Sohail Inayatullah, who eventually became my doctoral supervisor. Sohail is a brilliant academician, working via three different universities in Australia and Taiwan. One of them, the University of the Sunshine Coast, had a program suitable for me. The university was less than ten years old, and had little name in academic circles. It couldn't grant me academic status, but it would enable me to pursue my dream. I enrolled.

I could have gone with the call of ego and enrolled in the most prestigious school that would take me. I could have gone with market forces and studied whatever the education market was demanding. Instead, I made a decision to follow my excitement. I decided to study the frontiers of human intelligence, including the interface of rational and intuitive ways of knowing.

As I embarked upon my doctoral studies, I discovered something wonderful. Because I was studying knowledge that I had a deep passion for, the entire process became almost effortless.

Life become much less of a struggle when you listen to the heart, when you tap in to your intuitive intelligence.

As I read and wrote my dissertation, I found I had more words and thoughts than I could ever possibly use. I began to publish some of these in journals, mainly in the area of futures studies. That began a period of prolific output. I completed a 110,000-word dissertation, wrote a book based on it (which gained publication), wrote more than a dozen peer-reviewed articles, several book chapters, delivered conference papers and quite a number of critical reviews, all in less than six years—and all while working full time in education.

I even developed a specific intuitive research process called Integrated Inquiry, which I later outlined in two academic articles. Integrated Inquiry involves following the heart and applying several of the INI tools during research and writing.*

The way I initiated and conducted my academic research is almost unheard of in academic circles, though it is not "nonexistent." It is well known that many academics and scientists work with their intuitive feelings, and the history of science is dotted with anecdotes of synchronicities that have assisted the evolution of human knowledge. It is just that they do not talk about it much in public.

I have discovered that life becomes much less of a struggle when you listen to the heart, when you tap in to your intuitive intelligence. You guess less, and know more. INI connects the human spirit with something greater than the individual self. The entire process is quintessentially spiritual.

All energy readings have a degree of complexity.
Sometimes there are multiple considerations; then you
just have to open your heart to Spirit, and go with it.

To do this yourself, take note of your intuitions, dreams, and visions. Actively seek guidance, and do what you are being prompted to do. Use energy readings like the Quick Check and the Feeling Sense, but keep in mind that any reading you take, via whatever method, has a degree of complexity. Sometimes there are multiple considerations; then you have to open your heart to Spirit and choose as wisely as you can. At

---

*You can see one of the articles at www.benthamscience.com/open/toiscij/articles/V003/SI0001TOISCIJ/80TOISCIJ.pdf

other times the choice is clear, and the guidance will be definitive. Some choices will lead you toward your bliss, others away from it. Certain decisions may require a lot of courage, such as ending a relationship, changing jobs, or moving to another location. If the ego resists, denial can come into play.

READING ENERGY

Every action that you conceive of taking has a degree of alignment (or nonalignment) with your bliss, and with your spirit. This is why it is possible to sense and read the energy behind an intended action. The same is true for any decision you take in your life.

Let's say you see a poster of Thailand in the window of a travel agent, and a sudden tingling excitement fills you. It suddenly strikes you that your Internet-based business could operate perfectly from Thailand, where living and labor costs are cheaper. Each time you walk past the poster on the way to work it catches your eye, and you feel that excitement! A desire rises within you to travel to the Land of Smiles. Should you fork over the several thousand bucks for the trip and risk a great deal, or stay put? Here is where the INI tools are invaluable.

In Practice 9.1

℮ Using the INI Tools for Decision Making

The INI tools allow you to sense and measure whether a given choice or action resonates with your soul journey.

You can use meditative reflection, simply by relaxing deeply and allowing yourself to enter a Light Trance state, putting out the question to the universe.

You can then breathe deeply and, using the Feeling Sense, allow yourself to merge with your future self in the new setting or position or relationship.

What does it feel like? Does it feel right, wrong, or something in between? You can then use the Quick Check to confirm your feelings.

Then, write down what you saw and felt in your Intuitive Diary. That way, in the hours and days that follow, you can review what Spirit has told you. It is all too easy to quickly forget what we see in moments of intuitive connection. The ego often cuts in when we get back to living and working in the day-to-day world, and then we go into doubt and fear.

Here is the key. If the feeling and the reading are strong, take positive action—immediately. If they are weak, let go of the desire. When the feeling is uncertain it usually means there is no definite energy about your intention or wish. In such circumstances, wait. You will usually find the desire will drop off if there is no genuine excitement. Some synchronicity may also follow in the days ahead, which will assist you in the decision.

When you are seeking guidance, the way you frame the question is crucial. The feedback that you get from your higher self or spirit guides will differ according to the precise query. "What is the energy on asking this person out on a date?" is not the same question as "What is the energy on having a sexual relationship with this person?" There may be strong energy on asking the person out, simply because you might become good friends, despite the fact the person is already married. There may be energy on dating the person, but not on making the relationship intimate. Therefore, you can try changing the question to see what happens.

When you are using the Quick Check I recommend that you do not invest a lot of time and effort in doing the reading. Usually the first reading is the most accurate. If you doubt the reading, and the question is important, then use a Light Trance state and the Feeling Sense to double check. You might find the feeling or reading is not straightforward. Your ego might be resisting, or an external energy field, such as from a loved one or someone trying to stand in your way, may be influencing the reading. In that case, you need to back off a little and let things settle. Return to the question when you feel relaxed and are in presence.

ONE DOOR OPENS,
ANOTHER ONE CLOSES

When making important choices using INI, you need to be aware of certain distinctions. You will recall in a previous chapter that I mentioned a school where I chose to work in Hong Kong because it felt right. At that time the Feeling Sense gave me intuitive information about that school's general environment. I felt it was easy-going, with a much softer energy than most schools in Hong Kong. I felt I would fit in. But that feeling told me nothing whatsoever about whether it was right for me to resume teaching and living in Hong Kong. Even though the position turned out to be a very good one for me, allowing me to work and write at the same time in a pleasant environment, it was just one of the many choices I could have made.

The universe is only as smart as the questions you ask it,
and your openness to listen.

In fact, I chose to ignore some guidance at that time which suggested that it was a good time to get out of Hong Kong. There was some guidance suggesting I return to Australia, and energy readings that confirmed this. However, the guidance and the energy were not imperative. I was getting nudges and hints, but it felt like either place would be okay. In the absence of definitive options in Australia, I chose Hong Kong.

There was some suffering involved in this choice. My wife was unable to join me in Hong Kong, and I experienced a degree of loneliness and isolation. My decision to remain in Hong Kong may also have delayed my getting a university position in Australia at that time, as it is more difficult to entice employers while applying for jobs from abroad.

In short, you need to be aware of the contexts within which you employ the Feeling Sense, the Quick Check, or any other divination tools. The universe is only as smart as the questions you ask it, and your openness to listen. If you use the Feeling Sense to find which butcher's shop is the best to work with in town, when the bigger picture is that

Spirit is calling you to be a baker in the town across the river, then your "reading" will lead you away from your bliss.

At times there is no perfectly correct choice within a given scenario. Whatever the choice, there will be positives and negatives. As one of my friends used to say, "solutions are problematic." This is why presence is so important. There is no pot of gold at the end of the rainbow. In fact, that idea is an ego trap. There is only your walking in presence, enjoying the beauty of the rainbow as it appears before you. All this is testament to why getting on the right path is vital. To borrow from *The Seven Habits of Highly Effective People* author Stephen Covey, it's no use making great progress cutting through the jungle, when after completing the job you realize that you were in the wrong jungle all along.

TESTS

The universe will test you. The interplay of light and dark energy means that you will constantly be asked how strongly you believe in your vision and how committed you are to it. This is often quite subtle, and synchronicity may play a role.

In the prelude to this book I told you about a lecture I attended by Professor Ronald Laura at the University of Newcastle. That lecture occurred right at the very beginning of my spiritual journey. It changed the course of my life because I listened to the great excitement that rose from within me as I heard the words of Big Ron.

Your bliss will not be gift-wrapped. The interplay of light and dark energy means you will constantly be tested.

But here's something that happened in that lecture that I didn't tell you about. For the entire lecture I was sitting beside a student named Steve. Steve was a large, loud-voiced young man who was returning to study after a stint in the army. He was a real down-to-earth kind of guy. As Professor Laura began to speak about some of the more extraordinary implications of an intelligent cosmos, Steve suddenly slipped a piece of folded paper into my hand. I looked down and opened it, even as Ron Laura was continuing to speak. It had just one word written on it, in big, bold letters: "BULLSHIT."

Now, recall that I then held a skeptical mind-set, and this was the first time I had been exposed to the kind of alternative philosophy that Professor Laura was presenting. That note was perfectly in tune with certain beliefs within my psyche, and at that precise moment the universe offered me a choice. It was a choice between two competing worldviews, two competing energies: the patriarchal, controlling, skeptical military mind-set; or the gentler, more playful, and adventurous ways of Spirit. Who would I listen to: Big Ron, or Big Steve? This was the test.

For me it was no choice at all. I put the paper aside and allowed myself to be drawn into the universe that Professor Ron Laura was presenting. From that decisive moment, my cosmos began to expand, till this point twenty years later, where I live within the world of Integrated Intelligence every day. Big Steve, I suspect, is probably somewhere back in Australia, looking at a world that goes no deeper than a can of beer. But who knows?

> *The Feeling Sense makes life so much simpler and can save a lot of hassle, time, and money. It helps you see through the BS that is served up on a daily basis in the consumer society.*

FEELING YOUR WAY TO BLISS

The Feeling Sense is vital for you as you turn your vision into actions. It makes life so much simpler, and can save a lot of hassle, time, and money. It helps you see through the BS that is served up on a daily basis in the consumer society. It also allows you to know what to buy, what experiences to live, and what you really need.

Today, for example, I got a generic e-mail from a self-help guru selling his latest program. I like the guy and respect his work. He had a deal going whereby he was selling his program at half price and throwing in lots of goodies to boot. The program probably had a lot of valuable information in it. I felt somewhat inclined to buy. It was a good deal, after all. Yet I almost never buy stuff without using the Feeling Sense, and all the thoughts above came from the intellect. So, I simply calmed my mind, and projected my feelings into the program. I got an immediate feeling, which I can only describe as neutrality. There was no excitement. I checked again, with the same result.

I did not buy.

There are many occasions when I have done the opposite, and bought books completely on the basis of gut feeling. In fact I never buy books these days unless I intuitively read the energy on them via the Feeling Sense or the Quick Check. When I first heard about Timothy Ferris' *The Four Hour Work Week,* for example, I felt the strong pull of excitement. I bought the book, and it turned out to be extremely useful for me. It inspired me to take my own writing and work with Integrated Intelligence in new directions.

Using the Feeling Sense is part of the co-creative path to manifesting your dream. You listen to your excitement, choose your bliss, and the universe and your guides work through you to help get you there. The excitement helps you choose your bliss, and it helps you to make the big and small choices along the way.

THE WISDOM CYCLE

In chapter 1, I said that wisdom is one of the outcomes of successfully using INI. Wisdom is the deep knowing that comes from the accurate and useful knowledge that you glean from your life, from your spiritual journey. It is a profound and relaxed knowing. It comes to us in the peace of presence, and we communicate it in the spirit of generosity.

The key is to develop a strong relationship with your Sage and the Feeling Sense, trust whatever reading you get, and take action. Ultimately, it is the actions that will provide the best feedback about the readings you take. The actions also help to build a bridge between the conscious mind and Spirit. If you take readings and then go into fear and doubt and fail to take action, you will sever the link with Spirit. Unable to learn from the feedback the universe gives you, you will end up spinning round in a circle of confusion. You have to learn to go with it. The Wisdom Cycle contains the essence of the way of Spirit. Figure 9.1 shows the process in a nutshell. While the order I have given is generally ideal, it is not necessary to follow it step by step, like a robot following a computer program. You can shift the six steps around according to need.

Figure 9.1. The Wisdom Cycle

Step 1. Check Energy

Read the energy on the intended action using the Quick Check, the Feeling Sense, a Light Trance, or Free-Form Writing. If you feel it is necessary, check the reading for interference from the ego by Connecting with the Ego. If you get a sense that the voice you connect with is not yours, whose do you feel it is (parents, spouses, lovers, friends, competitors)? Later in this chapter you will learn how to deal with such interference.

Step 2. Take Action

When you get a strong reading—very positive feelings and images, or above 60 percent energy on the Quick Check—take some action as soon as possible. Usually, this will be a small action, even as you wait for the situation to unfold in the coming days. With big decisions you may have to wait for the right time. There are times when there is a lot of energy on making a move, and there are times when there is little energy. Check the timing before you make major choices, again by using the Quick Check or the Feeling Sense, to see if it feels right.

Remember, your actions also help to shift energy. They can initiate a creative consciousness that becomes self-perpetuating. This is why in the previous chapter, I suggested that you write out sub-goals and actions that you can take to begin to actualize larger goals. Once you have decided upon a goal, a good strategy is to commit to taking at least one concrete action every day, moving you toward your goal.

When *Chicken Soup for the Soul* authors Jack Canfield and Mark Victor Hansen decided that they would create and market their book, they committed to taking five actions every day. They encountered a lot of resistance, and endless rejections. At one point their agent, after a long and fruitless search for a publisher, told them the book was simply not publishable. They did not give up. Eventually they got the book into print and turned it into one of the most successful marketing franchises in the history of publishing.

Step 3. Release the Outcome (but Visualize)

Use Creative Imagination to regularly see and feel your intended goals as already accomplished in the present. Use Affirmations for the same purpose. However, after the visualization session is complete, release your dream to God, relax, and enjoy the journey.

Step 4. Observe the Result

This is perhaps the simplest part: Take time to assess your progress. Have you achieved your intended outcome? To what degree? A little honesty may be required. If something is not working, admit it.

Step 5. *Evaluate the Process/Listen to Guidance*

Here is where you place a value on what happened. How satisfactory was it? Is the result a perfect reflection of your bliss in action? Or does the result suggest that there is something quite wrong with the whole process? What does your intuition tell you? If things are on track, move on to the next step.

However, there are usually things to deal with, and sometimes we miss the mark completely. The causes can include misreading the energy at the beginning, letting the ego interfere, and taking action that was unwise or at the wrong time. Perhaps your negative beliefs, self-doubt, and fear are mitigating factors. Another issue could be physical or psychic influences of parties who are opposed to what you are doing. However, the evaluation phase is not only about left-brained analysis. As you evaluate things, take note of the voice of Spirit—intuitions, dreams, visions, and synchronicities. Your intuition will provide you with a sense of why problems are occurring.

At this point in the creative process you are playing a game of fine tuning: surfing that wave of high-vibration energy toward a more joyful reality, or conversely sinking into the muck of low-vibration energy of a murky future. At the evaluation stage it is therefore important not to invest negative energy in the results you have produced thus far. Remember the distinction between discernment and judgment? Discernment is a detached acknowledgement of the truth. Judgment is a rejection, and involves a destructive psychic energy.

The reality you invest energy in will expand, and that means that if you give things a negative spin you will tend to perpetuate that. Thoughts like "I'm frustrated and hate that my widget hasn't sold a damn unit" invest energy in what you don't want, not what you want. Keep your focus in the present moment and on the vision. Keep listening to Spirit.

Step 6. *Integrate and Learn*

The spiritual journey is about integration, the merging of light and shadow, of the ego and the Spirit. It is at the final point of the

Wisdom Cycle that this integration becomes clear. You are aligning yourself with a greater wisdom, a greater Spirit. You are learning to love. Integration is the process whereby awareness and deep understanding emerge within your mind. Integration lies at the heart of the development of spiritual wisdom. It is how you learn without fuss, without drama.

Integration is a receptive process, mostly about letting go and allowing the mind to process the experiences and the self-work that you have done. You cannot force integration. It is about patience, about loving what God has given you, and it is about self-love. Give thanks for whatever you find before you, for it is a perfect expression of Spirit.

> *You cannot force integration. It is about patience, about loving what God has given you, and it is about self-love.*

Sometimes you simply have to accept that you are not ready for a particular outcome, because you don't have the power, the energy, to pull it off. That is perfectly okay. This does not necessarily mean that you cannot manifest your dream. It may be that it is not the right time.

You can start the process over from the beginning. Check the energy and decide whether to keep steering the same course, and at what speed. Perhaps it is time to release the goal, or put it aside till your energy is stronger. Perhaps it is time for some new goals, or simply a time to rest.

In Practice 9.2

℮ The Wisdom Cycle in Action

This exercise provides you with a chance to put the Wisdom Cycle into immediate use. Use it for a large goal that takes at least a couple of weeks to complete. Use your Intuitive Diary to record your goals, path, and results. Order the steps to suit your situation. Eventually, the Wisdom Cycle will become second nature, and you will get into the habit of aligning your actions with Spirit.

1. **Read the energy.** Use the Quick Check or the Feeling Sense. Write what you get in terms of percentages, feelings, images, and so on.

0% _____ 100%

2. **Take action.** List the actions and time frames.

I	Time

2	Time

3	Time

4	Time

5	Time

3. **Release the outcome** (and visualize). Write down what you intend to visualize, and the present tense Affirmations to go with them.
4. **Observe the result.** What happened? Did you get what you envisaged?
5. **Evaluate the process** (listen to guidance). Why were you successful or unsuccessful in attaining your goal? Evaluate without judgment.
6. **Integrate and learn.** What have you learned? How have you grown?

THE ZOMBIES THAT EAT YOUR SPIRIT

The Wisdom Cycle and INI decision making can also be applied equally effectively with groups, institutions, and corporations. This can be an invaluable process, saving time and money. It also saves the soul, or at least the connection with Spirit.

Not long ago, an educational institution I was working for decided they wanted to buy a new learning program, as there had been some significant changes in the curriculum. Four major publishing companies were selling materials and all four were invited to give a presentation.

I found myself sitting in the meeting room, along with the rest of the department staff, one Thursday afternoon, listening to four successive sales pitches. About three hours into proceedings, while listening to the third sales pitch, I assumed full zombie status. By that time I was sticking toothpicks under my eyelids just to keep awake, and the rest of the teaching staff was equally comatose. When I roused myself enough to look at the pile of materials on the large meeting table before me, the Feeling Sense told me that there was just no energy on our purchasing the materials being shown to us by the third speaker.

At that point one more publishing rep remained to give us the big sell, from a very prestigious university press. I did a Quick Check on the energy for our buying his gear, and again got nothing. Then I did the same for the other three companies. There was no energy at all on any but the first. In my stupor, I wondered what the hell we were all doing there. I re-fastened my toothpicks and tried to think of my next holiday. At the end of four excruciatingly dull hours, it was decided that the staff would return the following week for another meeting to make a final decision.

Fortunately, I was not invited to that meeting. I was later told that they chose the first publisher, as I had foreseen the week before.

Yawn.

Those meetings were a testament to the raving cluelessness of the alienated mind. They were a total waste of time and energy for all concerned. After an hour of verbal drivel and PowerPoint pointlessness, everyone's brain was fried in true zombie fashion, and our spirits had been sucked dry. The energy of Spirit had dissipated, because we had rejected it. Another way of saying this is that the excitement of Spirit had evaporated. In fact, it had vanished long before those meetings. For most of the people there the excitement had died in childhood, many years before, extracted from the soul by a system that refuses to honor Spirit.

A meeting involving intuitively adept people could have completed the entire process of choosing new texts in just a few minutes, and in one sitting. All that was required was for the publishing company's materials to be placed on the table, and for the group to use the Feeling Sense to pick up the energy on the best option. The choice could then have been double-checked by everyone doing a Quick Check and comparing readings. Finally, by flipping through those texts and using a synthesis of intuitive and rational intelligence, we could have confirmed our choice.

> *There will come a time when corporations and*
> *institutions will choose to use INI in their decision*
> *making. The abilities and the tools are here already.*

Then we could have gone outside and swung from a tree, or done something else that was half human. And the energy of Spirit, the excitement of creation would have been flowing through us. But no. We did the "zombie shuffle."

In the situation I described above, the process was simple because there was one clear choice. All the energy was for the first option. In some other cases, there might be a similar energy reading on more than one option. In such a scenario, the process might take a little longer as the group weighs up the pros and cons of each. Even so, half an hour would see it wrapped up.

Unfortunately, groups of Sages gathering to make key decisions for mainstream institutions and companies isn't part of the current social or economic paradigm. Yet there will come a time when human beings will choose to use INI in such a way. The abilities and the tools are already here, as I am making clear in this book. All those years ago, my spirit guide was spot on when she told me that I was only using 3 percent of my mental ability. And I was only slightly more dull than average, I'm sad to report.

I have since participated in spiritual groups that have made major choices using INI. Mainstream organizations could also do so today, if only they were willing to invest time and energy in training staff to employ Integrated Intelligence, or alternatively, to hire people adept at INI to help them make decisions.*

KEEPING THE DREAM ALIVE

It is one thing to find out what you are passionate about. It can be more of a challenge to maintain that passion and enthusiasm over long periods, and through difficult times. This is where you have to become very aware of the kind of energy you are aligning with and putting out to the cosmos. The human mind is not one-dimensional. It is a bit like an old radio (remember those?). At any one time you can listen to only one tune, but just out of range there are numerous channels fighting for airspace. The mind is similar. Your conscious mind is but one level of consciousness, and the other levels of mind will cut back in when circumstances resonate with their belief structures. And that creates a problem. Even as you pursue your dream, there may be a part of you that is putting out a lot of doubt and negativity.

You will need to note the negative parts of your mind, and—like a parent nursing a child who has stubbed his toe—take the time to reassure the psyche that things are okay. If you pay attention, you will catch the psyche in action. Watching your dreams is important. Record them in your Intuitive Diary. You will start to see some common themes, ones that tell you a lot about what you really believe. Take note also of what you are thinking about in your spare moments, what you are saying to your friends, writing in e-mails, or on anonymous Internet forums. These are great ways to see your shadow. Until you acknowledge what lies beneath, you cannot work with that energy, and it will control you. This is why so many of the

---

*I should state clearly that the process for groups is more complex than I can relate here, because the process can be greatly affected by the interaction of individuals' energy fields, and the potential for egos to manipulate and distort the energy readings is great. I advise any organization wishing to pursue possibilities in this area to first seek the help of someone who understands the problems involved. In the back of this book I outline some of the services I offer in this area.

issues of the human oversoul template are about assuming higher levels of responsibility.

Take note of what you are thinking about in your spare moments, what you are saying to your friends, or writing in e-mails and on Internet forums. These are great ways to see the shadow.

THE VOICES THAT SAY "NO!"

You can be certain of one test that will definitely come to you as you live your bliss: the messages that will be sent your way by those around you. This interference will come in both the literal words that enter your ears, and in subtle, psychic voices traveling on waves of consciousness. The voices will be of competitors, enemies, and those who want to keep you small. They will also come from the mouths and minds of friends, family members, and loved ones. It is a real challenge to acknowledge the possibility that someone you love and respect is trying to sabotage your bliss.

Clairaudients—psychics with a gift for extrasensory hearing—can sometimes hear these messages, or channel them. Some people who are diagnosed as insane are actually clairaudients. In most cases, they simply do not know the source of the voices, cannot disentangle their inner voice from that of external minds, and become deeply confused.

But whether we are conscious of them or not, these messages affect us all. They claw at your mind and soul and can be deeply damaging to your self-confidence. They can affect your capacity to make clear and accurate decisions.

There are always a million reasons why you can't or shouldn't do something, and sometimes only one or two significant reasons why you should do it. When there is doubt and fear in your mind, it opens a psychic doorway for the voices to start telling you about a few thousand of those negatives. The question is whether or not you are going to let those reasons, those voices, lower your self-belief, sap your energy, and destroy your bliss.

The psychic messaging that people (including you) send out to manipulate and control others—the constant metaphysical hammering—is potentially more destructive than the negative words of those around you. At least friends will shut up after a while if you don't back down. But their psychic messaging may go on twenty-four hours a day. The key is not to tune into their channels. As soon as you let doubt and fear enter your mind, your consciousness shifts into a lower vibrational energy, and suddenly the monsters are crawling under the bed again.

Unfortunately, that fear and doubt is typically related to your soul issues, to the pain and negative beliefs held by the wounded child. If a woman's father imprinted upon her psyche that women are weak and untrustworthy, for example, any messaging that resonates with this consciousness structure will affect her deeply. If she wants to stand more firmly in her power as a woman and remain impervious to the psychic projections of others, she has to assume responsibility for that damaged part of her mind. Otherwise, the demons will keep scratching away under her bed.

If you want to stand more firmly in your power and remain impervious to the psychic projections of others, you have to assume responsibility for the damaged parts of your mind.

Here is where the Connecting techniques of INI are useful. They allow your fear-centered ego and the wounded child to speak. From there you can work with that part of yourself and re-parent it. When you find that the inner voices are getting the better of you, use the immediate level exercise, In Practice 5.1, to move back into alignment. If necessary, and if you are experienced in doing emotional work, also use the in-depth exercise, In Practice 5.2, to pull the hurt part of yourself closer, for it is through this split in your psyche that the negative energy enters your consciousness field. Reassure the doubtful parts of yourself that everything is okay. Then use Affirmations, and Creative Imagination and Feeling to build your energy back up. If you want to get an idea of the kind of energy that is cramming the human psychic airwaves, just take a look at the judgment, blame, spite, and pure hatred that dominate many chat sites on the Internet. People post their psychic crap online because they can do so anonymously and for the most part without fear of recrimination.

When the Sage meets the tiger on the path, she simply steps aside.

The hate and the haters are out there; and the truth is that there is an inner hater in most of us who will all too readily engage them in battle. Do not feed hate—within or without—with its daily requirement of hatred and blame. Unless absolutely necessary, do not engage those who message you, and that includes all of real-world, online, and psychic messaging.

Real-world haters rarely have the awareness to assume responsibility for their projections; and by definition psychic messaging is unconscious. You will simply be sucked into that negative energy field if you engage with it. It doesn't matter if you are right. It doesn't even matter if you are the rightest person in the history of sure things. Just leave it. When the Sage meets the tiger on the path, she simply steps aside. The focus of the Sage is firmly within the present, and upon the path unfolding toward her bliss. Avoid drama.

There are of course times when the Nazi wannabes and psychopaths of this world have to be confronted. But even then, a subtle confrontation usually works best. You will recall my tale from the prelude, where I described my treatment by the head teacher at the international school in New Zealand. When that drama evolved, I used the INI Connecting tools to assume responsibility for my part in the drama. This mostly involved my coming to terms with some hurt I'd experienced in childhood, involving my relationship with my mother. Much of it involved allowing myself to get very, very angry. That anger was not projected: it was owned, and in the acknowledgement of how hurt I was, I was able to stand more fully in my male power.

However, real-world action was also required. The head teacher was a genuine bully, and was like a dog at a bone. I had to approach her on a few occasions and ask her to clarify the stories I was getting from students and other staff members about things she was saying about me behind my back. I did so firmly, but respectfully. She denied all charges. I told her that I would prefer her to speak directly to me about any problems she had with my teaching. Eventually she backed off, and began to bully another staff member. Bullies go for the wimps, not the empowered.

HOW THE "HOWS" FOLLOW THE "WHYS"

You don't need to know all the "hows" to get to where you want to be. If you have a big enough "why," Spirit will show you the "hows." After that it is a matter of putting the Wisdom Cycle into full swing. Follow through, listen to the feedback the universe gives you, and be determined.

I knew a guy when I was an undergraduate at university in the '80s. John wanted to be a doctor. As a teenager he had scored a modest 250 marks out of 500 for his Higher School Certificate in New South Wales, Australia. He went back to high school at age twenty-four to get the high marks he needed to get into medical school. After a year of further study, he got a very high, but not brilliant score of 394. This put him into the top 10 percent of all HSC candidates, and meant that he was eligible for an interview to the medical degree at the University of Newcastle. But they turned him down. He was very disappointed. Still, he didn't give up. He went back for a third try, studying a further year and sitting the HSC yet again. Can you imagine being a twenty-five-year-old high school student telling the world that you want to be a doctor? It must have been slightly humiliating for him.

The third time round he did better—by a single mark, scoring 395! He returned for an interview at the University of Newcastle, and this time they accepted him. John told me that his determination had finally swayed the selection committee. He started his medical degree at the age of twenty-six. What a testament to persistence! The last time I saw him he was in his early thirties, and in the final year of his five long years of university study. I have little doubt he is now a practicing doctor.

John knew what he wanted. He had a big "why," too. He just knew that he was meant to be a doctor. He kept knocking and sure enough, the door eventually opened.

If your dream is true, if it resonates with your soul template, then there is a way to reach it. Your higher self will find it, and your guides will assist you along the way. However, this does not negate the necessity for intelligent planning. Nor does it entail passivity. You will have to do stuff, and lots of it. Yet, if you are on the right track, the path of least resistance will open up to you.

Just as for my doctor friend, John, patience is required. In every journey there are steps along the way where you cannot see around the next bend. Then there are moments when things are not terribly exciting at all. Many bits will be quite mundane. Problems will need to be faced. During these times you have to practice a little self-discipline, and keep your mind present and on track.

THE IMPORTANCE OF MEANING

Many times on the journey the game is one of waiting patiently. There will be times when you will be floating in the sea of potential, not quite sure if you are going to arrive at your goal, or knowing how you will get there. This is the limbo state between imagination and manifestation. The key at these times is to remain relaxed but alert.

It is a bit like being an astronaut in the emptiness of deep space. Imagine our space friend installing part of a new space telescope. After completing his work, he must launch himself across an empty divide of about ten yards, from one part of the space station to another, in zero gravity. He sets his goal, gives a short squirt of his little air gun, and lets go. Now, because of the physics of the situation, the astronaut will be propelled in a line from one point in space to another, at a uniform speed and in a single direction. There is effectively no resistance or external force affecting his little journey across space. As he moves across the void between the two hulls, he is helpless. There is not much he can do but wait to see if he arrives at his intended destination. He just has to wait the ten seconds or so as he drifts across space toward the opposite hull of the space station.

The meanings you attribute to the things that happen during the limbo state are critical. If you panic and start kicking and screaming, bemoaning that "This stuff never works!" or "Look at the unemployment figures, we're all stuffed!" then you set up a cloud of negativity in your psyche. This type of negative thinking not only robs you of the presence required to read situations intelligently, it sends the signal to the cosmos that you believe in suffering and failure. It tells the universe that you don't really believe you can do it, and the universe is only as smart as what you ask for.

For your mind, it's garbage in, garbage out. So you have to stay centered and strong, and keep believing, even when there is no hard evidence that belief is warranted. Don't assign neutral situations with negative meanings. The bird may have flown the coop, but that doesn't necessarily mean it is pigeon soup in Chinatown. Maybe your bird needs to get a bit of exercise and will be back later. Or maybe it's time to get a canary. Off you go to the pet shop, where you stumble into a business acquaintance, perfect for your new "pet" business project, pardon the pun.

> In the limbo state between action and outcome,
> do not assign neutral events with negative meanings.
> This will lock you into low-vibration energy fields
> and push your bliss away.

You often do not know the way the universe is working. Just be patient, trust, observe your psyche, and work on the "issues" and beliefs that the situation brings forth from within your mind. And expect the best. Use the Nonjudgmental Reframing INI tool to keep your inner doubter in check.

The path of least resistance is a key understanding. Life brings things to you, and the ideal relationship with this creative process is to allow "what is" and work with it. In presence, your intuitive discernment (not judgment) allows you to make intelligent and wise choices in harmony with your soul. Peace and joy are as much a part of synchronicity as light is part of day. When you add emotion-laden judgment to the life process, it is like throwing a tree trunk into the stream of life, and expecting the water to keep flowing smoothly. Use the Wisdom Cycle. If an action does not create the result you want, simply accept the creation, and move back into the nonjudgment of presence. Who is to say that this is not merely a stepping-stone to where you want to go?

ten

Inspiring

Giving Birth to the Ideas
That Empower Your Journey

As a Sage you are a creator, living in love and without judgment. You create your bliss in alignment with the cosmic mind, with Integrated Intelligence. Your task as the conscious personality is to understand this creative process, align your life with the correct energy, and take the right actions.

When you are aligned with your soul and your purpose, and when you are in a state of presence, the creative energy of the cosmos flows through you. You become inspired. This is why Inspiration is one of the core operations of Integrated Intelligence. In this chapter, I am going to tell you about spiritual inspiration and how to tap in to it. This will include the idea of aligning your life with Spirit and living as a creator.

Creation born of your bliss requires love. For love drives
spiritual life, spiritual journey, and spiritual vision.

AN IDEA IS BORN

Before any act of creation, before any action is taken, and before any product or service hits the market, there is a corresponding idea born

202

within the mind. Every dream, therefore, requires ideas and imagination. Dreams need inspiration.

But creation born of your bliss requires one more thing: love. For love is what drives the spiritual life, the spiritual journey, and the spiritual vision. This love emerges from presence, from healing. It is ultimately due to the permission of Spirit that your dream is empowered, and it is the grace of Spirit that takes you home. In the context of the law of attraction, to be attracted is to feel drawn to something, to long for union. Therefore, dreams born of your bliss are dreams born of love.

Inspiration can come from mundane sources, and it can also come from the higher self and spirit guides.

Conversely, dreams born of ego are dreams that take us into separation. They are a movement away from something. That something is often the pain of our soul issues. Instead of moving toward healing and integration, the ego moves away from the wounded child, and sets an agenda that it feels will anesthetize the pain. This leads to delusion, because self becomes broken, split, and part of us becomes hidden in darkness. This creates the shadow, the unconscious part of us that ensnares us in dense energy fields centered on fear, shame, guilt, blame, and so on. Then we attempt to establish goals that are often not reflective of Spirit, and to reach them using control and power over others and life circumstances. A spiritual fall is inevitable when the stubbornness of ego can no longer sustain the charade.

Once you have found and committed to your bliss, Spirit will step in to help you along the way. You will experience grace. If your aim is true, if you are working toward a dream that expresses the needs of your higher self (and is therefore in alignment with your soul template) then Spirit will fill you with excitement. This is a kind of love where mind, body, and soul are in perfect alignment. And from that grace inspiration flows, enabling the creativity that empowers your dream.

WHERE CREATIVITY COMES FROM

There are several sources of creativity. First, there is mundane human intelligence. The brain is a self-organizing system, and even when you are not paying attention, it will process and organize information, and go about solving problems. It is well known that the most creative people in terms of excellence of performance tend to be those who have mastered a domain through years of deliberate practice. Once the elements of a domain have been thoroughly learned, the person can then innovate to produce outstanding innovative performances. This background skill is required in most kinds of creative acts. No matter how inspired I am, I am not going to win the Fields Medal in mathematics. I simply lack the skills to do advanced mathematics.

Most creativity experts assume this is the limit of creativity, and work within the restrictions of this model of mind. Yet inspiration and creativity are not the same thing. I see inspiration as an excitement that leads to the generation of ideas. Innovation is what potentially follows when those ideas are put to work in creative endeavor.

However, there are sources of creativity beyond the physical brain, and you can learn to tap in to this inspiration. The higher self is involved in creativity, and has access to the extended mind. The higher self is that part of you that is an expression of the soul. It is an established pattern of energy, with certain soul aptitudes. If your soul template moves you to express yourself in the intellectual realms, it may guide you in researching subjects you are passionate about, finding the solution to mathematical problems, or identifying causes of neuroses in clients (psychologists). If your soul template moves you to express yourself in more grounded ways, it might assist you in repairing old cars, redecorating the house, or even fixing broken table legs. If you are in textiles, it may plant the seeds of knowing within you about where to find suppliers and customers. The creativity of the higher self is impersonal. Just like mundane inspiration, it involves an unconscious processing of information. Your higher self organizes information for you, and brings answers to questions that you are asking or thinking about.

*You need to be aware of your ego's role in what you are
trying to create. If you are not conscious of what your ego
is up to, you may steer yourself in the wrong path,
or even become a channel for dark energy.*

Spirit guides are another source of inspiration. These spiritual aids plant ideas in your mind, sometimes even entire story lines, melodies, solutions to problems, and so on. Many of your ideas, dreams, and intuitions are actually ideas planted in the mind by your guides. They will also work through you when you are in a relaxed state, such as when daydreaming or during meditation.

Just as with Free-Form Writing, during acts of creation you can invite your guides to assist you with ideas and inspiration. As you quiet the mind, simply put out a prayer to Spirit for inspiration. If what you are aiming to create or the problem you are trying to solve is aligned with your higher self, then inspiration will flow.

Spirit guides can also help you in your healing journey. When you are ready, they will release images into your mind. This information helps you to see what your soul issues are. But they will not assist you when your creative endeavor is not aligned with Spirit or it contains an ego-centered agenda.

In fact, where there is unbalanced ego, you may be influenced by negative energy. This may include the messages and projections of others around you, or perhaps discarnate entities. These can really lead you astray, and take you away from your bliss if you are not careful. As an extreme example, Hitler was greatly affected by very dark spiritual forces. Sometimes he would awaken in the middle of the night, vaguely aware of entities in the room, and begin shouting at them. Because of his manic lust for attention, power, and control, Hitler was a magnet for dark energy. It's true that most of us will never embody that degree of darkness. However, many people do harbor quite dark spiritual energy within their consciousness field.

You need to be aware of your ego and its role in what you are trying to create. Use the Connecting with the Ego process to check the real intention behind your actions. If you are not aware of what your ego is up to, you may end up steering yourself along the wrong path, or, in a worst case scenario, become a channel for dark energy.

WHEN INTUITION GOES DARK

Well over a decade ago I was going through a real bad patch. It was not long after I had been kicked out of a spiritual group in New Zealand for being a drama queen. I lost face big time, and it was all terribly embarrassing for my ego. After about twenty-four hours of deep despair, I started to think about how I could get my life back on track. Within a few weeks, I decided that I wanted to run a workshop, teaching people about the kinds of ideas you find in this book (though a little less developed at that time).

I used the Quick Check to determine the energy on doing the workshop. However, I could not get a consistent energy reading, and remained locked in self-doubt and confusion. Being asked to leave the spiritual group had affected me deeply, as belonging to that group meant the world to me. I also knew that self-doubt and uncertainty was a doorway through which negative energy was prying at my mind, and I wondered whether this was affecting my readings.

So, I decided to use a Light Trance to seek clarification, and put the word out to Spirit. I sat down and slowly relaxed until I knew I was in the drowsy state where visions flow. I then asked the question: "Spirit, what is the energy on my conducting this workshop on spiritual development at (such and such date)?"

I repeated this question over a period of ten minutes or so, and a faint voice kept saying "No." Yet I still felt there was something not right about it. So I relaxed even more, and continued putting out the question. Suddenly, a short vision came to me. Looking down from above, I saw my personal teacher from the spiritual group. She was half-obscured under a black umbrella, as if she was trying to hide from my view. She said very clearly: "No, there's no energy on it at all."

After the meditation, I reflected on the vision. The meaning seemed clear. My spiritual teacher was generating a lot of dark energy, "messaging" me, and trying to stop me. Psychic messaging occurs when someone unconsciously sends a stream of negative thoughts to you to try to manipulate your mind. It happens to all of us every day, but some messaging is stronger than others. This was the very strong kind.

I had trouble believing what I had seen. It didn't make much sense. After all, this was the woman who had taught me so much of what I knew. She was one of the good guys. Why would she be trying to hurt me in my darkest hour? That would be the "behavior" of a rather devious personality. Nonetheless, I had experienced enough such visions to know that this one felt right—and it was the Feeling Sense that I trusted. Still, there was no way for me to confirm or deny the vision's content in an empirical way, for I was completely excluded from contact with the group, and I wasn't able to talk to my teacher or anyone else in the group about it.

I went ahead and did the workshop. Just a few people attended it, but that was fine for me, and I got some positive feedback from those who did come. Nonetheless, the truth is that my self-belief was so low that I was being greatly affected by dark energy throughout the workshop.

Meanwhile, I continued to work on the soul issues that had led to my exclusion from the group, the same issues that were allowing my mind to be affected by dark energy. I figured that even though I would probably never be able to work with such advanced souls again, what I was doing would benefit humanity as a whole. For whenever any of us heals a part of the wounded child, when we raise the vibration of our consciousness, we add a little more light to humanity and cosmos. The issues are then prevented from being passed down to our children, as unresolved soul issues tend to become imprinted upon the minds of our descendants.

Some inner voices are misleading. They come from
external sources and their goal is to try to mess you up.
You need to distinguish the darkness from
your genuine guidance.

A month later, I got a surprise phone call from one of the spiritual group members. To my great joy, I was invited back into the group. As they had the capacity to read my psyche from a distance, they had been observing my progress. I was even more shocked to learn that my former spiritual teacher had been asked to leave the group. It had been discovered that her negative energy was adversely affecting other group members, and she was unable to deal with the ego states and soul issues that lay behind the problem. These issues were about power and control over others. The vision about her that I had picked up the month before had been spot on.

There are several things to note from this. First, some inner voices are misleading, and are not yours. They come from external sources, and their goal is to try to mess you up. You need to distinguish the dark energy and projections from other minds from your genuine guidance. If you are experiencing a lot of fear, self-doubt, and confusion, you can be pretty sure there will be dark energy around. Dark energy is attracted to fear like ants to sugar. However, it is a chicken and egg situation. The dark energy is coming in through the wounds within your psyche, including your self-doubt, self-destructive thoughts, and negative beliefs. So, in a sense, the darkness is a mirror of your soul. If you turn and face whatever is permitting the energy to enter your mind, you will come to a deeper awareness of yourself and your soul issues, and will in turn experience a greater degree of healing. This is one of the reasons why I say that you must work on your healing as you live your bliss. If you don't, you will be vulnerable to manipulation from negative energies.

PROTECTION

Thus, part of the answer to the inevitable question about how we can protect ourselves from negative energies is that we have to do healing work and reign in the lost parts of ourselves that dark energy uses as doorways into our psyches. Imagining white light around you (as some naive New Agers believe) is useless, as it does nothing to shift the energy of the psyche. It's about as effective as imagining a wall in front of you as an army tank is about to run over you.

White lighting also does nothing to close the second doorway for dark energy: the human ego and its pomposity. One thing that dark energy will try to do is build up your ego. It will tell you that you are the next great one, that you are so strong, so beautiful, and so special. If I were you, I would be very suspicious of any spiritual teachers who try to build up your ego, who use flattery, or who give off a lot of sexual energy. In fact, I'd get the hell out of there.

The way around all this is to constantly monitor your ego. Make it your friend by doing Connecting with the Ego. Talk to your ego, and gently remind it that it is not half as big as it thinks it is. If that doesn't keep it quiet, try a good smack on the bum. If you don't, life will give you a good butt-kicking, sooner or later.

GOOD IDEAS

The good news is that there is also a team of good guys helping inspire you to live your bliss. These are your spirit guides. Your higher self is also a great source of inspirational energy, too. When you are in presence, when you are balanced and aligned with Spirit, and when you actively seek guidance, you will be able to draw upon these sources of knowledge and wisdom.

It is, however, really hard for you to hear your guides when you go into self-doubt and fear, when you are running around like a peacock, all full of yourself, or just complaining and fighting with the rest of humanity.

Each human psyche is different. Although there are archetypal symbols and meanings, all dream images have to be understood in context.

Imagine yourself stuck at the bottom of a rugby maul, your face is pressed to the turf (been there, done that!). You see and taste nothing but dirt, and hear only the huffing and puffing of a dozen big guys stomping all over you. There is a lot of pain as the sprigs from their boots bite the flesh in your back. Meanwhile your mother is on the sideline yelling, "Come on, get on with it!" Chances are Mum's voice is the last thing you are going to hear at that moment. You are just there eating dirt, and complaining about how bad it tastes.

Unfortunately, the situation for most of the human race is not too far removed from this analogy. The human collective energy sphere is like a psychic rugby match, with people stomping all over each other trying to get what they want, even as the voice of Spirit is drowned out. However, as you work on your energy, bringing your spirit into presence and doing your healing work, you will slow down and be able to listen. You will notice that you are not alone, spiritually speaking.

CONNECTING WITH THE CREATOR

Whether it is your higher self, your guides, or the intelligence of the cosmos, getting in touch with Spirit is an act of co-creation. It is about letting go, and allowing the energy to pass through you. Your Intuitive Diary is really important to this process. It will help you establish a deeper connection between your personality and spiritual realms. As you remember and acknowledge more dreams, mental images, and intuitive prompts, and commit these things to paper, you will begin to understand the language of the psyche and the language of Spirit.

I did this diligently for many years. I put my diary beside my bed, and would awaken numerous times during the night to record what came to me. Over time, I learned to decipher the language of my psyche. I suggest you do the same. If you do not want to interrupt your sleep, use your Intuitive Diary first thing in the morning, when you awaken.

I have given you a bit of a head start in learning this language in the appendix, which explains how to interpret common symbols from dreams and visions. When you use it, keep in mind that each human psyche is a little different. Although there are archetypal symbols and meanings, any specific dream image has to be understood within the context in which it appears. A very helpful way to understand psychic symbols is to *feel* them. Get to know them via the Feeling Sense. This will often tell you more about them than an intellectual interpretation. You cannot simply say that an old man represents wisdom. He might just as well represent the local exhibitionist, especially if he is wearing a musty raincoat. In that case, you'd be better off ignoring his advice.

WRITING FROM SPIRIT

When it comes to really allowing yourself to be a channel for Spirit, I know of no better process than Free-Form Writing, which I also sometimes call "automatic writing." For it, you can use a pen, a computer, or any medium you feel comfortable with.

Much of this book has been written using Free-Form Writing. I simply sit and focus upon the subject matter. Often, the prose seems to write itself. The ideas come, and I allow the energy to take me downstream. Later, I come back and tidy it up.

It is much the same for any creative endeavor where you connect with Spirit. Most of the inspiration occurs in the initial stage. After that, the process will become more left-brained, as you dot the i's and cross the t's. Yet, even in later stages of the creative process, when more left-brained thinking is usually required, inspiration may continue to flow. You can continue to actively pursue it as you make decisions about the final form of your project.

The key with Free-Form Writing is to release the need for control. You have to appreciate that it is not "you" who is doing the writing. You are connecting with something much bigger than your personality. Be careful not to overmanage the content. The process is like snowboarding down a mountain of smooth, dense snow. Ideally, it should be just as effortless and just as much fun.

*With Free-Form Writing you release the need for
control. It is like snowboarding, and it should be just as
effortless and just as much fun.*

The secret to letting go of control is nonjudgment. You do not stop to find out if what you are writing is any good, or whether it falls in line with the views of the Democrats, the Republicans, or the women's movement. You are just going with the flow. You open up and out comes the message. As you begin to write, you can imagine a light coming down through your head, and passing out through your heart, moving from your chest and onto the page or computer screen. The light is the energy of Spirit, of love, and perfect love involves no judgment.

To facilitate this state of nonjudgment, relax and let go of the outcome. Whatever you produce at the end of the sentence, the paragraph, or the book is perfect. If you insist on a particular outcome (the quality, quantity, or even subject matter), you impose control and block the flow of Spirit, the flow of energy, and the flow of love. Nonetheless, Free-Form Writing can involve structure. You can begin by writing the heading, or putting out a question to Spirit. An Affirmation often helps. You can ask for guidance. But after you begin writing you just need to get out of the way and let the words flow.

One statement I like to use to begin goes something like this: "Dear Spirit. Please guide me as I write these words. Let me be a channel for your thought and your love, so that what I write may be a true expression of Spirit."

The voice of Spirit is an excitement, a love, and you can feel that love and excitement flowing effortlessly through you. There is a blissfulness; an experience that is as much feeling as thinking. The voice comes through of its own accord. If you listen closely, with your heart, it is saying, "I love you," and all you have to do is accept the embrace. You let go.

You can stop for a moment now and then to quiet your mind, focusing upon your breath. This allows a space for the next thought to catch you, or for you to catch the idea. It's a soft and receptive process, like a child catching butterflies. It is harmonic, a wave of light that moves inspiration through your soul and engages your spirit in a dance of consciousness.

When you write free-form there is no immediate editing. If you want, and the writing is something serious (say, if you are a writer, or you want to polish it for future reference), you can come back later and correct it. But don't do this during the Free-Form Writing phase. The left-brained, analytical mind has to be put aside, or used very sparingly during this process. You will find that if you begin to analyze, or if you become overly "rational," you will lose the flow of Spirit.

In Practice 10.1

℮ *Free-Form Writing: A Story of Love*

In this practice you are going to write a love story in your Intuitive Diary using Free-Form Writing. I encourage you to resist any judgments about love stories and just go with it! The experience will help your future Free-Form Writing and spiritual creativity.

Begin by relaxing deeply. Take some deep breaths and quiet the mind. Allow yourself to fall into a pleasant state of relaxation.

Put out an Affirmation to Spirit, asking for guidance: "Dear Spirit. Please guide me as I write these words. Let me be a channel for your thought and your love, so that this love story may be a deeply meaningful expression of wisdom."

Close your eyes and imagine a white light coming into your mind from above and filling you. Feel the love and inspiration of Spirit flowing through you. Just rest in that space for a minute or two, or for as long as you feel is necessary. If any ideas come into your mind, just observe them.

When you are ready, open your eyes and begin to write. If it comes to you, fill in the name of the story first. If the title doesn't come right away, that is fine; just move straight on to the writing of the story, and fill it in later.

Begin with the first thing that comes into your head, and keep moving. You can stop for a moment and quiet the mind here and there, focusing upon your breath, and feeling the light flowing through you. Do not judge any idea, word, sentence, or plot line. Just go with it. Still, if something important comes to you in a flash of inspiration, and you have to go back and change something from a previous sentence, that is fine. Keep going till you feel the story come to an end.

If inspiration begins slowly, ask a few questions, such as those given below. First read through the questions and let the answers come into your mind, but don't start writing again until you have read all of the questions. Your psyche will go about answering them, even if you are not sure of the answers straight away.

> What is the setting?
> Who is the main character, and what is she/he like?
> Who is the object of her/his love, and what is she/he like?
> Where do they first meet, and how do they feel?
> What separates them?
> What obstacles do they need to overcome?
> What problems does their relationship have?
> What is special about their love?
> Do they stay together, or part?
> What happens in the end?

When you have finished reading the questions, you will have plenty of ideas, and you can begin writing. When you finish, give thanks to Spirit. What you have written is perfect. Allow it to be. However, you can reread the story if you wish, or even tidy it up.

Then consider the meaning of the story for you. Is there a message for you in your own life, or the life of someone you know? Just allow the answers to come, and if they don't, that is okay.

———

You can repeat this exercise as often as you like, to facilitate your connection with Spirit. If you like, you can change the theme from *love* to other archetypal themes such as *redemption, wisdom, transformation, salvation, grace, honor, betrayal,* and so on.

Academic Writing

Free-Form Writing can be used in the drafting phase of even the most academic writing. For my doctoral thesis, I channeled the first drafts of all of the chapters, using Integrated Inquiry. I continue to channel the drafts of almost all of my academic writing.

However, academic writing involves a great deal of editing and rewriting. So I come back later to rework it again and again. For my thesis, this process involved about fifteen drafts per chapter. As I mentioned earlier, using daily Free-Form Writing, my writing output over the five years I worked on my dissertation was prodigious: about 350,000 words of publication.

It was all relatively effortless; it just took an awful lot of work! The only papers that were really difficult and painful to write were the ones that I did not channel from the word go. In one paper, for example, I took ideas from one of my previous papers, reworked them into another form, and added some new ideas. It really did not flow well. It did get published, but I wasn't happy with the result. Yet, in the end it was perfect. It was a lesson from Spirit. I now know better what works and does not work for me in terms of my writing.*

> *Free-Form Writing will help open your third eye, the doorway to the psychic realms, and especially psychic inspiration. You can then transfer that channeling process to other creative pursuits.*

---

*If you want to learn more about how to use Free-Form Writing for research, read my book *The Professor's Other Brain.* I also wrote a paper on this topic for the journal Foresight, called "Futures Research at the Edge of Mind." It is also available on www.mindfutures.com, and at www.scribd.com.

OTHER PURSUITS

Writing is not everyone's cup of tea. Nonetheless, I encourage you to persist with Free-Form Writing to help develop your connection with Spirit. Becoming proficient at Free-Form Writing will help to open your third eye, the energy center that lies approximately in the space between and just behind your eyes, near the pituitary gland. The third eye is the doorway to the psychic realms, especially psychic inspiration.

My third eye opened at the age of twenty-six, at precisely the time I began to meditate. It was also the time I began to write my first book. This was no coincidence. The act of writing helped to open that channel. One day, while I was meditating, I suddenly noticed a dark bluish spot of light right before me. I didn't really know too much about chakras or psychic energy at that time, but I intuitively knew what it was. Every time I closed my eyes, it would be there (and still is).

Whether you see the light of the third eye or not is not important. Just trust that as you engage in intuitive creative processes such as Free-Form Writing, this energy center will respond.

There are few limits as to how you can employ the creative energy of connection in your work and play.

Once the third eye is open, you will develop some proficiency at letting information flow through you from Spirit, not just in the realm of writing. There are few limits to how you can employ the creative energy of connection in your work and play. You can connect with inspiration to plan meetings, lessons, and performances, to write poems and songs and to deliver them, and to decorate your home.

I have used spiritual inspiration for public speaking, acting, dancing, and even face-painting. Several years ago, when I was living in Taiwan and working in a school for primary-aged students, I was asked to do some face-painting for the kids. The children were mostly aged four to ten years old. I wasn't too keen on the idea, and was even more taken aback when I noted it was the little girls who started to come to me to have their faces "done" (strangely, little boys are not quite as keen on that!). After a bit of an awkward start, I soon fell into a Light Trance state, and simply painted what I felt, using precisely the same consciousness state as I use for Free-Form Writing. The child would come, I would see an image form in my head, and I would paint his or her face. I had never thought of myself as being artistic, so I was amazed that I was actually quite good at it. And the kids loved it.

Soon, they were running off to show their parents, and to tell their friends to come over and have their faces painted. I did this nonstop for about three hours. Despite the fact that it required a great deal of concentration, it was an ecstatic and effortless experience.

One advantage that connecting with Spirit for inspiration has over other methods is that the ideas are more likely to be connected with your soul purpose, because you are deliberately aligning with Spirit.

If an artistic dufus like me can channel creative energy for face-painting, you can connect with inspiration too—and for many more tasks than you realize. The key is to allow yourself to fall into that effortless state of flow and grace that psychologists like Mihaly Csikszentmihalyi have written about. We have all felt this state of flow at one time or another. It is a state of relaxed but disciplined joy, and requires relaxed concentration. In this state, the breath is full and deep, and ideally you feel your abdomen moving in and out without resistance. By deliberately relaxing and breathing deeply, you can mirror the state of flow, and this process permits the state of creative connection to emerge without resistance.

Recently, I was watching a video about Australian soft pop band, Air Supply. I was very interested to hear their guitarist and songwriter Graham Russell say that he simply did not know where his songs came from. He said that he hears chords and songs in his head all the time, and that he considers himself to be merely a medium for the music. Graham always knew that he wanted to be a songwriter and play in a band. He became a living channel for his dream. Many times in his life he was knocked down, but he kept getting back up. He compares himself to the cyborg in the movie *Terminator 2*. The cyborg keeps getting smashed and bashed, but just keeps coming back again.

I highly recommend that you take note of highly creative people like Graham Russell. Graham's determination is exemplary. You need persistence to actualize your dream. You need commitment. You need to know who you are, and who you are not. And most of all you need to nurture the inner love of the Sage.

SETTING THE SCENE AND GENERATING IDEAS

Generating ideas is a creative act, and connecting with Spirit is just one of many ways to enhance creativity. There are numerous other ways that are effective. Experiment with them and find the ones that you prefer. There is no reason why you cannot combine spiritual inspiration with other ways of creating.

One advantage that connecting with Spirit for inspiration has over other methods is that the ideas are more likely to be aligned with your soul purpose, because you are deliberately aligning with Spirit. It is inevitable that flow experiences come with activities that you are proficient at, and which are aligned with your soul aptitudes. It is hard for a writer to enter a flow state when he is learning to type, when he is all fingers and thumbs. Later, as he approaches mastery of the skill of typing, he will be able to effortlessly enter the state of flow.

It is important to create a safe, gentle, nurturing environment when connecting with the inspiration of Spirit. Being close to nature is ideal. You might take a notebook to the park, sit by the sea to think, write, paint, dance, or sing. Find a quiet coffee shop, or perhaps a church or monastery. Generally speaking, environments with a lot of clutter, noise, and people coming and going are poor places for connecting with Spirit.

You can also play some appropriate music. I find gentle music best for meditative states, but sometimes faster-paced music can work if you want to create an excited state. If you like, use other ways to enhance presence and relaxation, such as flower essences, aromatherapy, or burning incense. Soft eye-level lighting is best at evening or night. You can also try dancing, singing, whistling, juggling, or whatever gets you in the mood! Experiment, and be creative when you are being creative!

After inspiration arrives, you have to trust it, and you have to act on it. The more you act, the greater will be your connection with Spirit. In this way, the creative act will continue to spring forth from you. Ignore it, and it will weaken. The action in turn has to emerge from the intuitive mind.

The modern scientific worldview has sold us the lie that we are a bunch of biological nuts and bolts. Nothing could be further from the truth. We are magic becoming. In Practice 10.2, Using Inspiration in My Life, will help get you into the habit of connecting with the magic of the universe as you work and play.

In Practice 10.2

℮ Using Inspiration in My Life

In what ways can you connect with spiritual inspiration in your work and play?

List three situations in your life where you feel you might be able to channel the creativity of Spirit. Describe how you will do it. For example, you might write, "While creating this month's newsletter, I will relax deeply at the office and allow the inspiration to come to me."

Then, apply spiritual inspiration to each situation at least once (but preferably several times). Soon you will develop an easy habit of coming up with multiple ideas, the first step in creativity.

Finally, record your results, and think of ways to improve next time.

SITUATION	HOW I WILL DO IT	THE RESULT AND HOW TO IMPROVE NEXT TIME

YOUR LIFE AS THE GREAT PORTRAIT

For the vast majority of humanity, life is a series of reactions to external events—but not for the Sage. As you become more conscious, as you align with Spirit and live your bliss, you will begin to see your life as a creative act. In that sense, your life becomes a process of connection and of integration with a greater intelligence. This is why it is called Integrated Intelligence. For the Sage, life is a process of connecting with inner worlds, taking actions that build a dream, and dancing as he allows it all to unfold.

The meanings that you assign to things are central to the creation of your life. They move out from you and determine the vibration of your energy field.

Part of the creative act of alignment is to allow what is, without judgment, and to see what unfolds before you as an act of Spirit. This is a natural result of the state of presence. Judgment robs you of presence and steals your bliss. Some judgments are worse than others: the negative ones. This is why some of the meanings that you assign to things are central to the creation of your life. Meanings are judgments, and they have great power. They move out from within you and determine the vibration of your energy field, of your universe. They create your life experience.

Meaning in, energy and experience out.

You can walk down the street with a smile on your face, noticing with awe a small plant struggling through the crack in the pavement, and feeling love and compassion for the people you pass. Or you can walk down the street grumbling about a piece of litter at your feet, feeling contempt for the people who won't smile or greet you, and wearing a grumpy frown. Same time, same place, different energy. Different life. In effect we are talking about two different universes: universe misery and universe bliss. You can choose which one you prefer.

Meaning in, energy and experience out. Never forget that.

*If you want to be a creator and not a hater, if you want
to be part of the transformation of humanity,
begin assuming responsibility for your
judgments and projections.*

THE CREATORS AND THE HATERS

To put it simply, there are two expressions of energy in this world: creating and hating, or the acts of creation and destruction. They represent the same polarities as light and darkness, nonjudgment and judgment, love and fear.

Not that long ago, after I wrote a post on an education website, I received an anonymous e-mail response from somebody calling himself (they are usually men) "youprick@......com." Just quietly, he wasn't contacting me to offer his compliments. Here was a man who felt so powerless, and was so full of anger and discontent that he had taken out a special e-mail account for the sole purpose of spreading hate in the world. A classic hater, he has lost the plot and fallen off the page of the Book of Spirit.

Every act of judgment (and all the various projections of ego) testifies to your separation from Spirit. At times all of us project our feelings of fear and anger onto other people, objects, ideas, or things. It might be a politician, political party, religion, musician, nation, race, pop figure, media group, profession, or so on. Another expression of this occurs when we complain to a friend, the guy behind the counter, or vent on the Internet.

You might think venting is harmless, but you are creating a stream of negative energy in your psyche. You are creating meaning, writing the plot of your life.

The thing to remember is that the thing you hate or are complaining about is not real. That's worth repeating. The thing you hate is not real. Objects of blame or hate are constructions of the ego. You create judgments about things, situations, and people, and then you invest the energy of destruction in your "relationship" with them. Every act of judgment contains a desire to destroy. It takes you out of alignment with Spirit, and brings you into alignment with dark energy fields.

If you want to be a creator and not a hater, begin assuming responsibility for your judgments. Own them fully, then take responsibility for them. Let's say you intensely dislike the president, and you want to take responsibility for that energy. Imagine him or her standing before you, and say whatever comes into your mind when you think of him or her. Then, after a minute or two of ranting (the ego's favorite game), go to a mirror and begin a conversation with yourself. Parent that judgmental part of yourself, as with the Connecting with the Ego tool. State an intention to be responsible for the blame and hate you have just expressed. There is no need to be ashamed; bringing the ego out into the open is an act of love and acceptance. You are loving your shadow.

Next, move away from the mirror and bring yourself into presence using either of the presence techniques mentioned in chapter 3. When your mind has gone quiet, return to an image of the president, and look upon it in silence. If you are fully present the projections will have ceased, or at the very least, you will simply witness them as they arise, and they will have no power over you.

If you engage in this kind of process regularly, you will soon no longer need to go through the whole series of steps. It will require just a moment of mindfulness to witness projections as they arise in the mind, and release them. The hater will have made space for the creator.

All judgment robs you of presence and your
connection with Spirit.

What you see and hear in public discussions, at the local supermarket, or on the Internet are projections going head to head, and egos spending vast amounts of energy fighting each other. All for stuff that isn't real. All judgment robs you of presence and your connection with Spirit. It sends your Sage packing for the next train out of town.

Changing the way you see the world takes some degree of self-discipline. We have been conditioned to judge and blame. In some of my academic papers I have written about the confrontations of opposites that have been central to Western logic and education systems since the time of the ancient Greeks.* We are taught to think this way. Western societies are also individualistic. This confrontation and individualism means that we are unconsciously programmed to aggressively challenge what we see and hear. That's great for independent thinking, but it can cut us off from Spirit.

The connection with Spirit requires a gentle and receptive attitude. One of the reasons why academics have such a hard time with Integrated Intelligence is that the ego-centered intellectualism of the academic system is the antithesis of receptivity.

There is a good chance that your ego is starting to party hard as you read this. Time for a hard slap to the frontal lobes! Yes. I am suggesting you allow many of your opinions and intellectual viewpoints to gently

---

*See my "Harmonic Circles" articles in the recommended reading section, and on www .mindfutures.com.

fade into the background. The truth is that they are not that important. Many of them are based on partial truths, and a lot of them are utter rubbish. They weigh a ton and are a pain to carry around. They get you into dramas.

I am suggesting that it is better to value presence more than the intellectual mind. Listen to the voice of Spirit and discipline the voice of the mind. Spend time in meditation or in the silence of nature. Even a few minutes will help.

When you find yourself in a confrontation of some kind, go within and ask yourself why you are fighting, and what you are fighting against. If you like, use In Practice 10.3, Rising Above It All, given here. It is a transformative process, which will enable you to put yourself outside of the drama and to connect with the knowledge and wisdom that is potentially there.

In Practice 10.3

℮ Rising Above It All

This exercise can be done when you find yourself in an intellectual conflict with someone, or you can also use it for a long-standing difference of perspective on a certain topic, such as if you are a "greenie" with a dislike for corporate greed. The purpose of this exercise is not to find agreement with your opponent, but to develop deep empathy for him and move beyond ego space and out of the drama that projection brings.

See yourself facing your opponent, and listening to his side of the debate. Listen for a minute or so without interruption.

Then give your perspective in equally brief form.

Now, imagine your spirit coming out of your body, and moving into the body of your opponent, so that "you" are now facing yourself from within your opponent's body. Begin to speak and feel as your opponent.

Allow the new "you" to keep talking for at least a minute.

When the new "you" has finished speaking, from that perspective (from within the body of your opponent), observe your true self sitting opposite, speaking and arguing your original perspective on the debate.

Just watch with detached interest, and avoid judgments. You should be able to witness yourself from a unique perspective, and you may even gain some insight into the way you think.

Next, imagine your spirit rising out of your opponent and above the two figures below. See and hear them talking about the issue. Remain detached. Allow any observations or insights to come to you. These can be about you, your opponent, or the interplay between you.

Then begin to project love at the two people you are seeing below you. Make sure you love both equally, and forgive them for their humanness. If you like, you can say a prayer to Spirit asking for forgiveness and for wisdom, praying that all parties can learn and grow from the experience.

See and feel yourself moving back into your true body, and give thanks to your former opponent. Say another short prayer to Spirit, affirming your intention to refrain from judgment and to love, such as: "I am now willing to allow a space for love and nonjudgment within this situation. I release the need to be right, and commit to my bliss."

Wish your opponent well and imagine yourself walking away.

Last, you need to reaffirm your intention in the period following the exercise, as the ego will try to reassert its agenda. Repeat this exercise whenever you feel the need.

This process is not simply an act of imagination. All minds are connected, so when you imagine yourself in your opponent's body, you are connecting telepathically with his energy field. Honor what you sense. And when you project love and forgiveness, you initiate healing.

In this chapter, I have encouraged you to write, dance, and sing your way through life. Create it the way you see it, the way you feel it deep within you. You have that choice. Don't waste it. It's never too late. Your creative energy is precious. Conserve it for creation, not destruction.

One day in the presence of Spirit and living your bliss is worth more to your spirit and to God than all the ego-generated achievements on the planet. Many people never experience that joy. You are one of the blessed ones.

In the next chapter, you will learn more about creating relationships that are aligned with your bliss and are filled with the love of Spirit.

eleven

Love Matters

Creating Relationships That
Sustain Your Soul

Integrated Intelligence is not merely great for deepening the relationship with yourself and with Spirit, it is also a fantastic capacity to have for developing and deepening relationships with others.

I would like to state from the outset that I consider myself a student of human relationships, not a master. The scars of my childhood left me with deep wounds that have required much attention in adulthood. Yet, I used these scars as a means to develop a deep awareness of inner worlds and human consciousness. Further, my work as a spiritual counselor has helped me develop a high level of perceptual acuity. It has permitted me to develop a great deal of knowledge about the dynamics of relationships.

All relationships have both a primary or surface dimension as well as a secondary or deeper dimension. Developing Integrated Intelligence will enable you to gain a good deal of understanding about the deeper dimension. You will be working with the essential causes of relationship problems and dynamics, not just surface behavior.

Using Integrated Intelligence within relationships not only makes you more aware, more responsible and more loving, it deepens your understanding of Spirit. This is too great an opportunity to pass up.

EASY LOVING

You might recall from a previous chapter that before moving to New Zealand, I was living in Newcastle on the east coast of Australia, about two hours drive north of Sydney. I was studying part time toward a doctorate.

I was also experimenting with Integrated Intelligence, but not quite to the degree I have developed today. I was not exactly on my spiritual learner's license—more like the provisional license. Fortunately, I was getting a lot of spiritual guidance through the Light Trances and Active Dreaming tools. This helped address some, but not all, of my general lack of understanding about the subtleties of human relationships and the spiritual journey.

I was single throughout most of this time, but one particular week I got some spiritual guidance that raised my hopes regarding a possible relationship. I awoke on a Wednesday night, and there was a song playing very clearly in my head. It was "She's an Easy Lover" by Phil Collins and Phil Bailey. Then, as I was falling back to sleep, the old song "Wild Thing" by the Troggs came through. This was too much to ignore, so I did what I always did at that time: I switched on the light and recorded the song titles and lyrics I had heard in my Intuitive Diary.

The next night the same thing happened, with the two songs coming through again. I knew that this was more than a coincidence. Spirit was trying to tell me something. Going to my diary, I speculated that my guides were trying to get me together with some bimbo. Was I about to get lucky?

On Friday my friend Gary rang me up and suggested we head out on the town to one of his favorite dance venues. Later that evening as Gary and I entered the club and forked over the entrance fee, the doorman thumped a stamp on our wrists (which is how they checked to see who had paid). I looked down at my stamp under the glittering lights. My eyes nearly popped out of my head. There I saw two words on my lower arm, bright in fluorescent ink: "Wild Thing."

As it turned out, I did meet a rather "wild thing!" And I didn't have to try too hard at all. Now why would Spirit guide a person toward such an encounter? For me, it served the evolution of my Spirit. That little encounter shook me up a bit. And just as quietly, I needed a bit of shaking!

I had a lot further to go on my spiritual journey than I realized at that time. It is just as well I didn't know the true distance I had to travel. Spirit only gives us the knowledge that we can handle. If I had known what lay ahead, I probably would have quit. Instead I was the Fool, stepping naively toward the future, and experimenting with Integrated Intelligence as a creative process in my life journey.

As time went on and I began to deal with my soul issues, my perception expanded and I came to rely less on direct spiritual guidance to assist me in making choices. I developed other INI tools, and found them to be invaluable.

THE GIFT OF FEELING

One of the greatest blessings of Integrated Intelligence is the gift of feeling. It is the Feeling Sense that allows you to see deep within yourself, to unveil your soul template, and thus come to know who you really are. It will also assist you in finding the motivations that are really driving your behavior. It can help you find out what it is holding you back from bringing the love that you want and need into your life.

Integrated Intelligence is the mental capacity that brings
you to greater awareness that you are one with all
people, with all of nature, and with the entire universe.
It is awareness of ultimate love.

Ultimately, Integrated Intelligence is the mental capacity that brings you to greater awareness that you are one with all people, with all of nature, and indeed with the entire universe. And what is that, if not awareness of relationships, of ultimate love? Love is honesty. Perfect love hides nothing. Integrated Intelligence is the spark that will help you to ignite the flame of truth. It will not do so in a blaze of glory (pardon the cliché and pun). The complete truth will most likely arise within you slowly.

One thing I have learned as I have explored the human psyche is that you have to be patient and humble. You can learn only so much at any given time. If you attained total truth and were healed instantly, it would blow your mind. To heal you have to not only see the truth, but also feel it. While in theory we can heal immediately and forever, the reality is that we are governed by certain laws of consciousness. Just as in physics, energy is never destroyed. It is simply transformed. The same occurs after the death of the physical body. The overall energy of the psyche does not shift greatly in most people when they die. In particular, for the deeply wounded and those who have unloved parts of themselves ensnared in the shadow, death simply relocates the problem to another dimension.

As a person sensitive to the psychic energy of people, I have seen very clearly that the deceased retain psychological issues and mental scars even after passing. They continue in many cases to have "relationships" with those they left behind on the physical plane. There are continued exchanges of consciousness and energy, and many of the dramas—the unconscious projections—continue unabated.

There is no escape. There is but the reality that you are being asked by Spirit to live here and now, and assume complete responsibility for your mental energy.

A great many people are largely controlled, and even possessed, by their dead family members.* The most common possessions involve parents. Since my own father passed away over a dozen years ago, I have had to fight really hard to ward off his psychic energy. He retains much guilt for his time on earth, and due to his sense of isolation on the other side, tries to manipulate me and other family members. His

---

*Here the term *possession* refers to an individual's consciousness field being subsumed by another's.

prime goal is to retain a psychic connection with the family, as his sense of "self" still retains the idea of being head of the family and in control.

This is not an unusual situation, and it often gets worse as people age. Many of the problems involved with senility and dementia involve possession by long-dead family members. As people age and stop living life forward, their psyches tend to revert to the relationships that founded their identities and gave their lives meaning. Almost inevitably, this process involves increasingly entangled psychic relationships and dramas with those they grew up with or lived their lives with. It makes no difference whether those people "live" here or on the other side.

This is bad news for those wishing to get out of here as quickly as possible and to be whisked away to paradise when they finally keel over. When people lament, "I just want to go home" (i.e., go to heaven), what they are really wishing for is escape, to relinquish responsibility for themselves. But there is no escape. There is but the reality that you are being asked by Spirit to live here and now, and to assume complete responsibility for your mental energy. You are not going to be elevated to the Great Hereafter on a golden chariot; there is no bevy of vestal virgins awaiting you there; and Big Daddy is not coming to save you.

Right here, right now is the best place and time for you to be, not "Up there, later on." A genuine misconception of many religious philosophies is that of placing peace, happiness, and healing in another dimension to come later. This is a complete inversion of the crucial truth that it is only through presence that we come to peace. Bliss is now, or it is never.

You are already in heaven. Your mind is just too stuck in remembered pasts and imagined futures to see and experience the immense joy and beauty of life. Don't despair. This is actually great news, for it allows to you to begin to understand that you have complete responsibility for your own energy, and therefore, complete power to change the way you feel. This can be done by quitting all the moaning and groaning, disciplining your thoughts, and changing the meanings that you grant the events of your life.

THAT LOVING FEELING

Having a loving relationship with a special someone, and forming strong friendships and professional relationships are important for just about all of us. This is where Integrated Intelligence can be invaluable. It helps cut out a lot of the guesswork about who to hang out with, and who to ditch. And it enables you to be more honest with yourself and your acquaintances, for if used diligently it quickly gets to the bottom of things. INI can assist you in identifying the motivations of those you love or are dating. Looking into the soul of the person sitting opposite you at the restaurant isn't really cheating! The essence, once again, is to develop your capacity to use the Feeling Sense.

I know this concept will be an affront to some. Who wants to know what another person thinks about you? Or worse still, who wants to date someone who can read your mind?! First of all, it is not so much reading minds as it is reading *feelings*. While specific thoughts of others are difficult to determine, a developed Feeling Sense, and your ability to channel, will allow you to sense the emotional body of the other person. This ability develops naturally as you let go and do your healing work. As you move more deeply into your own emotional body, you will start to feel things within yourself that you barely knew existed: both repressed emotions and subtle intuitions. In turn, you will be able to perceive the feelings of others.

CONNECTING WITH THE BLOND

In my late twenties, I learned that Integrated Intelligence could assist in the dating game. I was beginning to experiment with other ways of knowing. It was at this time that I had an interesting experience after I joined a singles group. It was a "no lose" situation for me. My potential dates would be captive at the dinner table of prearranged group outings. Now they wouldn't be able to run away screaming.

My first group dinner was on a Friday night at a local restaurant. My hopes rose, because a particular song had kept playing in my head all week: the Melissa Manchester song with the lines, "You should hear what she thinks about you, you should hear what she says . . ." Since my guides often communicate to me via placing song lyrics in my mind, I figured that they were encouraging me to meet someone who would fancy me.

I rocked up to the gig in my best shirt and shiny shoes, and waited for the girls to begin drooling. But things did not go quite according to plan. When I walked into the large room, I saw about fifty people of varying ages, and some of them had a decidedly well-worn look. I reassured myself that I could not possibly be as desperate as they were. After a little searching, I found my allotted seat, and sat down with three women and two other men. The idea was that we would flirt with each other, pair off, and someone would get dragged back to the pad for an evening of Scrabble. Or something like that. Sadly, I didn't feel particularly attracted to any of the women at my table.

Then I spotted her at a distant table: all long blond hair and curves. A gong almost went off in my head—or perhaps in some other body part. There was definitely something about her, and it was not just that she was easily the most attractive woman in the room. There was a *connection*. So I ignored her—a well-practiced move widely adopted by losers worldwide. I made no eye contact with her whatsoever. She was quite a distance away, so that would have been impractical. I did, however, hook up with her energy field, deliberately using the Feeling Sense to "see" who she was.

> *Human relationships are the perfect testing ground*
> *for INI. You might make a lot of errors, but persist*
> *with it. It's a bit like learning a new language:*
> *you feel like a moron at first, but a whole*
> *new world opens up before you.*

What happened next was quite unexpected. As I was chatting with the folks at my table, I became aware of an energy field of light connecting the attractive woman to me. I didn't see the light directly, only when my head was turned away from her at about forty-five degrees.*

I again recalled the song, "You should hear how she talks about you." I didn't see anyone else around who fit the bill. It had to be her. But how could I bridge the gap between us? I got up and went to the toilet to think about my dilemma. What should do? I didn't have the courage to walk up to her and introduce myself. I headed back to my table—only to find that someone was sitting in my chair. The gorgeous blond!

"Oh, sorry," she said. "Is this your seat?"

"Oh, not to worry," I said. "You can sit here, no problem." My ability to spit out a full sentence without dribbling surprised me.

Somehow I managed to ask her to dinner and she agreed. We started dating.

Cathy was not the love of my life. Far from it. In fact, it was quite a troubled little affair. But our relatively short relationship turned out to be a very important one for me. It got me in touch with some of my soul issues, especially those related to abandonment and giving my power away to women.

When I dated Cathy, I was relatively inexperienced with using Integrated Intelligence. I did not have the array of INI tools that I have now. Nor did I understand the function of the human ego and its tendencies toward self-deception, and how this is related to the wounded child. The truth was that I had dealt with very few of my psychological and spiritual issues.

I was a beginner.

If you are unfamiliar with Integrated Intelligence, and have never tried to employ the intuitive mind in your life, you too will have to go through the beginner's phase. Human relationships are the perfect testing ground. You might make a lot of errors, but persist with it. It's

---

*It is easier to see psychic energy with your peripheral vision than straight on, possibly because the cells at the outer rim of the iris are different from those at the front.

a bit like learning a new language. You feel like a moron at first, but a whole new world opens up before you.

Using the Wisdom Cycle, as I described in chapter 9, is ideal for relationships and dating. Let's say you are a single guy and see an attractive woman working in a retail shop down town. Each time you go there, she smiles at you, and you feel something tingling inside! You decide you'd like to ask her out for a date.

First, you read the energy. Since it is a relatively light decision, you can simply trust your feelings, or use the Quick Check to get a reading on the energy percentage. Let's say you find that the reading is good, and it feels right. You feel a little nervous, but you relax as you release all expectation of the outcome. The next day you walk up to her and ask her if she'd like to grab a cup of coffee after work.

There are several possible outcomes. In the first scenario, she is delighted, and says yes. You have achieved your goal. You probably read the situation correctly. But you don't know for sure, of course, as getting what you want is not necessarily the same as following your genuine guidance. Nonetheless, you begin to date the girl, and continue to use the Wisdom Cycle again as the relationship progresses.

The other scenario is that she rejects your advances. Then you need to go away and reflect on whether the reading was accurate (Spirit will often not warn you if you are about to make a mistake, if there is a lesson in it for you). Did your desire interfere with the process? Feelings of anger and rejection may arise, and you might feel the need to do some inner work to keep the ego in check, and work with the hurt of the wounded child. You record the whole process in your Intuitive Diary. The experience provides you with an opportunity to refine your ability to read energy and make wise choices. It will bring you into close relationship with Spirit, and facilitate awareness of the role of ego.

Although you did not get what you wanted, you got what you needed. The Wisdom Cycle has provided for a little growth and healing.

I highly recommend that you apply these processes to your existing relationships also. Friends and lovers are the greatest sources of personal drama and thus represent the greatest opportunities for you to grow spiritually. When drama arises, you can simply use the kinds of processes I have mentioned here and in previous chapters to get to the bottom of things and take responsibility. Keep an eye out for the dynamics of the karmic triangle. When you find yourself playing the role of persecutor, victim, or rescuer, acknowledge it and pull out of the drama.

THE SAVIOR DELUSION

The greatest delusion of the human race is that we are going to be saved: pulled up by the bootstraps by another. The Savior comes in many forms but is always disempowering: It is the lover who is coming to take away my pain. It is the time that is coming to transform me (the promotion, the retirement, or the year 2012). It is the deity who will protect and save me (Jesus, the angels, the guides).

Sorry to tell you this, but none of this is going to happen, at least not in the way you think. The lover to whom you give your power away has major control issues (otherwise why would she bother to take you on?); 2012 arrives and they are still blowing each other up in the Middle East; and those folks waving the "He's coming!" signs look a little older and sadder with each passing year He postpones the big day. He breaks His promise yet again and doesn't show up for the press conference.

In short, the Savior is really the Enslaver in disguise, because you are desperate to give your power away to her. To be saved by the rescuer, you have to give yourself away. You have to play the role of victim. Happily, it is never too late to save yourself—it just takes more work.

The best way to know the ego is to develop a close
relationship with it. Befriend it. Love yourself.

All those pop singers were right when they sang "Love is just the best thing going." They just defined it wrongly, and turned the truth upside down. "Relationships" are one of the greatest gifts—even those that we may consider negative. In a sense there are no positive or negative relationships. There are merely relationships that reveal to us who we are—if we are willing to assume responsibility for them. Just think about that. All relationships are an expression of love, regardless of how they may look on the surface. There is only one thing that stops you from drawing from them the lessons that will transform you, and bring a more positive expression of love. That is not taking responsibility.

RESPONSIBILITY AND RELATIONSHIP

Responsibility is the key to transformation in relationships, and in bringing more love into your life. Responsibility is the secret of presence and healing.

If you were to estimate the percentage of responsibility that you are presently taking in your key relationships (from 0 to 100 percent), where would you place yourself? Here 0 percent responsibility would indicate totally giving your power away to the other person. This would include a total victim state where you are basically being a doormat. At the other end of the spectrum is 100 percent responsibility, where you use the relationship to reflect upon yourself, and at every turn look within yourself to identify your role in whatever problem occurs.

Stop for a moment now and estimate your general level of responsibility. Give it a percentage. Then read on.

Here's the truth. Presently on earth the average level of responsibility people take for their relationships and life in general is well under 10 percent. You read it right. Of the people reading this sentence, the mean level is around 20 percent. The higher level is because this book would not be in your hands, and you would not have read this far, if you were not willing to assume a greater level of responsibility for your life.

So, how did your self-estimate compare with the average for readers of this book? Chances are you estimated much higher, and this is perfectly normal. The ego nearly always overrates itself. The tendency of the human ego is to go into denial when life tells it the truth. And when it gets really upset at the news, it enjoys beating up the messenger. Some of you will feel indignant at my telling you this. "Who the hell do you think you are? I've been working on myself for twenty years! I already know all this stuff anyway." And so on. The ego likes to feel indignant. It builds delusions in order to preserve its elevated sense of self, protect the stories that establish its sense of specialness, and perpetuate its belief in separation.

Unless you are willing to assume a higher-than-average level of responsibility in your relationships with others, and in the relationship with yourself, you cannot relax into the divine presence that lies at the heart of the spiritual journey.

SPECIAL ME

Divine love is incompatible with specialness, for love is about integration, while to be special you have to be better and above everyone else. It is a power game. This does not mean that you are not better or worse than others at specific things. You might have a higher level of responsibility and consciousness than anyone else on your block. Yet it would still be true that you are one with all those folks in the neighborhood.

The key is to be able to acknowledge differences, and observe distinctions between yourself and others without judgment. Remember, discernment, not judgment.

Specialness tends to be destructive. It destroys genuine love. In order to maintain the sense of specialness, you have to make sure that others stay below you. If you conceive your specialness to be, say, being more beautiful than other women, then one day you may end up like the wicked witch in the story of Snow White, trying to destroy those who threaten to become the next in line to the throne of beauty.

Specialness destroys genuine love. In order to maintain the sense of being special, you have to make sure that others stay below you.

You may not literally try to destroy others, but there is a strong possibility that you will be emitting a destructive energy at them. The Sage can acknowledge her beauty. She will undoubtedly catch herself being vain at times, as all egos are want to do. But she won't buy into the story. And when she matures and the time comes to let go of the idea of being beautiful, she will be able to do so with minimal fuss.

To really experience love within your relationships, you have to release the need to be special. You can begin by Connecting with the Ego. Be gentle with yourself. We are all pompous and vain at times, and we are not trying to condemn ourselves for being human. After a while, you will get the hang of it. You will observe your ego in action, and you will realize that it is not "you."

THE DARK MASTER

Spiritual narcissism is what develops when a person uses their "spirituality" to establish a sense of superiority over others. Once you develop a little power and perception, there is a tendency for the ego to go to town with it. I am no exception. The more a person has been abused or damaged in childhood, the greater is the likelihood of developing a big spiritual ego down the track. As a child I was neglected, along with my brothers and sisters. I developed very low self-esteem and a sense that I could never be loved by anybody. In order to compensate for the illusion of worthlessness, I developed a compensatory sense of specialness. I wanted to be loved, famous, the great one. Though the spiritual journey made me more aware of this, it did not diminish this tendency.

Today, I still work with this part of myself. I call it the "Master." It is the part of me that thinks itself superior to others—smarter and wiser. I recall vividly a dream I had a few years back which pretty much summed up my spiritual ego. I was standing in a field when a great spiritual light descended from above and filled me with its vibrancy and ecstasy. Even as the divine light poured down upon my little soul, I was looking around in the hope that others could see what was happening.

That was all there was to it, but that simple dream revealed an obvious ego agenda, an intention. The seeking of the spiritual light was, at least in part, not for the sake of healing or the betterment of humankind, nor for the evolution of the cosmos. It was for the sake of attention.

It takes one to know one, as they say. Nowadays, whenever I come across a spiritual teacher who is coming from ego but not assuming responsibility for it, I can spot it quickly.

> *"Ego goes with us all the way to God," as Leonard*
> *Jacobson is fond of saying.*

In itself, narcissism is not "bad." We have a tendency to judge and shame ego as if it is something wicked, so most of us try to hide it. Yet, in the long list of horrors committed by humanity throughout history, having an ego hardly rates! "Ego goes with us all the way to God," as Leonard Jacobson is fond of saying. So, let's stop judging it and start loving it—with a little discipline. Pretending you have no ego is a short-cut to self-delusion.

Nonetheless, egotism, and spiritual narcissism in particular, has a potential to thwart your spiritual development, or even create havoc if left unaddressed. In fact, if left to its own devices, ego is a magnet for dark energy. The demonic loves the spiritual ego. All spiritual teachers are susceptible to this, even those who at any given time may seem to have risen above it.

> *As you raise your consciousness you will punch holes in*
> *the darkness, and that will be a threat. Dark energy will*
> *try to exploit your ego as sure as night follows day.*

There is a real battle for the soul of humanity occurring at this time of human consciousness evolution. As you lift your consciousness, you will be punching holes in the darkness, and that will be a threat to unconscious folks, both physical and discarnate. Dark energy will try to exploit your ego as sure as night follows day. This occurs at an unconscious level. You join a group, and before you know it, the guru is taking you aside and telling you that you are the new Silly Lama, all the while making sure you never get too big for your boots and threaten his power.

The narcissist (extreme ego) emerges from the pain of the wounded child. When the ego is particularly stubborn (and egos by nature are stubborn), you have to be a very forceful parent to it. Otherwise, it will run amok, like an uncontrollable child. Working with the ego does not have to be a great burden. The potential is there for great love and healing. For me, each time the Master appears, I employ Connecting the Ego, and where necessary, Connecting with the Wounded Child.

A WARNING

When you work with spiritual teachers, you need to trust your dreams, your visions, and your gut feelings, but watch for interference from the darkness. A dead giveaway is when sexual energy is being bandied about. The most manipulative teachers (and people in general) use sexual power to wield control over others. This is because people are so vulnerable in this area; it is very, very difficult to resist sexual energy. We are naturally attracted to sexual stimulation.

I want to be clear that I am not necessarily talking about something happening physically (although it may occur that way). I am referring to energy that is primarily being projected psychically. Somebody batting his or her eyelids at you is obvious and relatively harmless. Yet the projection of manipulative sexual energy at an unconscious level can be highly destructive.

Sexual energy is not the same thing as sexual attraction. It can take different forms. It may involve an excitation of the sexual regions, or conversely, a negative, repressive energy projected at the sexual regions, for the purpose of shaming the individual and keeping him from empowerment.

Remember Robert, the spiritual teacher whom I referred to in chapter 5? I said that over time I became less interested in Robert's teachings. However, there is a little more to it than that. At one point, I had started to explore his work again. However, as I read more and more of his stuff, including from his regular online writings, I began to feel a discomfort rising from within me. My Feeling Sense was giving me messages about manipulation and control. There appeared to be more fear around him, and more forcefulness in his words. Some things happening in his life were really pushing his buttons, and he wasn't fully taking responsibility for his soul issues. In particular, he has certain abandonment issues, a great distrust of people, and a lot of anger at the unreliability of people, all of which are pretty much my own soul issues. As I said, it takes one to know one.

Then I had a vision that settled it for me. In this dream, I was sitting opposite him, and suddenly he reached a foot over and started to rub my crotch with his big toe! That was it. I saw that he was using sexual energy to entice people to follow his teachings. Note that I never had any direct contact with the man, nor have I ever met him personally—although I have heard him speak in public. The energy I perceived was thus not directed at me personally. It was a perception of a generic energy he was employing, albeit unconsciously. Robert is not a spiritual write-off, any more than I was a spiritual reject when my spiritual teachers kicked my butt out of my beloved group in New Zealand. But at the time of this writing, he does need to address the soul issues the universe is waving in his face.

Spiritual delusion is often a product of the intention behind something. When choosing a teacher or philosophy you need to be conscious of whether or not things are aligned with truth. Once you begin to develop your power of perception, you will be able to see beyond the words people use, and look directly into their souls. You will be aided in this by using In Practice 11.1, Checking Another's Intention. You will be able to see the intention that lies behind what they say and do. That's not just cool. It's vital.

In Practice 11.1
_____

℮ *Checking Another's Intention*

How can you know someone's intention within a relationship? Here we might be talking about a lover, a friend, a relative, a spiritual teacher, or anyone else. Besides keeping your wits about you and trusting your gut feelings, you can connect with the other person's ego. Because all minds are connected nonlocally, the Connecting tool works just as well with others as it does with yourself.

Begin by relaxing and breathing deeply, just as you do when Connecting with the Ego. However this time, imagine and feel yourself as the other person. Feel yourself sitting in their skin.

Now, as you imagine yourself as the other, look back at the real "you." Move your awareness into the solar plexus of the other, and connect with the feelings that person has toward you. Then, just allow those feelings to form words. What does the other person want to say to you? Go deep, beyond the personality. Remember, people are often unaware of their own true intentions, and you are connecting with something much deeper than their surface personality.

When you feel that there is nothing left to say, stop. Record what you have felt and seen in your Intuitive Diary. Later you can return to read it again. The meaning may be obvious, or it may make more sense later.

Don't be surprised if what you have observed is something embarrassing. It may involve projections of sexual energy, shame, anger, blame, or a desire to be beaten and abused. Normal human intentions typically involve power and control issues.

This process is not simple. Human minds are deep and complex. They are multilayered, and in theory it is a complicated process to connect with the precise part of the other's mind that you want to connect with. However, with a little practice this is not too difficult to master.

How do you know that what you channeled was correct, and not just a product of your imagination? The truth is that short of asking the other person to confirm it, you can never know empirically (and even then, if you have channeled their shadow, they may be unaware of its contents).

However you can and should continue to observe the relationship at a deep level, trusting your feelings. You will intuitively know whether your reading was on the mark or not. You will get better at this Connecting exercise over time, and soon you will be reading people's energies without even trying.

But it doesn't end there, and you know it. In the eyes of Spirit there's no such thing as the good guy versus the bad guy, the victim and the bully. You too are playing a part in all this. You can complete the process by Connecting with the Ego to check your own intention. What are you really "saying" to the other person? What do you really want? Let go, imagine the person standing before you, and just do and say what you really want to say and do. Once you have seen it, dialogue with that part of yourself. Send it love. Now that you have seen it, it will have minimal power over you, and you can stop blaming the other person. Instead you will see it as a dynamic interplay of power between two egos.

Think very carefully before saying something to the person, especially if it involves an intuitive perception of their energy or their intentions. People do not react well when they are forced to confront their shadow. The shadow lies within the deep psyche precisely because people don't want to look at it. You do not have a right to force consciousness on people. That's a contradiction in terms. People gain consciousness when they are ready for it, not when you march in with all guns blazing and tell it like Dr. Phil. If you tell the truth, tell it very, very gently, and check your own intention, to see that you are not playing a power game yourself. Even when you are checking another's intention, the focus of consciousness work is 99 percent about you, 1 percent about the other.

Finally, you need to decide what you are going to do. Are you going to stay in the relationship, or walk away? If you stay, what are you going to change about yourself or about the relationship? What is the best way to go about it without blame or anger?

MEASURING CONSCIOUSNESS

You can also do a Quick Check to measure the consciousness level at which a spiritual teacher, book, or teaching resonates. This may well vary from time to time, as teachers can shift consciousness depending upon several factors, including their responsibility levels, intention, and the degree of conscious or unconscious fraudulence. When I measure level of consciousness of the video *The Secret,* for example, it measures around 15 percent overall. This means that it is a very worthwhile philosophy for much of the human race today. However, more than 80 percent of it lies in shadow. This is the "delusion."

My spiritual teachers used to call this "the lie," but I think this term is a little misleading, as what I am talking about is usually unconscious, whereas a lie is deliberate. The delusion is often a product of the intention that lies behind the thing or idea. In the case of *The Secret,* there are certain ego agendas that remain just behind the cameras, so to speak. I'm not going to tell you what they are, because I don't think it is my prerogative to go round telling people what lies behind every spiritual idea or movement. Besides, I can only afford one lawyer.*

Instead, I invite you to use In Practice 11.1: Checking Another's Intention to examine this for yourself. Instead of imagining yourself in the emotional body of an individual, simply imagine yourself as the hosts of that program, as a collective. This will be a great opportunity for you to develop your perceptual power.

All philosophies have a certain degree of delusion.
The key is to be aware of what that lie is.

---

*As a collective whole, the level of consciousness of those who made *The Secret* has dropped since that program was made (at the time of writing). This is not an uncommon problem for spiritual entrepreneurs when they taste success. Because of their new-found influence and power, they become attractive targets for manipulative energies. The effect is not the same with all of the presenters of the video, of course.

When we see the delusion, there is always a tendency to judge the people involved as bad or wrong, but this is unnecessary. Further, if you are directly involved with the people, judgment will tend to create drama, particularly psychic drama. Almost any philosophy will have a certain degree of delusion, and that includes the one you find in this book (although I have the advantage of being able to check it, to the best of my own wisdom and intention). The key is to be aware of what it is. In the case of *The Secret,* you would thus first make a decision whether to apply that philosophy in your own life. Secondly, having distinguished truth from delusion, you could then apply those parts of the philosophy you felt served you on your journey.

If you are a beginner on the spiritual journey, and your Feeling Sense is not so well developed, you need to be extra careful. Take note of your feelings, and what is drawing you toward the philosophy or teacher. Watch your dreams and visions, and take a look at the way the teacher is using body language—that is a real give away.

The Sage needs to take high levels of responsibility in his relationships. It's part of the evolution of his soul, and the evolution of the human oversoul. I have simply provided you with certain specific processes you can employ. Whatever tools you choose, there is no escape. You are here to love, and that means to be responsible.

twelve

Sage Teachings
From Wisdom to Global Transformation

If you recall all the way back to chapter 1, I listed two core outcomes of Integrated Intelligence: wisdom and transformation. This book is about a particular way of enhancing wisdom; using the innate ability of the mind to draw upon intelligence beyond the boundaries of self, and then applying that intelligence to make decisions, take action, and then reflect upon the whole process. This is the Wisdom Cycle.

This is a pivotal moment in human consciousness evolution. We are now at a time where we can consciously make the choice to be conscious.

Once you stand in your power as the Sage, your wisdom cannot help but assist in the transformation of human consciousness. As you detach your individual psyche from the ego-driven world of common humanity, and take more responsibility for your energy, your light will brighten the world a little. Even if you do not realize it, the energy of your consciousness will help to bring humanity forward. Those within your group soul will benefit first and foremost. The inner work that you do will release some of the karmic energy from the group oversoul. They will not be consciously aware of it. They might even think you are a bit wacky if they know about your commitment to Spirit. But at a deep level, they will take on a little bit of the consciousness you develop.

When you stand in the energy of the Sage, in presence, in your own power, you will be able to see at a deep level. When you talk to people, you will be able to sense their mind-set, their attitudes and beliefs, and their pain. Much of the time this will happen automatically because you will perceive not just the physical reality, but the energy of the situation, the thing, the person. When you see celebrities on television, you will be able to see past their image and into their hearts. When you listen to politicians blabbering away to the masses, you will be able to see past their lies to their true intentions.

That's some power.

Such intelligence—the capacity for perception, and the ability to glean knowledge from beyond the surface of things—is potentially of great benefit to humanity. We are now at a time in human history where we can make the choice to be conscious, and we can make it consciously. This is, therefore, a pivotal moment in human consciousness evolution.

TO TELL OR NOT TO TELL?

There is another way in which your light will shine. You will become a teacher, whether you like it or not. Your awareness can be of great benefit to the people you meet—friends and strangers alike. The question that follows is whether or not you should tell people about your ability. Should you tell them about what you see in them, or the wisdom of the decisions they are about to make? The answer is that it depends on the person and the situation.

If you are dealing with a stranger, then you have to be cautious. Nobody wants someone they don't know to be in their face. In the book *Grace and Grit,* Treya Wilber relates a great example of how not to give consciousness to a stranger. She reports that, while attending a New Age convention with her famous philosopher husband, Ken Wilber, she was approached by a woman who suddenly blurted out, "Do you know you have a very angry child inside you?" Ken, who has a reputation for not suffering fools too gladly, was unimpressed. He exploded and told the woman off, rather unambiguously. The woman got what she deserved. Even if her insight was correct, it was a violation of Treya's privacy and her dignity.

> *Never force your perception on someone, and don't share*
> *consciousness without their permission.*

Never force your perception on someone, and don't share consciousness without their permission. Ask for permission by asking their soul. Focus for a moment upon the inner world of the person, and ask, "May I give you this piece of consciousness?" If you feel it is right, go ahead, but if it feels wrong or indifferent, let it go. If you do proceed, do so with a gentle touch. And check your intention. Do you have an ego agenda? Are you trying to impress the person, change them, or gain power over them? If the answer to any of these questions is yes, again, let it go.

Not long ago, I was on a public bus, and a young man and woman were sitting just ahead of me. We were the only people on the bus, so I was able to hear everything they said clearly. The man looked very tired and listless. He began to complain to his female companion that he always felt tired, and that he could easily fall asleep anywhere, anytime.

I saw straightaway that he was badly possessed. His energy field was completely subsumed by his mother. I would have loved to explain to him that he needed to work on his mother issues, but—not wanting a punch in the face—I decided against it. There is just so little understanding in the world about spiritual awareness that talking to people about such things is about as useful as talking to an indigenous hunter about French postmodernist thought. Most people are just not on the same page, and it runs completely counter to the materialism of society and education.

With friends, the situation might be different. Where friendship is involved, personal boundaries are more fluid. Yet once again, there should be discretion. One thing to consider is how open the person is to the idea of spiritual and intuitive perception. Many of my casual friends have absolutely no idea what Integrated Intelligence is, and would probably quickly become ex-friends if I suddenly blurted out that they needed to deal with their tendency to rescue others and possess them.

If the person is also on a spiritual journey, then there may be a greater degree of receptivity. I once had a date with a woman who was a decade or so older than me. We had contacted each other through a newspaper dating service, and it was clear that we both had a passion for the esoteric. Over lunch I suddenly decided to scan her body intuitively to check for any problems. I immediately felt a problem with her hip. Wanting to impress her with my astounding psychic abilities, I asked her if she had some problem there. She told me that she had had surgery in that area, due to a complication. Then I put my inner twit away, and we ate lunch.

Now, this comment was perfectly acceptable for a person with an understanding of medical intuition. My date was not offended by my intrusion, but neither was she impressed or particularly interested in my reading. But you can imagine the problem it might cause for someone who had no awareness of such things.

HOW TO LOSE FRIENDS AND INFURIATE PEOPLE

While in New Zealand, I had a friend who worked at the international school with me. Wayne was a bit of a hippie, although a rather hard-working one. I used to visit him and his wife often, dropping by after school for dinner and a yarn. We often talked about my experiences with my spiritual group, and how we read energy and worked with the deep mind. Wayne was fine with my perceptive ability, but I could see his wife Tina was terrified of me.

It was not long until I began to have a few problems with her energy. After my visits, Tina would give me a real psychic beating. This was unconsciously done, of course, as are almost all psychic attacks. I got bad headaches from the negative energy she projected at me, attacking my third eye, which is the center of clairvoyant ability. What's more, she was coming between Wayne and me. I don't know what she actually said when I wasn't there, but energetically she was creating drama between us, by psychically messaging Wayne, telling him that I was some kind of devil and couldn't be trusted. I saw this projection clearly from the personal Connecting work I did on the drama.

I knew that Tina would destroy the friendship between Wayne and me unless I did something about it. So the next time I went around to their place, I mentioned the fact that she seemed scared of me.

"You are right!" she blurted out. "You can read minds! I don't like you looking at me!"

I told her that I couldn't read her mind, just sense her emotions, attitudes, and psychic energy. Strangely, telling her that I could look into her soul didn't seem to placate her.

You might think that once you have developed INI the world will beat a path to your door. Yet most people will be disinterested, and of those who acknowledge your ability, some will feel threatened.

The situation didn't improve, and I was eventually forced to let go of the friendship with Wayne. It was a pity, as I really liked the guy. But I could not allow myself to be subjected to the kinds of psychic attacks I was experiencing from his wife. I felt genuinely sad about the whole thing, but there was not much I could do about it. It's hard to say how I could have approached that situation much differently. I was respectful of Wayne and Tina's privacy, and didn't try to force consciousness upon them. And if I had not told Wayne about my spiritual experiences, our friendship would not have developed in the first place.

The Wayne and Tina saga should tell you something. While you might think that once you have developed a good level of perception the world will beat a path to your door, the truth is that most people will be disinterested. And, of those who care to acknowledge your ability, some will be threatened by it.

GENTLE CONSCIOUSNESS

There are times, though, when you may feel that it is really important to tell somebody what you have seen psychically, but are unable to tell them how you came about the perception. In such cases, after asking for soul permission and checking your intention, you can communicate the consciousness while simply disguising the fact that you cheated and peered into their soul. That is okay.

If you have a certain perception that you feel is important to share, you can ask a question to encourage the other person to speak, or begin by saying, "My feeling is that . . ." Strangely, despite the fact that the psychic realm is largely taboo in modern society, this phrase is perfectly acceptable. In fact, many cultures use the verb "to feel" as an acceptable prelude to talking about an insight. In northern China the Mandarin Chinese is *Wo juede*, and in the south the Cantonese say *Ngoh gok duk*. So, while talking about where intuition comes from may be inappropriate under many circumstances, the good news is that intuition is perfectly valid as a means of knowing, right across the world. You can, therefore, use the phrase to open up dialogue about something you feel is important.

Of course, the nature of the insight you provide is just as crucial. There are some things that are just too personal to communicate. One of the most painful visions I ever had involved a relative of mine. I saw that psychically she was being raped by an ex-boyfriend of hers. It was clear that he had completely possessed her, and that this had been key in her steep psychological decline to the point of insanity. But what could I do? She had no understanding or awareness of such things, and was hostile to all attempts to help her, by others and by me.

The other factor was that the energy surrounding her was so dark and destructive that I simply could not deal with it. Even some of the great spiritual teachers I have worked with were unable to work with certain individuals who came to them for help because of the destructive energy fields in which they were embedded.

THE JESUS COMPLEX

Ultimately, it is unnecessary to go round telling people about your perception. Be observant of yourself, as you may be looking to get recognition or attention. It's a slippery slope down to the murky stuff from that point on. One of the real dangers for the Sage is getting too carried away with it all and getting a big head. In this case, you become not so much the Sage as the Jesus Wannabe.

Mr. Jesus Wannabe experiences a little bit of power, and then he thinks he's the Second Coming incarnate. He thinks he's special and above others because he has had a few visions, an out-of-body experience (OBE) or two, and can sense a bit of energy.

> *One of the real dangers for the Sage is getting too carried away with it all and getting a big head. He then becomes a magnet for the darkness.*

When I first started meditating, I was hopelessly ungrounded. Because I was extremely dissociated spiritually—cut off from my shadow and my pain—I started tripping out all over the place. I would lie down for a nap, and suddenly, I'd go flying out of my body. In my naïveté, I thought that this was evidence of some kind of spiritual advancement. Here I was, cosmic superstar wannabe, tripping all over the universe. I recall telling another New Age chap about my OBEs, and he congratulated me on my spiritual superiority, and that I had advanced so far so fast.

In fact, my out-of-body experiences were testament to the fact that I was totally out of touch with the here and now, my inner child, and my body. I was dangerously close to making a permanent exit from this plane of existence (i.e., snuffing it). Luckily, my desire to gain power over others was not so great, so I didn't do any real damage to anyone.

The truth is that because we all have an ego, we have a Jesus Wannabe just waiting to bust out to try and seize a slice of the glory pie. Some folks are just a little more prone to the Jesus complex than others.

The great difficulty with Jesus Wannabes—besides making you want to throw up—is that many of them don't go round sporting a cool beard (especially the women) or lugging a cross over their shoulder. They get all sneaky on you, and may even do a good job of coming across as all nice and spiritual. The other complication is that ego is such a trickster that many spiritual teachers are seduced by ego without realizing it themselves. These are the ones you have to be careful of. If you don't watch yourself, you'll get sucked into their muck.

Others are easy to spot at first glance. The John Wayne swagger just doesn't go with the saffron robes. Or after the show, he parties hard with the babes. Just remember to make sure that you do not get carried away. Use the Connecting with the Ego tool to keep an eye on your inner twit. For me, I know that this is an ongoing issue. If I am not careful my inner twit becomes an outer twit. We all have to be vigilant.

The problem with the Jesus Wannabe is that when his ego becomes inflated, he becomes a magnet for dark energy. This means that spiritual entities with a low-density vibration can start to go to work on him, and possibly possess him. Because he is a leader, he will then infect many of those around him. Spiritual leaders have a lot of responsibility—responsibility to keep their energy in check, that is.

RETURN OF THE EGO, RETURN OF THE DARKNESS

I can talk about this less-than-appealing aspect of the spiritual journey from firsthand experience. In the little tale I am about to tell, I play the bad guy, the Jesus Wannabe who falls flat on his face just at the moment he was preparing to climb the stage to give his acceptance speech at the annual Spiritual Twit's award night.

It occurred in New Zealand during a time of intense emotional stress for me. In May 1997, my father died suddenly of a heart problem. I flew back to Australia for the funeral, and then my young brother Jerome committed suicide the same day we buried the old man. When I returned to work in New Zealand, I had a lot of work to do on myself to keep my energy in check, quite a bit more than I realized.

Just a few weekends after my return from Australia, I attended a retreat with the spiritual group that had become an integral part of my life. The event was held over a long weekend, at a country estate. On the Friday night, we all met in the conference hall and played a few games and basically had a bit of fun. To be honest, I was not paying much attention to my energy field. This was a big mistake in a group where absolute responsibility for your emotional and psychic energy was expected. I had no premonition of the "ego fall" that was about to unfold for me.

What I am about to write may be an affront to some who prefer the "love 'n light" version of the spiritual journey, but I will relate it here because it will help you appreciate that things are not always all sweet and nice on the road to bliss.

After the meeting in the hall, I went to bed. It was a terrible night. I was repeatedly assailed by dark energy, which attempted to enter my body. No sooner would I lie down to try to get to sleep, then an entity/energy would attempt to penetrate my energy field. Dark energies are simply energy forms that resonate with lower expressions of consciousness: fear, hopelessness, shame, guilt, hatred, and so on. These feel very different than higher vibrations of consciousness, which center on love and nonjudgment.

There is a constant interplay of dark and light energy around us like a weather map with areas of high and low density circling about each other, influencing each other's movements. Once a person becomes aware of psychic energy, it is very easy to be conscious of such things as they are happening. The development of awareness of these dimensions of mind is like developing a sixth sense. It is not just a feeling—there is a definite physical aspect to this. Some energy can be felt physically within the body. For example, psychic attacks to the head are very easy to pick up. Quite often these target specific areas of the brain, or at least register in specific areas of the brain or the head. As a person who once had no consciousness of these realms at all, I can only compare this awareness to the sensitivity one feels when stepping outside in different weather conditions. You do not need a thermometer to tell you that below zero degrees Celsius is cold, or that above forty is very hot. I can just as easily feel psychic energy when it is entering my consciousness field, and can sense whether it is "light," "dark," or something in between.

That night in New Zealand, it was Dark with a capital "D." I slept very poorly. In the morning I awoke feeling very heavy and extremely drowsy. This should have told me that something was wrong, as this is a common symptom of being embedded within a dark energy field. I went to join the group in the meeting hall in a kind of dumb stupor. Little did I realize that I was in for a rather nasty surprise. As we sat down in a big circle, the group leader, Tracey, told us that there had been a lot of dark energy invading the group. I listened attentively, not expecting what was to come next.

Tracey said, "There is a lot of fear here, a lot of darkness. I really have not been able to work out why." She related that out of desperation she had rung up Jessica, who was the most powerful seer in the group, but absent on that day. Tracey said that Jessica was able to pinpoint the cause of the problem straightaway. Tracey then turned toward me. "And the truth is that the energy is coming through you, Marcus."

I was totally shocked. And terrified. All eyes of the group fell upon me. I felt like the bad boy again—and in truth I was. For a person to work with others at an advanced level of consciousness, taking responsibility for one's energy is required. And I wasn't doing the necessary groundwork.

There is a constant interplay of dark and light energy around us all. To put it another way, all energy fields have a particular density, and they are in constant interaction throughout the collective consciousness field of humanity—and beyond it.

In his book, *Power vs. Force,* David Hawkins compares consciousness fields to attractor fields in physics, and this is a good analogy. It is very, very difficult for a person to shift from a low-density energy field to one of a higher vibration, or greater light. Further, once a shift has occurred, it is very easy to get pulled back down into dense energy fields—into the darkness, so to speak. Dark energy circles around the light, waiting for ways to penetrate the light and suck away its power. I have been observing this process for a long time, and not all the dynamics are clear to me. It may be due to an impersonal dynamic—energy simply tends to even itself out, much like the atmosphere systems "try" to balance air pressure about the globe.

But at an individual level there are more personal dynamics involved. Ego states tend to attract dark energy. In fact, as stated previously, dark energy attempts to build up the ego, so that it can more easily manipulate the psyche of the individual involved. It likes to whisper: "You are special." "You are the great one." "Power and riches are coming your way soon." And so on. Once your inner Jesus Wannabe buys into the power and greatness lie, you are spiritual toast.

Just like me with my spiritual group.

In all fairness, they gave me a chance. Some group members used Connecting with the Ego to show me what my unconscious projected energy was doing to other group members. I was psychically attacking certain individuals, trying to stop others from seeing what I was doing, and generally attempting to thwart the goal of the group—to heal and develop spiritually. The reason I was doing this unconsciously is that the forward movement of the group—the healing that was occurring—required that I also fully address my healing process. And within myself I had "decided" not to deal with the pain that stood between me and my further healing. Therefore, my psychic energy was projecting through to others and trying to stop them from moving forward.

Because of certain ego states I had developed, I had become a channel for some very dark energy. What I—and eventually the others in the group—would come to see was that my energy field had been occupied by a particularly malevolent entity. In layman's terms, a dark discarnate spirit had possessed me.

It was incredibly confronting. Besides the sheer terror of it all, I felt deeply ashamed of myself. But I was also outraged. This is where my inner victim cut in, and my thoughts turned ugly. "How dare you say these things about me! Don't you know my father and brother just carked it, you heartless bastards! I'm not a bad person! Why would I want to hurt anybody else or stop their spiritual journey? It's all bullshit!"

In short, I didn't get it.

Unfortunately for me, among my peers thoughts were as good as spoken words, such was their ability to sense consciousness. I was told in no uncertain terms that I would have to leave the group until such time as I was able to deal with the massive issues I was facing. They sent me packing.

Sounds awful, doesn't it? And it was. In fact, it was worse than you can probably imagine. The next day I had to go to work, and I was so scared I was shaking. My head was being bombarded with so much dark energy that it felt ready to explode.

But my teachers were right. They saw the truth and gave it to me. When it didn't register, they kicked my butt outa there. And it was the best thing that ever happened to me. I had to take a really long, hard look at myself. I had to acknowledge how much I gave my power away to others, how deeply hurt I really was, and I had to learn how my ego plays games for attention and power at an often unconscious level. And I did get it. It took me a few months, but eventually it got through my thick skull.

HOW TO SLAP YOURSELF AWAKE

I have had the good fortune of having spiritual teachers who were willing to give me a good slap in the face when I deserved it. I was told when my ego was out of control. My teachers had the perception to be able to spot the trickster; and just as importantly, the courage and commitment to tell me the truth. As a result, I had a few ego falls like the one I mentioned above, falling flat on my butt just as I was about to congratulate myself about how well I was doing. At the time I had these falls, I experienced a lot of pain. I got angry and ranted and railed against the injustice of it all. I threw tantrums till I got really tired and cried myself to sleep. Eventually, however, I was able to rise above my need to play victim. I returned to the group after each fall from grace, usually after a break of a month or two.

Many readers will never have the good fortune to be slapped awake by a hard-case spiritual teacher. That means you just have to slap yourself awake now and again. Listen to your guides and to the feedback of the cosmos. When you see your Jesus Wannabe popping up, stand in front of a mirror, wind up, take a good swing at yourself, and tell the face in the mirror to wake up. During such times, you need to get disciplined. Meditate, fast, pray, hike, run, or do whatever you need to bring yourself back down to earth. Avoid alcohol, drugs, and drama. Remember, though, as far as giving consciousness to others, the slapping part doesn't work for 99 percent of humanity. Most people are far too insecure to be told the truth to their face. You need to be gentle and subtle when dealing with most folks. Drip-feed your average Joe and Josephine the truth if you feel he or she can take it.

TEACHING SPIRIT

If you want to go the whole hog and set yourself up in business as a spiritual teacher or counselor, then there are some important things to consider.

A spiritual teacher is called upon to serve Spirit. If you are not doing that, if you have no intention to do that, you are not a spiritual teacher, but a spiritual fraud.

First, you have to ask yourself why you want to do it. Clarify your intention by Connecting with the Ego. Chances are the ego will go along for the power trip and the attention. That does not mean, however, that you are not suitable for the calling. All human beings and all spiritual teachers have an ego. Your job is to keep an eye on that part of yourself so that it does not dominate your work. Above all, listen to the voice of Spirit. It will guide you. It will tell you if your ego is starting to party hard, and will often let you know whether you are ready or not, and whether to stop, go, or wait.

Regardless of all other considerations, a spiritual teacher is called upon to serve Spirit. If you are not doing that, if you have no intention to do that, you are not a spiritual teacher, even if you call yourself one. You are a spiritual fraudster.

At a very practical level, you have to decide what it is you are selling. This may not seem very spiritual, but actually there is nothing unspiritual about selling or making money. Remember, in the end it is all an exchange of energy.

*Once a certain level of delusion is reached, you have to
invest more and more energy in maintaining the charade.
Inevitably the whole thing comes crashing down
like a house of cards.*

I highly recommend that you begin part-time. I have met more than a few naive wannabe teachers who think the cosmos will reward them for the generous act of offering their grand wisdom to humanity. That's not how it works. You have to honor the language and the realities of the marketplace. You have to offer a product that has some kind of business worthiness. Someone out there is going to have to want to buy what you are selling. And then you have to let people know about it.

Another approach is to make your teaching into a pastime, rather than a money-making venture. You might see it as a chance to share your wisdom with humanity. This is a perfectly noble ambition. One point to keep in mind, however, is that people often do not value what they are given for free. Scientific studies have confirmed this. When people are charged more for a service, they tend to report more positively about it, and when it is cheap they tend to dis it. If you write a book, print off a thousand copies, and give them away on the street, you can bet a lot of people will not value it. If you charge market prices, only people who really want it will buy it. If you overcharge people, they will think you are a crook.

Jessica, the woman who was the original inspiration for my theory of Integrated Intelligence, charged hefty fees. She earned about five times more per hour than I did at the time, and I was an education professional with a university degree (she had no degree). But she was so brilliant that she had no trouble attracting clients. She was also very generous. One time I had a one-on-one session with her and at the end she laughed playfully like a little girl and said that Spirit had told her to give me the session for free. And so she did.

As I mentioned in an earlier chapter, every time you step forward out of your comfort zone in an act of creativity, it will draw out the resisting beliefs and energies from your psyche. As a Sage you will need to work on your consciousness, as well as deal with the day-to-day running of your business. This takes time and discipline. Don't overestimate how quickly you can set things up, because it usually takes longer than you think. Creating unrealistic expectations places unnecessary stress on yourself.

Money pushes buttons too. If you put yourself under financial pressure, you may, ironically, cut yourself off from Spirit. Think about it. You open your little spiritual center and nobody comes. Suddenly you can't pay the rent, and you are asking all sorts of questions of Spirit, and demanding some answers. The ego will tend to get scared and angry and then go into blame and judgment. Fear takes you away from presence and away from Integrated Intelligence and the wisdom of the Spirit. This situation can turn into a self-perpetuating cycle of poverty and poverty consciousness. You go into business believing that the cosmos owes you a living. You have a bit of a hard time, and suddenly the negative beliefs within the psyche come forward, and before you know it you are broke, bitter, and screaming, "I told you so!"

This is precisely what happens to a lot of wannabe spiritual teachers. Mostly, we overestimate our level of spiritual development and our faith in the cosmos. Nothing will bring out doubt and fear faster than the rent notice when you haven't got a penny to your name.

Remember the concept of being a spiritual fraud? I call it *frauding,* when you believe you have gained a level of spiritual development that you have not. Frauding involves a rejection of certain parts of your psyche that you are not willing to look at, and this usually means that there is some personal pain that you are avoiding. My ego fall at the country retreat, which I mentioned above, is a classic example. My ego fall came early, as the lie was exposed by perceptive people. In day-to-day life (as opposed to doing spiritual work), a fall also inevitably comes when we fraud. It may just take longer to happen.

An awareness of the trickster and its tendency to fraud, is crucial for your business and for the manifestation of your bliss in general. When your estimation of your attainment exceeds the reality, it creates a metaphysical wake. A critical instability emerges when the delusion becomes too great. Even as you think you are putting forward positive energy into the world, your psyche will be working against you and against your bliss. Once a certain level of delusion is reached, you have to invest more and more energy in maintaining the charade. Inevitably, the whole thing comes crashing down like a house of cards.

Everyone frauds from time to time, because everyone has an ego. It's just a question of spotting the lies as they pop up, and gently and lovingly correcting them. When you are frauding, Spirit will send you signals. We have to be on the lookout for the signs. Within my own psyche, I have always gotten a particular symbol in my dreams and meditations at such times: Mickey Mouse! To say that something is "Mickey Mouse" is to imply that it is false or simply of poor quality.

For you the symbol you are given or the way Spirit lets you know you are going into delusion will most likely be different. Your life experience is different from mine, and the symbols within your psyche are particular to you. You have to learn that language.

It is also important to remember that, though the Sage is always a teacher of Spirit, she does not necessarily have to become a spiritual teacher. As long as you are living your bliss and in presence you will be serving Spirit. You will be part of the light, pushing holes through the darkness. I trust that this book has shown you that this is not as easy as some popular versions of spiritual development make it out to be.

Keep in mind though, that beyond the price you pay, the reward is the joyful discovery of your soul, and the knowledge that your time here on earth has been of service to all humanity.

SURRENDER

All this may appear to be quite a burden to carry. Yet the truth is that you have to be self-disciplined and committed to the spiritual process if you want to be an instrument of light.

Despite what is mentioned here, if there is one key process that will simplify everything and keep you on the right track, it is the process of surrendering into full presence. This is why I suggest making presence the single "discipline" that you return to again and again each day of your life. This was revealed to me via a vision one morning when I awoke. In my mind's eye, I saw a single page on a computer screen. It was a document full of numerous words and phrases, most of which I could not make out. However, there was a single word written over and over again in bold type, throughout the document. There were several random words in lighter standard font, then this word would appear, followed by another few words, and then that same bolded word again. That word was *now*. I instantly and intuitively knew what the vision meant. Spirit was telling me that through-out the course of every day, I needed to keep bringing my mind into silent presence at regular intervals.

In presence you don't need to concern yourself with solving prob-lems or resolving anything or finding closure. There is only this moment. Surrendering to presence automatically brings the ego into check and delimits power games. Equally, fear dissipates in presence, and the human energy field is able to fill with love. Suddenly the joy and beauty of the world begins to spontaneously unfold. It is as if even the most simple thing has great beauty. As judgment ceases, the light within all people becomes visible.

For several years during my time in Hong Kong, I commuted to work and back three hours every day, on top of a nine- or ten-hour work day. To get to work involved a short bus ride, a twenty-five minute ferry trip, and taking two subway trains. This daily schedule might seem impossibly demanding; however, most mornings I arrived at work feeling light, blissful, and centered.

How? I used the commute to bring myself into mindful pres-ence. In particular the time on the morning ferry was used to allow mental silence. I meditated, or regularly used the Five Breaths tool and Oneness Technique. By the time I got onto the subway train, my energy field was usually light, relaxed, and open. There were often many people crushed together on the trains, but in my nonjudgmen-tal state of mindfulness, they appeared quite beautiful. Sometimes I had spontaneous and euphoric spiritual epiphanies sitting on subway seats. I would close my eyes and a great light and love would come pouring through me. Even though my eyes were closed, it seemed as if a great sun was shining directly through my skull and into my body. At times I actually had to pull myself out of these blissful states, because I became concerned that I would lose all capacity to function. One does need to be conscious of time and place to get to work!

Regardless of where you find yourself on your journey—no mat-ter what the drama or the soul issue you might be dealing with—

remember that in simple presence you are home, and all is perfect and all is peaceful. That is the grounded awareness that will bring forth the joy and light that is within you. It will transform your life, and you will be a catalyst for the global transformation of humanity. Your life will be a gift to Spirit.

Conclusion

What Next?

I want to be clear on what INI is not, and what it won't do. Developing Integrated Intelligence is no guarantee of great riches, high romance, wisdom, or a successful life. It isn't a guarantee of anything. But if you care to take the time to develop it and to actually listen to your intuition, it will certainly assist you in all these areas.

Integrated Intelligence is not a linear, systematic process like, say, mathematical intelligence. If you have a quadratic equation to solve, you know that if you apply the same process every time, you will find the one right answer. With INI it is a whole different ball game. It is a fuzzy intelligence. Often there is no single, correct answer, but multiple paths to choose from, all with differing outcomes. The information you work with is not always transparent. It could be that your mind is not clear, or there might be psychic interference, or your ego may be getting in the way. What's more, Spirit often thinks it best you not be given a clear set of instructions, because the main purpose of the whole exercise is not fulfilling the ego's definition of success, but facilitating wisdom and transformation.

Sometimes you just don't know. You just have to let go and wait. Or just let go, period.

While INI is no guarantee of riches or success in business, I can tell you that if you will take the time and develop the self-discipline to work with INI, you will have a true ace up your sleeve. The energy, timing, and outcomes of life and business decisions can be sensed by employing Integrated Intelligence.

Using Integrated Intelligence in your life is not a recipe for enlightenment, any more than using the Internet is going to turn you into the next Buddha. Both the Internet and Integrated Intelligence allow you to "download" a lot of information in an instant, but what you do with the information is up to you. Sometimes people confuse the psychic and the spiritual. While there are certain overlaps, they are not the same thing. The cognitive abilities involved with INI can be seen as a stepping-stone toward enlightenment—the very highest stages of spiritual evolution on this planet. If you employ INI wisely and with a commitment to presence, enlightenment will naturally arise.

A little warning, however: You can misapply Integrated Intelligence to create suffering for yourself and others. Just as people sometimes use their intellectual brilliance in the wrong way—consciously or unconsciously—to mess up their lives, INI can be misused. Integrated Intelligence is a powerful tool. Be careful.

Make no mistake, though. Having a well-developed Integrated Intelligence is invaluable for you on your spiritual journey. Most crucially it will allow you to see and feel firsthand that the society you live in has perpetrated the lie that the material substrate of existence and the ego's demands are the prime focus of life. INI will allow you to know that there are spiritual dimensions of mind and cosmos that situate your existence in a far more profound context than what you were told at school or by the mass media. You have a soul template, and its information pattern contains the seeds of your bliss.

More importantly, you are part of the evolution of the human collective. You are responsible for a small part of that progression, and your thoughts and actions affect everything. It is only through allowing unconditional love to enter your being that you will fully realize your part in all this.

INI will also allow you to see that there is a spirit world, and that consciousness is not confined to the physical form. You will understand, through direct experience, that the mind is not contained within the head, but it embraces all of existence. You will appreciate that life does not end with the physical death of the body, but is simply relocated. And, just as consciousness is always being transformed from moment to moment (if only you allow it), death is also potentially transformative. Once you understand these things, you will never be the same again. You will not need to read spiritual or New Age tomes to be reassured that there is "more to it than just this," because you will be experiencing it and living it.

Finally, Integrated Intelligence will help you better understand the relationship between mind, spirit, and ego. But in order for you to evolve as a conscious being, you have to commit to something greater than the cravings of the ego.

Now that you have finished reading *Discover Your Soul Template,* you are probably wondering where you should go with all this, or whether you should go anywhere at all. I cannot tell you the answer to that query. Every soul journey is different. However, I will predict that the universe will give you some solid hints. It will then be up to you to decide whether you are going to listen to the universe.

To help you develop a better capacity to listen, I suggest strongly that you immediately and regularly begin doing In Practice 2.1: Listening to Spirit First. Make it a discipline. Do it every day for a month (preferably for the rest of your life!) without fail. This exercise only takes five minutes a day, and will get you into the habit of listening to the voice of Spirit.

The second step is to get an Intuitive Diary. Record your dreams, intuitive feelings, the decisions you make using intuition, and the results of any meditations or use of the INI tools. Set yourself the goal of writing in your diary for a minimum of two minutes a day. Yes, just two minutes. That will create the habit. Always write something, even if it is only that you are confused about how to use INI, or that you didn't use your intuition, or that you had no dreams. You can manage that, no problem.

Next, I suggest that you go back through this book, reading it slowly. Complete as many of the In Practice exercises as possible as you go through. These are really important, as they will help you to bridge the gap between the rational and intuitive parts of your mind.

And remember to immediately begin using INI for little decisions in your life: such as which coffee shop to go to, which movie to see, or what book to buy. Do that for a couple of months. Then gradually build up to more important decisions.

Once you have accepted that Integrated Intelligence is real, and developed some mastery over it, you will be tested by the universe to determine whether you can use it for better or worse. The more you use it for good, the more the power opens up. Such tests will never stop.

Discover Your Soul Template is my way of helping the shift back to our rightful nature—the world's and yours—where reason and intuition are rebalanced. May the winds of change carry you safely along your journey.

Appendix

Interpreting Dreams and Visions

If you are going to develop your Integrated Intelligence, you have to get to know your inner world, and to do that you need to read the language of the psyche. This appendix is meant for those just starting to try to understand their dreams and visions. However, it will still be useful for those with a little more experience who are trying to deepen their awareness. There isn't room to give an exhaustive account of the subject here, but this will get you going in the right direction.

When you try to understand a piece of scientific writing, you rely on logical and rational cognitive processes. When you try to comprehend a story or movie, you rely on a wider range of cues. Besides analysis, you rely on images, symbols, feelings, music, and so on. Understanding dreams and visions is closer in nature to the process of understanding stories. The psyche speaks in all sensory modalities: visual, auditory, and kinesthetic (both intuitive/emotional and physical feelings in parts of the body).

This is why many in mainstream scientific culture have almost completely lost the capacity to understand dreams. I have read papers by scientists arguing that dreams have no actual meaning, but are merely random stories the brain makes up from patterns of light on the eye.

Give or take a degree or two, this theory is approximately one hundred and eighty degrees from the truth about dreams, and testament to just how estranged many individuals within mainstream science have become from their inner worlds.

All you have to do to see the truth for yourself is begin to record your dreams and visions. The most important part of understanding dreams and visions is to take them seriously. So start recording them in your Intuitive Diary. This act alone will take you a long way toward becoming aware of what your psyche and your Integrated Intelligence is trying to tell you.

The dream types listed below are just a few common types of dreams. There are many others that I will not outline here. Often these dream types occur together in a single dream, such as when you see something about psychic energy that will affect you in the future. In one dream I found myself walking out of the house to see a huge black tornado approaching. A day later I was hit by a very dark mass of psychic energy from some relatives of mine, related to some unresolved issues among us.

Precognitive Dreams

Some dreams outline future events, although not always literally. One morning in my twenties, I awoke with a fresh image in my mind. I saw two tall bottles of tomato sauce with the sauce coming out of the top. Later that day, I played a game of rugby, and the two tallest players in the team suffered head wounds and were bleeding profusely (one was me!).

Energy Projection

I remain surprised that nobody I know of has worked out that many dreams depict projections of psychic energy between and among minds. Sometimes these will be fairly literal, such as a dream I once had where a female spiritual teacher of mine suddenly transformed into a kind of monster, reached over and grabbed my crotch with her bare hands, and squeezed very hard. I screamed in pain. This dream told me that my teacher was trying to control me via sexual shame and suppression of my male power.

Other times the identity of the person who is projecting psychic energy toward you will not be so clear (and remember, you can be the one projecting energy too). In your dream it might take the form of a celebrity, for example. Sometimes I have dreams of the pop singer Madonna, and it nearly always represents projections involving my mother. Other symbols can be more vague. King Kong in my dreams and visions usually represents my father and his energy. Usually he is chasing me or is very, very angry, just as my own father was during much of my childhood. To a little boy, the masculine energy of a grown man is often a physically threatening thing.

Not all projections are so nasty. Some can be kind of sweet. I used to have dreams that I was hugging the female teacher who sat beside me at work. We were attracted to each other in an innocent, childlike kind of way.

Needless to say, energy projection dreams can be very helpful. They tell you about the real-life and psychic dramas that you are entangled in. They can really help you become aware of your soul issues, especially unresolved childhood issues and how you give your power away or how you project it at others in order to control them. If you see such projections and feel a need to work on the problem, you can initiate a dialogue with the part of yourself that is engaging in the drama. Use the Connecting with the Ego or Wounded Child tools to do this.

Collective Issues

These are basically a larger version of energy projection dreams and visions, only more minds are involved. They can involve small groups, such as your family, or large groups, such as ethnic groups, nations, and all of humanity. They can be quite useful, as they can help you to see how your mind is being shaped by broader influences.

An example at the time of writing relates to the death of Michael Jackson. Just after he passed away, I kept getting images of MJ, as well as images of tidal waves and earthquakes. Earthquakes are an archetypal dream symbol, usually representing massive changes that threaten the ego's sense of control and power. Tidal waves tend to represent masses of emotional energy coming through. Water typically symbolizes grief. MJ's death triggered a huge wave of sadness, and pushed a lot of buttons for his generation (including me). In particular, it triggered awareness of mortality. This destabilized the human collective energy field.

Spiritual Guidance

Here there is an interaction or a dialogue between you and a spiritual guide. My experience with the female guide who told me I was only using 3 percent of my mind (mentioned in the Personal Prelude), is a classic example. Typically you might see yourself sitting with, listening to, or talking with the guide. You may not be aware that it is a guide, as they rarely arrive with trumpets blaring or strut around like a peacock.

Another form of spiritual guidance dream is impersonal in form. The guide simply directs information to you, but you do not see him or her. This may create an entire dream or visionary sequence, or the information may become entangled in the narrative of an existing vision or dream.

Quite often guides will just whisper in your ear, so you will hear a word or a phrase. As I have mentioned throughout this book, my guides use songs to communicate with me, as I have quite an auditory inner processing system.

Soul Issues

These dreams feature recurring stories. They often relate to events in your personal or karmic history. The stories contain a theme and belief structures that you need to acknowledge and rise above. One recurring dream for me involves not being permitted to play in a game or activity. This stems from my childhood, and the belief is that the world is not fair and that "they won't let me join them." Remember, you attract what you are, so these stories will tend to play out in your real life until such time as you have integrated your consciousness.

Anxiety Dreams

When we worry about things, they often show up in our dreams. These are rather common and mundane dreams. The way to deal with them is to acknowledge your worry, and then either act to stabilize the real-life situation, or simply dialogue with yourself to calm the mind.

WHAT IMAGES MEAN

When I first began to analyze dreams, I bought a dream dictionary, and used it to interpret dream images. I would not discredit this approach entirely, but you should be aware that dream images cannot be interpreted literally like words are in a language dictionary. First, you have to look at the context. Running for a train (anxiety) might mean something entirely different from seeing a train going into a tunnel (possibly a sexual image). You have to look at the big picture.

Secondly, symbols mean different things to different people. For some reason Mickey Mouse means fraudulence or faking it in most of my dreams (when I am kidding myself). But for someone else it might represent playful laughter, because they had a great time at Disneyland as a kid (I'm Australian and never went to Disneyland).

As you spend time with your psyche, the meanings of its symbols will become clearer.

Ken Wilber, the well-known transpersonal philosopher, once said that dreams are really difficult to understand because they are so vague. I disagree somewhat. I suspect Wilber employs a little too much of the analytical mind in trying to understand dreams.

I like to use the Feeling Sense as an integral part of dream understanding. You should acknowledge the overall feeling of the dream. Is it pleasant, joyful, fearful, or anxious? Secondly, you can use the Feeling Sense to get a sense of the meaning of any particular dream image. What does that computer represent? Imagine that you are pulling the computer into your chest, and feel it. Let it speak to you.

ONE FINAL POINT

Do not become overly obsessed with dreams and visions.

Dreams and visions are a useful tool only, not the prime goal of spiritual development. Far more important to the spiritual journey is the capacity to remain in presence. People who become obsessed with visions and dreams may lose presence. When this happens they live life in a kind of dissociated state, never quite in the here and now. They become chronically confused, as the visionary state is a rather perplexing place. It's a bit like using the Internet. If a web user finds himself spending a large chunk of his day obsessing over his online life, then it is time to cut back, or just walk away from it altogether.

Take from the psyche what you can, and just leave the rest.

Glossary

Note: In this glossary I have attempted to stick to common usage for all terms. However in some cases my definition will vary slightly from the usage that others may apply. Some terms have multiple subtle meanings, and the way I use them is therefore quite specific. For example, the word *intuition* has dozens of common usages, while I use it in the "classical" sense, as you will note below.

℮

Alienated mind. Consciousness that is unaware of its mystical roots, and unaware that it is deeply connected to others, nature, and cosmos.

Computer rationality. This is the cognitive mind-set that evolves from an extended usage of computers and computer data. It typically involves dissociation between the "observer" and the thing being observed or studied, as the data and images are mediated by a computer. It can thus exacerbate the problem of the alienated mind.

Consciousness field. These are bodies of psychic energy that exist within, around, and beyond individuals and groups of people. They contain information about that person or group. They each have a certain vibration or density, and function like attractor fields in physics. Those that are "heavier" contain more fear, shame, and deluded belief structures, while those that are "lighter" are more closely aligned with the truth of the divine: love, light, forgiveness, compassion, and so on.

Critical rationality. The predominantly Western approach to knowledge based upon logic, reason, and the scientific method. The key ways of knowing are classification, analysis, experimentation, verbal/linguistic, mathematical/logical intelligences, and computer rationality.

Critical/rational worldview. This is the worldview that emerges from critical rationality.

Deep knowing. Knowledge that comes to an individual in a state of receptivity, where the ego is silenced and mind chatter ceases. It is closely related to the core operations of Integrated Intelligence, especially integrated perception, integrated diagnosis, integrated recognition, and foresense.

Ego. The human mind/self as a single, isolated, and discrete entity.

Extended mind. The state of personal consciousness whereby individual awareness is infused with a transpersonal awareness that transcends the confines of the individual mind and the limits of the sensory organs.

Foresense. The capacity to sense what is going to happen in the future, arising from the application of Integrated Intelligence.

Integrated Intelligence. The deliberate and conscious employment of the extended mind, so that an individual might function successfully within a given environment.

Integrated mind. The human mind in awareness of its spiritual and transpersonal knowledge base, and of the deep connectedness of all things.

Karmic child(ren). Karmic children are not really children as such, but packets of nonintegrated energy left over from previous lives.

Karmic issues. Soul habits that are carried over from one lifetime to the next.

Karmic triangle. An archetypal situation that develops when we feel disempowered. It is composed of three common positions: the victim, rescuer, and the persecutor.

Mechanistic paradigm. Also known as the Newtonian or Cartesian paradigm, this is the paradigm that emerged from the Enlightenment; it represents the universe as a great machine, with mechanistic contents and processes. Newtonian science describes a universe of solid matter, consisting of atoms that operate on the principles of determinism, with fixed laws governing the phenomena of a cosmos consisting of chains of independent causes and effects.

Mystical intuition. This incorporates sources of intuitive knowledge that involve transcendent, extrasensory, or metaphysical dimensions. It contrasts with mundane intuition (tacit knowledge), which is normally construed as having sensory sources of information. Within this book it is interchangeable with the term *intuition*.

Paradigm. A paradigm is a way of looking at things: a set of shared assumptions, beliefs, dogmas, conventions, and theories.

Psi. This is the term used by parapsychologists to describe the seemingly mysterious process behind so-called paranormal phenomena such as clairvoyance, telepathy, ESP, precognition and psychokinesis. What lies behind such phenomena, however, is debatable, and it may be several different "forces." *Psi* is not so much an explanation as a description, which is a common criticism of skeptics.

Receptivity. The open state of mind that allows for the possibility of receiving thoughts or ideas from subtle levels of the mind and from "external" sources beyond the brain.

Soul aptitudes. The various abilities at which you excel.

Soul issues. The soul's self-limiting behavioral habits.

Soul template. The essential character of your soul, which has three components: soul issues, karmic issues, and soul aptitudes.

Synchronicity. Amazing and deeply meaningful coincidences.

Worldview. A way of looking at the world, including a tendency to employ preferred ways of knowing. This term is interchangeable with the "paradigm" concept. However, it can also be employed with reference to an individual as well as systems of knowledge.

Wounded child. The total of all the unexpressed pain energy within a person's psyche, from this life and from others.

Recommended Reading

OTHER WORKS OF MARCUS T. ANTHONY

Books

Integrated Intelligence. Rotterdam: Sense Publishers, 2008. Based upon Anthony's doctoral thesis, this book is for the more academically inclined. It outlines the interplay of Integrated Intelligence and critical rationality throughout Western history and looks at where we can take things from here. In particular, the focus is upon the hidden power structures within society, culture, science, and education, which have created a deep ignorance about Integrated Intelligence.

Extraordinary Mind: Integrated Intelligence and the Future. Hong Kong: MindFutures, 2010. Integrated Intelligence is the natural human ability to connect with a greater universal mind. This book shows why the secret of Integrated Intelligence is a crucial part of human futures. Anthony draws upon decades of research and his direct experience in activating extraordinary mind in his own life and in the lives of others. In *Extraordinary Mind* you will discover why the power of Integrated Intelligence is widely misunderstood in modern science; what Deep Futures are, and how they can help us survive the crises of the modern world; and the six key abilities of Integrated Intelligence, and how to apply them in your life.

Academic Articles—All available at www.mindfutures.com

"A Genealogy of the Western Rationalist Hegemony." In *Journal of Futures Studies,* 2006. This article is an overview of the interplay of rationality and Integrated Intelligence through Western history from the time of the ancient Greeks to the turn of the twenty-first century.

"The Case for Integrated Intelligence." In *World Futures,* 2006. This article provides an overview of the empirical and anecdotal evidence for Integrated Intelligence, including some key examples of the core operations of the theory.

"Harmonic Circles: A New Tool for Futurists." In *Foresight,* 2007. Harmonic Circles is an innovative inner process that encourages researchers and opposing groups to assume greater responsibility for their psychological projections at others.

"A Personal Vision of the Integrated Society." In *Journal of Futures Studies,* 2008. This gives an overview of how Integrated Intelligence might be used in a hypothetical society and its education system in the future.

"Futures Research at the Frontiers of Mind." In *Foresight,* 2009. This paper is a basic introduction to the use of Integrated Intelligence in research—what I call "Integrated Inquiry."

EMPOWERING RESOURCES BY TOPIC

The following books may be helpful for you on your journey. I have categorized them according to several knowledge domains that I feel are important for creating an empowered life and living your bliss.

Healing

Bradshaw, John. *Healing the Shame that Binds You.* Deerfield Beach, Fla.: Health Communications, Inc., 1988. For anybody wanting to know more about how shame becomes embedded within a child's mind and the ways it can be healed.

Dossey, Larry. *Healing Beyond the Body.* Boston: Shambala, 2001. Dossey is a well-known medic who details the healing potentials of prayer.

Myss, Carolyn. *How People Heal, and Why They Don't*. New York: Random House, 1997. Myss is a medical intuitive with a fine knowledge of consciousness. She understands the psycho-spiritual causes of many illnesses. Myss argues that many people do not heal their emotional scars because their wound gives them certain advantages— especially a way to connect with other wounded people.

Philosophy of Science

Grof, Stan. *Psychology of the Future*. Albany, SUNY Press, 2000. Grof is a veteran writer and researcher in depth psychology and transpersonal human experience. This volume illuminates fifty years of research into human consciousness. Highly recommended.

———. *When the Impossible Happens*. Boulder, Colo.: Sounds True, 2006. Here Grof recounts many incredible and poignant stories from his half century of research into consciousness and extraordinary human experience.

Laszlo, Ervin. *Science and the Akashic Field: An integral Theory of Everything*. Rochester, Vt.: Inner Traditions, 2004. Ervin Laszlo is one of the finest exponents of new paradigm thinking. This book details some of the science and philosophy behind the Akashic Field—the Hindu idea that the universe contains an intelligent reservoir of knowledge that we can tap in to.

———. *The Akashic Experience*. Rochester, Vt.: Inner Traditions, 2009. This book continues where the previous book left off. This time Laszlo focuses on the experience of connecting with the Akashic Field. Contains many anecdotes from those with experience.

Loye, David. *Darwin's Lost Theory*. Carmel, Calif.: Benjamin Franklin Press, 2007.

———. *Bankrolling Evolution*. Carmel, Calif.: Benjamin Franklin Press, 2007.

———. *Measuring Evolution*. Carmel, Calif.: Benjamin Franklin Press, 2007.

Loye argues that Darwin's theory and message have been greatly distorted by modern science. Challenging mainstream scientific concepts such as "survival of the fittest" and the "selfish gene," Loye states that it is time for a new understanding of evolution and, ironically, it is Darwin to whom we can turn to for the inspiration.

Tarnas, Richard. *The Passion of the Western Mind*. New York: Random House, 1991. This book offers a detailed overview of the interplay of reason and mystical intuition throughout Western history. A book for those with an interest in how we got where we are today, and why Integrated Intelligence has been largely forgotten.

Mundane Intuition

Gigerenzer, Gerd. *Gut Feelings*. London: Penguin, 2007.

Gladwell, Malcolm. *Blink: The Power of Thinking Without Thinking*. London: Allen Lane, 2007.

Klein, Gary. *The Power of Intuition*. New York: Doubleday, 2004.

Inspiration

Bach, Richard. *The Bridge Across Forever*. New York: Dell, 1984. A rather romantic autobiographical tale of mystical love.

Canfield, Jack and Janet Switzer. *The Success Principles*. New York: Harper, 2007. One of the best "How to" success books around. Very compatible with what you have read in *Discover Your Soul Template*.

Synchronicity

Jung, Carl. *Synchronicity*. New York: Bollingen, 1973. Jung's short and readable original work on synchronicity.

MacGreggor, Trish and Rob. www.synchrosecrets.com/synchrosecrets. This website contains the best collection of reports of synchronicity that I have found.

Parapsychology

MacTaggart, Lynn. *The Intention Experiment*. New York: Simon & Schuster, 2008. This book summarizes, in a reader-friendly way, much of the scientific evidence for psi phenomena.

Sheldrake, Rupert. *The Sense of Being Stared at and Other Aspects of the Extended Mind*. New York: Random House, 2003. To my mind, Sheldrake is the finest scientist around who deals with this area of understanding. In this book he argues for the existence of the extended mind, which reaches out beyond the brain.

Radin, Dean. *Entangled Minds*. New York: Simon & Schuster, 2006. Radin is a parapsychologist, who presents a strong scientific argument for the existence of a universe where minds are not localized in brains, but are entangled with each other.

Other General Empowering Resources

Bashar. *Blueprint for Change* (channeled through Darryl Anka). New Solutions, 1990. I don't normally recommend channeled information, but Bashar is the exception. What I like about this book is that it gives far more concrete and usable methods for creating the life you want than any other New Age channeled material that I know of. There are also, at the time of writing, quite a few Bashar videos on YouTube. Highly recommended.

Bolker, Joan. *Writing Your Dissertation in Fifteen Minutes a Day*. New York: Henry Holt, 1998. This is the book that inspired me to develop my research using Integrated Intelligence. Bolker is not a mystic, but outlines a practical guide, informing researchers and students how to write fluently throughout the research process. Highly recommended for postgraduate students and researchers.

Colvin, Geoff. *Talent Is Overrated*. New York: Penguin, 2008. This is a good introduction to the topic of deliberate practice. Colvin outlines the significant features of deliberate practice and shows that it is what often separates genius from very good.

Ferris, Timothy. *The Four Hour Work Week*. New York: Random House, 2007, 2009. The author is not so much a mystic as a professional vagabond. Ferris writes about living an independent entrepreneurial lifestyle in the modern age. It is all about getting others to do the work, putting together your brilliant ideas. Full of helpful links and references on how to get started on your dream.

Jacobson, Leonard. *Words from Silence*. La Selva Beach, Calif.: Conscious Living Publications, 1997.

———. *Bridging Heaven and Earth*. La Selva Beach, Calif.: Conscious Living Publications, 1999.

———. *Journey Into Now*. La Selva Beach, Calif.: Conscious Living Publications, 2007.

All Jacobson's books are simple and readable. His message is that bringing the mind to presence is the essence of the spiritual journey.

Tolle, Eckhart. *The Power of Now*. Novato, Calif.: New World Library, 1999.

———. *A New Earth*. New York: Penguin, 2005. Tolle's books are also about the importance of presence.

Wilde, Stuart. *Whispering Winds of Change*. Carlsbad, Calif.: Hay House, 1993.

———. *The Sixth Sense*. Carlsbad, Calif.: Hay House, 2000.

These are only two of his many titles. Wilde is one of my favorite alternative philosophy authors. If you are looking for some mind-expanding takes on life on this planet, he might be just the author for you.

About the Author

Marcus T. Anthony, Ph.D., is the founder and director of MindFutures, and a futurist with a passion for the futures of Asia, consciousness, human evolution, intuitive research methods, and spirituality. His vision has been to balance scientific and technological futures with deeper human and spiritual futures.

Anthony's work is unique in that it blends professional scholarship and mystical insight, a result of combining intense training with spiritual teachers and advanced academic qualifications. His other books include *Integrated Intelligence* and *Extraordinary Mind*.

Marcus Anthony obtained his Ph.D. from the University of the Sunshine Coast in Australia. He is a member of the World Futures Studies Federation and the Darwin Project Council. His personal blog is www.22cplus.blogspot.com, and his website is www.mindfutures.com.

INTUITIVE ANALYSIS AND COUNSELING WITH MARCUS T. ANTHONY

For those readers with a strong commitment to move forward, and to learn more about Integrated Intelligence firsthand, Marcus T. Anthony conducts personal consultations and group workshops. He works with individuals, couples, and organizations. His goal is to help people create ideal futures. He looks at issues from many perspectives, combining traditional, rational methods with innovative and intuitive processes. He uses Integrated Intelligence to get right to the heart of problems. An important motivation for Marcus is to teach people how to find empowerment, and their soul purpose, using Integrated Intelligence. He does this by teaching people how to use the INI tools. Marcus does sessions in person, by phone, or via the Internet. He is also available for public talks.

One-On-One Personal Psycho-Spiritual Counseling

For people who wish to move forward in their lives, find their bliss, and develop personal empowerment. In particular, this one-on-one counseling will benefit you if you are at a crossroad in your life, or facing recurring emotional issues. This process centers upon:

- Identifying soul issues that lie at the core of your life journey
- Naming your bliss, and mapping the way to get there
- Connecting with and healing the inner child
- Learning to use your Integrated Intelligence—how to tap in to the wisdom of the cosmos to live your soul purpose

Psycho-Spiritual Counseling for Couples

For couples wishing to create more loving and harmonious relationships. This is particularly useful for couples who have recurring problems that they have been unable to resolve. It is for those couples wishing to continue their relationship and move it to a more blissful level. The process centers upon:

- Uncovering the psychic projections that prevent harmonious relationships from developing and that lie behind many arguments and conflicts
- Learning to use the INI tools, to help both partners take greater responsibility for emotional energy, with the goal of becoming more loving to one another
- Uncovering the trapped emotional energy from childhood and past lives that prevents truly loving relationships from developing

Consultations for Organizations

For organizations that wish to move beyond a sticking point and achieve a greater level of true prosperity and harmony. Here Marcus combines many of the tools of the academic discipline of futures studies (such as scenarios, visioning, and horizon scanning) with intuitive skills. The process he employs helps bring forward both factual and intuitive information about the group, and Marcus teaches participants how to intuit the results of the actions that individuals and the organization are intending to take. The process centers upon:

- Developing Conscious Leadership skills in your organization using Integrated Intelligence
- Mastering the INI tools to help develop your intuitive skills and those of your employees in order to enhance existing institutional decision-making processes
- Learning what strategies are best for taking your organization forward
- Developing a powerful vision that taps in to the core genius of everyone within your organization
- Shaping your organization's future by aligning with your strengths
- Getting straight to the heart of what psycho-spiritual issues are holding your organization back

To book a personal session, workshop, or talk, contact Marcus Anthony at **marcus.a@mindfutures.com**.

Index

Page numbers in *italics* indicate illustrations.

BOOKS OF RELATED INTEREST

The Science of Getting Rich
Attracting Financial Success through Creative Thought
by Wallace D. Wattles

Shamanic Experience
A Practical Guide to Psychic Powers
by Kenneth Meadows

Visionary Shamanism
Activating the Imaginal Cells of the Human Energy Field
by Linda Star Wolf and Anne Dillon

Shamanic Breathwork
Journeying beyond the Limits of the Self
by Linda Star Wolf

Shamanism for the Age of Science
Awakening the Energy Body
by Kenneth Smith

The Prophet's Way
A Guide to Living in the Now
by Thom Hartmann

New World Mindfulness
From the Founding Fathers, Emerson, and Thoreau
to Your Personal Practice
by Donald McCown and Marc S. Micozzi, M.D., Ph.D.

Your Emotional Type
Key to the Therapies That Will Work for You
by Michael A. Jawer and Marc S. Micozzi, M.D., Ph.D.

INNER TRADITIONS • BEAR & COMPANY
P.O. Box 388
Rochester, VT 05767
1-800-246-8648
www.InnerTraditions.com

Or contact your local bookseller